WHEN H[illegible]L

WHEN HEARTS HEAL

AN ANTHOLOGY OF THE POWERFUL RIPPLE EFFECT OF IMPACT AND SUCCESS WHEN HEARTS HEAL, OPEN AND RECEIVE.

BROUGHT TO YOU BY
SCHOOL OF HEALING MASTERY

A&Co.

First published in Great Britain in 2025
by Authors & Co.
www.authorsandco.pub

Copyright © School of Healing Mastery Ltd 2025

School of Healing Mastery Ltd asserts the moral right to be identified as the author of this work in accordance with the Copyright, Designs and Patents Act 1988.

ISBN 978-1-917623-10-0 (paperback)

All rights reserved. No part of this book may be reproduced or transmitted in any form or by any means, electronic or mechanical, including photocopying, recording, or by any information storage and retrieval system without the written permission of the author, except where permitted by law or for the use of brief quotations in a book review.

HeartHealing®, Ancestral HeartHealing®, Love Wound®, Enoughness Wound®, Trust Wound®, Safety Wound®, Worth Wound®, Voice Wound™, Receiving Wounds® are trademarks of Natasha Leigh Bray and School of Healing Mastery Ltd. All rights reserved.

DISCLAIMER

This book is intended for informational and inspirational purposes only. It contains a mix of personal stories, professional reflections, and insights from the main author and contributing authors, all of whom are trained in HeartHealing®. Some contributors may also hold professional qualifications (such as medical degrees, psychology credentials, or therapeutic licenses) in their respective countries; however, all contributions are offered in a personal capacity and do not constitute licensed medical, psychological, or therapeutic advice.

Each contributing author is solely responsible for the content of their individual chapter, including any views, personal experiences, or healing approaches expressed therein. The main author, other contributors, and the publisher accept no responsibility for the claims, opinions, or practices shared by individual contributors. These views do not necessarily represent those of the main author, publisher, or other contributors. These views do not necessarily represent those of the main author, publisher, or other contributors. Our contributing authors are from many countries. You may notice variations between USA/UK spellings and conventions: we have respected the language conventions standard to the regions of our writers.

The practices, opinions, and personal accounts shared in this book are not a substitute for professional medical or mental health advice, diagnosis, or treatment. Always seek the advice of your physician, psychologist, or qualified health provider with any questions you may have regarding a medical or psychological condition or before starting any new healing practice.

The results described by contributors are based on their unique experiences and should not be taken as typical or guaranteed outcomes. Each person's healing journey is different.

The publisher and main author cannot independently verify the extent of AI use, and each contributor remains solely responsible for the originality, accuracy, and integrity of their submitted chapter.

Some chapters may include case studies or References: to client experiences. In all such instances, names and identifying details have been changed or omitted to protect client confidentiality. Any resemblance to actual persons, living or deceased, is purely coincidental unless explicitly stated with permission.

By reading this book, you agree that the main author, contributors, and publisher disclaim all liability for any direct or indirect loss or damage that may arise from your use of or reliance on any material contained within.

The information in this book is not intended for use in jurisdictions where the distribution or use of such content would violate local laws or regulations.

CONTENTS

FOREWORD

JOE VITALE

There are moments in life when the world reminds us that healing is not only possible but inevitable – when we surrender to the wisdom of the heart. I have witnessed this truth in my own life, and I have been blessed to see it unfold in the lives of others. It is an honor to introduce this book and the remarkable force behind it—Natasha Bray, a true catalyst for transformation.

I remember a time I was at a crossroads, weighed down by the invisible burdens of past wounds, limiting beliefs, and self-doubt. I was broke, homeless, suicidal. Like so many, I had done the work—read the books, attended the seminars, practiced the techniques—but there was still something missing. The missing piece, I would come to realize, was not another method or philosophy but a deeper connection to the heart. My heart was closed and wounded. When I allowed myself to truly listen, to trust, to feel, I discovered that the heart carries its own intelligence—a profound, healing energy that can dissolve barriers and open the door to infinite possibilities.

Healing our hearts is not just about mending what feels broken; it is about stepping into a greater version of ourselves. It is about remembering who we truly are beyond the layers of fear, pain, and conditioning. This journey is one of courage, trust, and surrender. And it is a journey made infinitely richer when guided by those who have mastered the art of facilitating profound transformation. That is what Natasha and this book offer.

Over the years, I have had the privilege of exploring the limitless nature of the human experience. My journey has taken me to places I never imagined—both within myself and out in the world. I've written ninety books. I'm in thirty movies, including the famous *The Secret*. I have my own movie, *Zero Limits*, which Natasha stars in. Through my work, I have sought to dissolve barriers, open minds, and inspire change. I have learned that true transformation does not come from force or struggle but from an openness to something greater—a willingness to embrace the unknown with trust and curiosity. It comes from opening the heart.

I have seen the power of healing in many forms, but there is something uniquely powerful about the work Natasha brings to the world. She understands, at the deepest level, that healing is not just an intellectual process—it is a deeply felt experience. It is about resonance, alignment, and an unwavering commitment to truth. Natasha has an extraordinary gift for helping others access this power within themselves. She is a guide, a mentor, a teacher, and above all, a living example of what it means to walk this path with authenticity and grace. I know her. I love her. She is my friend.

This book is more than a collection of insights and techniques; it is a portal to something deeper. Natasha has brought together an incredible group of practitioners—each with their own unique wisdom, experience, and perspective—to offer something truly special to the reader. She has woven together a tapestry of knowledge that is not meant to be just read but to be felt, experienced, and integrated. This book by itself is a tool for healing.

If you have ever longed for healing, for clarity, for a deeper sense of purpose and connection, then this book is for you. It is an invitation to open your heart, to embrace your own power, and to step into the limitless potential that has always been within you.

Natasha is a force of nature—fierce in her commitment, boundless in her compassion, and unwavering in her dedication to helping others awaken to their own brilliance. She has created something truly extraordinary here, and I have no doubt this book will serve as a guiding light for all who are ready to embark on this journey.

Open your heart. Trust the process. And let the power of healing your heart transform your life.

INTRODUCTION

NATASHA LEIGH BRAY

A NEW PARADIGM OF HEALING

There was a time, long before modern history, across cultures and traditions all over the world, when the heart was revered as the body's most important and sacred organ. Ancient Egyptians believed the heart was the seat of the soul, crucial to their passage to the afterlife. In the ancient practice of Chinese Medicine, the heart is known as the 'emperor' or 'ruler' because they believed it ruled the body and had a key role in balancing body, mind and spirit. It is thought to be where the 'Shen' (spirit or consciousness) is stored. These traditional concepts are widely acknowledged in Chinese Medicine practices to this day.

Similarly, Ayurvedic texts from Ancient India describe the heart as the 'king' of organs, where a person's soul, self and intelligence were stored. Shamanism, one of the oldest healing practices of the world, recognises the heart as an essential source of wisdom and healing, a link to the soul and a bridge between physical and spiritual realms. There are records and archaeological findings of heart sacrifices to the gods beginning with ancient Mesopotamia and the Mayan civilisation thousands of years BC.

Ancient Greek philosopher Aristotle also believed the heart stored the soul. He found that it was the first organ to form after conception and that the body lived even if the brain was not conscious. Figueredo (2021) discovered that even early Christians believed the heart held the soul and a connection to God within its walls. For many thousands of years, the dominant paradigm of the world was profoundly spiritual and connected to the heart.

Then, with the seventeenth century emergence of modern science in the Western world, the paradigm shifted heavily from one that valued heart, emotions, intuition and spirituality to one that valued brain, logic, intellect and science. The brain became the most important part of the human body, while the heart became a long-forgotten friend. Logic replaced magic. Following our heads replaced following our hearts. Masculine energy dominated feminine energy in an increasingly patriarchal culture. Spirituality was shunned for science. We learned to disconnect from our hearts, the seat of our souls and our true selves. Separation formed – within and in the world. The pendulum, once to the left, now swung strongly in the other direction.

That disconnection never went away, it only grew into a deep feeling that *something was missing*. A deep hole inside that no matter how much money we made, how much success we created, whatever we achieved… it never felt filled. We sacrificed love for career. Sabotaged health for success. Believed we couldn't have both. A collective striving for more, more, more never felt enough, even when that more was achieved. Understanding how the brain works has its value; however, the plethora of mind-based approaches to healing this disconnection have never really filled the void.

The Missing Piece

A new paradigm has begun to emerge to fill the gaps and holes where modern science and the masculine paradigm fall short. It values both spirituality and science. Heart and head. Emotions and logic. Intuition and intellect. Feminine and masculine. It weaves the wisdom of ancient cultures and traditions with the innovation of modern science. The two halves of the whole, united as one, create a paradigm that is infinitely more powerful. In this New Paradigm, the pendulum swings towards balance in the middle – but it still has a long way to go.

That missing piece? It's your *heart.*

The heart has been neglected and forgotten about for centuries in the Western world – and now it's making an almighty comeback. As the great Renaissance philosopher and physician Paracelsus himself said: "The practice of healing lies in the heart." The modern world is only now realising… maybe he was on to something.

More recent research from Dr Andrew Armour (1991) discovered the heart stores its own memories independently of the brain and has its own complex nervous system, something he called the 'heart-brain'. Modern science is catching up with what ancient traditions have known for centuries. Recent decades have seen emerging schools of research set up purely to study the transformative power of the heart. A full circle moment is in action.

What Is HeartHealing?

HeartHealing is a revolutionary healing approach used within a meditative state. It uniquely merges ancient spiritual wisdom and cutting-edge science for a holistic approach to healing that is deep, fast, incredibly powerful and yet beautifully safe. It bypasses the rational, logical mind and accesses the hidden wounding stored in your heart. Beyond that, it activates the emotional, relational and spiritual intelligence hidden beneath those wounds. It is the missing link to wholeness and a new paradigm of healing and success that changes your world and the world for generations to come.

We have all had experiences that have impacted our heart, whether that's a loss or trauma, feeling rejected, betrayed, judged, unsafe, abandoned, not worthy or 'not enough' in some way. As a result, we put walls up around our hearts to stop us from feeling that pain so intensely again. In doing so, we also created energetic blocks to receiving the unconditional love, success, and abundance we truly desire and deserve. These are the Universal Receiving Wounds of the Heart.

Anatomically, your heart has a physical 'heart wall' called the pericardium (the 'Heart Protector' in Chinese Medicine) that keeps it safe from anything that could physically hurt it. There is an energetic heart wall, too, that protects it from *emotional* pain.

The more hurt you experience in life, the more you build up that energetic wall around your heart to protect yourself from being hurt again. But this also limits the power of your heart's magnetic field – and your ability to receive the healing, love, money and success *that same heart desires*.

HeartHealing safely breaks down that wall by expertly unveiling hidden wounds stored in the heart that have often been in place since childhood. It deeply heals the cycles of wounding passed down through families and relationships. Then it moves you rapidly towards a sense of wholeness and emotional freedom that ripples through every dimension and relationship in your life (including your relationship with money and success). This pioneering approach combines psychology and spirituality, using the heart as a portal to holistic mind-heart-soul transformation that HeartHealing Practitioners and their clients often describe as "more powerful than years of therapy."

It is very common for people on their healing journey to spend a lot of time trying to change the symptoms of their wounds instead of addressing the true root cause. That's where HeartHealing is different. It focuses on healing the heart and specifically from the *painful feelings* created by the person who wounded it, to rapidly free you from the sabotaging patterns and symptoms created by the wound.

We believe the more you heal these wounds, the better you *feel* and the more open you are to receiving the love, success and abundance available to you.

The Five Universal Receiving Wounds of the Heart

I have discovered the energetic walls we put up around our heart consist of five core Receiving Wounds of the Heart. They impact our ability to receive healing and our capacity to receive the good that comes from that healing – more happiness, more fulfilment, more love, more impact, more money, more success. *Everything.*

They are the Enoughness Wound, the Love Wound, the Trust Wound, the Worth Wound and the Acceptance Wound. Everyone has these wounds, just with different experiences and relationships at the root of them. I have personally witnessed thousands of clients dramatically transform themselves, their relationships and their lives as a result of healing these wounds. You will also tend to have one wound that is deeper than the others and this can change depending on what is happening in your life that may be bringing these wounds to the surface for you.

Think about which wound may be deepest for you and how it might be showing up for you in your life, work and relationships.

1. The Enoughness Wound

Have you ever felt not good enough? Not smart enough? Not successful enough? Not enough to have the relationships or career you want? Welcome to your Enoughness Wound, the deep wound of the heart that keeps us comparing ourselves to everyone else and deciding that we just don't match up. I call this the SuperWound because its sneaky long roots influence all the other wounds too. This wound leaves you feeling and believing that you are not enough unconditionally, not enough to have the success and relationships you desire. You find other ways to feel enough… like doing, pleasing or achieving and giving to others, because deep down you don't believe you are enough for just you.

How else does this wound show up? You may place exceptionally high expectations on yourself to be perfect and beat yourself up if you are not. It impacts how enough you feel as a parent or partner, like nothing you do is ever good enough. It impacts your confidence. You may find you struggle to love or like yourself and worry about what others think of you.

It is not always things we consider big trauma that lead to an Enoughness Wound. Maybe you had a perfectionist parent who expected you to be perfect too or a parent who struggled to give praise? Or an elder sibling or best friend you were always compared to or felt less than? When you heal this wound, you feel and believe you are enough on a deep level. This can dramatically shift your relationship with yourself and others, and what you believe you are enough to receive.

2. The Love Wound

Ever felt you are not loved just for who you are? Worry that your loved ones or friends will abandon you? Welcome to your Love Wound, the wound that keeps you feeling and believing that you are not loved unconditionally, just for being you. You overgive, people please, and sacrifice yourself and your needs for everyone else and theirs. It never feels like anyone else gives to you as much as you give to them… and it doesn't feel good. The word 'no' is very difficult for people with a deep Love Wound because their biggest fear is being abandoned by others. They do all they can to stop that happening, even if it comes at a huge cost to themselves.

In what other ways does this show up? You will self-sacrifice and self-abandon in order to receive love, connection and money from others. It keeps you chasing the wrong relationships and friendships – toxic ones, unhealthy ones, trying to rescue everyone else whilst neglecting yourself and your health. Secretly, you need to feel needed – it gives you a sense of control, and that control helps you feel safe.

This is a deep and often very hidden wound. So many of my clients with a hidden Love Wound say, "I know I was loved as a child, but didn't really *feel* loved." Knowing and feeling are two very different things. One comes from your head, the other from your heart. And feeling it in your heart is needed to truly heal it. Sometimes it comes from a simple mismatch of love languages between you and your parents or a home where love always felt like it came with conditions. Other times it can be more sinister. It is very common if you grew up in a home that was toxic, abusive or narcissistic. When you heal this wound, you shift from overgiving to opening your heart to receiving. The quality of the relationships in your life can dramatically improve in all areas.

3. The Trust Wound

Do you struggle with self-doubt? Constantly second-guess yourself and give power away to others rather than follow your inner guidance? Have a deep fear of getting it wrong or making mistakes? Say hello to your Trust Wound, the Universal Receiving Wound of the Heart that leaves you thinking and feeling you cannot trust yourself, others or the Universe. It leaves you feeling you have to do everything yourself, struggling to accept support and in constant circles of indecision and procrastination.

Other ways it shows up? You may even feel like an imposter, constantly worrying you will be found out. If you have a big Trust Wound, you put a lot of focus on evidence, research, facts and qualifications (you have a lot of them!) whilst ignoring your intuition, feelings and spiritual connection. You are too scared to trust where your heart leads, so you feel safer living from your head than your heart.

This wound comes from acts of betrayal, whether intentional or unintentional, which cause us to doubt ourselves and the intentions of others. You have probably experienced many betrayals in your life. It is a normal part of being human. Maybe your parent had an affair or constantly made promises they never kept. Maybe they betrayed you in the deepest way you can imagine through childhood abuse.

The energy of betrayal is metaphysically like being stabbed in the heart. Your heart will energetically build very thick walls of defence against its Trust Wound being triggered, because it feels so deeply painful. The double-edged sword is that we often blame ourselves for others betraying us, which leads to self-betrayal and a loss of self-trust. When we heal this wound, we repair our ability to trust in ourselves, others and the world around us. We feel safer and more able to listen to our intuition, follow our hearts and live a life true to ourselves. We trust that it is safe to receive.

4. The Worth Wound

Do you find that you sabotage your body, bank account or relationships when one area is going well? Do you believe you have to work hard or struggle for every bit of money you make? Struggle to relax and just 'be'? Welcome to your Worth Wound. This Universal Receiving Wound of the Heart leaves you believing and feeling you are not worthy and deserving unconditionally. This can block you from receiving success in *all* areas of life – relationships, work, money, health – without sabotage. Whilst all the wounds influence your relationship with money, this one has the greatest impact because your identity and worth tend to be built on struggle and hard work (a recipe for burnout!).

If worth is conditional, you believe you are not worthy for who you are. You only believe you are worthy for what you can do. You may constantly find yourself trying to prove your worth through your external achievements and external things, always hustling and on the go (work addiction, anyone?). You feel guilt and shame when you do receive good things like money and success because deep down, you don't feel deserving of it. You push it away, struggle to keep it, or feel you need to work yourself to the bone to receive it. When something is conditional, we always believe there must be some sort of trade-off for having it: work hard for success; be the best to be loved; sacrifice love for money.

So many of us have placed conditions on our own worth, or others have made us feel that way. It is the most common wound associated with the effects of being a 'scapegoat' child in a dysfunctional family, or of childhood abuse and in particular childhood sexual abuse. When you heal this wound, you feel worthy of rest, ease, fun and good things in your life. You feel worthy just for who you are, not what you do and can see shifts in receiving love, money and success with more ease and flow, instead of the usual struggle and hustle.

5. The Acceptance Wound

Do you worry about being rejected if people knew the real you? Feel scared of being seen or of public speaking? Hide parts of yourself to fit in and be accepted by others? Meet your Acceptance Wound. Do not underestimate this final wound – it is often one of the biggest hidden ones. The Acceptance Wound leaves you believing and feeling that you are not accepted by others for who you are. This can lead to self-rejection and rejecting the things you want to receive by pushing them away.

You avoid being visible as who you really are in relationships, socially and at work, and develop a high level of independence – a 'lone wolf' so to speak. It leaves you feeling lonely, isolated, misunderstood and like you don't belong or fit in anywhere. We learn to reject others before they do it to us, pushing away love. You seek safety through hiding, playing small, and avoiding intimacy and connection. Or the flip side, this wound can show up as hiding behind the mask of a false personality, an 'I don't need anyone' bravado.

To be rejected as a child literally threatens your very survival. A child cannot survive unless their parents accept and look after them (even if that care is poor or abusive). They have to learn to cope with the family they are born into. They do this by self-rejecting so they can survive until adulthood. This is a big wound because it is a survival wound.

You crave to feel you belong; you crave love, success and connection, but hide away and wear a mask to stay safe. The acceptance wound affects all our relationships, just like the other wounds, especially our relationship with self.

So many of us have experienced rejection in our childhood, with devastating impact on our adult relationships and our ability to feel safe to be seen for who we really are. Maybe you felt rejected by your caregiver as a child or experienced a humiliation at school in front of others. Whatever the root, it can be healed, and you can be free.

It takes energy to guard your heart. It takes energy to hide who you are. When you feel safe to let down those walls, be your true, authentic self and open your heart – all that energy goes into your success, abundance and happiness. It is a beautiful thing. Healing just one of these wounds creates a rapid and dramatic shift in your inner and outer world – but healing all five? That's the path to dramatically expanding your heart's capacity to receive everything it has ever desired and more. Love is possible for you. Healing is possible for you. Success is possible for you, no matter what you have been through or where you have come from.

The Five Dimensions of HeartHealing

HeartHealing is revolutionary in the way it works across the Five Dimensions of Healing to help people expand their capacity to heal and receive more.

Addressing each of the Universal Receiving Wounds of the Heart in these five dimensions can lead to incredible, profound shifts for you and those around you – since everyone who interacts with you benefits from the change in you; your family, your clients or colleagues and your loved ones.

1. **Psychological** - working with your heart/mind connection to identify and transform the thoughts and beliefs that are connected to and reinforce your heart wounds, healing on a heart level is actually the fastest way to change beliefs and thoughts too. This aligns heart and mind so they work in unison and not against each other.
2. **Emotional** - unveiling and releasing buried emotions that cause the heart walls and keep you stuck in cycles of self-sabotage, emotional numbing and disconnection so that you can reconnect to safety, love and trust and expand your emotional intelligence and capacity.
3. **Relational** - rapidly identifying and healing key life relationships at the root of the heart wounds to free you from them and expand your capacity to receive more love, money, success and inner peace. This reconnects you to your most important relationship: the one with yourself and dramatically expands your relational intelligence.
4. **Generational** - Your heart doesn't just carry your wounding. It carries the wounding of the generations before you, passed down through epigenetics. Generational healing is key as it breaks family cycles for you and the generations after you, creating a ripple effect of impact in up to seven generations.
5. **Spiritual** - The heart is used as a portal to the soul and the healing allows you to awaken your spiritual intelligence by becoming more of your authentic self – who you really are. You move close to wholeness, reconnect to your intuition, your higher self and a higher power that helps you make sense of and release the wisdom in your wound.

These five levels all work in harmony during a one-hour HeartHealing session, delivering a more powerful healing session than any one dimension alone, awakening the intelligences of the heart.

The Magic of HeartHealing

HeartHealing is informed by science on trauma, attachment and relational dynamics. We all have a relational blueprint, so to speak, stored within us and influenced by our early childhood relationships that creates the relational patterns and dynamics in our lives today. For example, if you had a parent who abandoned you in your younger years, you may find yourself in a pattern of adulthood romantic relationships where you are repeatedly physically or emotionally abandoned. Your blueprint for 'love' and relationships is shaped by the experience of abandonment you had with that parent.

If you experienced a lot of emotional pain as a child in your caregiver relationships, you may have a relational blueprint that creates patterns of painful relationships because a part of you carries the imprint Pain = Love. This relational blueprint is also known as an attachment pattern. My theory is that this relational blueprint or 'attachment pattern' doesn't just impact our love and family relationships but *every relationship we have*. With people, with ourselves, with money, with everything we interact with in the world.

Let me explain further by using the Love Wound and all the relationships it impacts as an example. Your Love Wound can hugely influence your relationship with food. It often triggers emotional eating or binge eating to fill the empty feeling inside; you may have used food as a child to numb the pain of feeling unloved; maybe you felt safe and warm and fuzzy inside when you had sugary foods. The imprint becomes: Food = Love.

This wound can impact your relationship with your body and self. You might struggle to love your own body or believe you are only lovable if your body looks a certain way. It can be hard to relate to yourself in a loving way if you have never been shown love or your emotional needs were neglected.

Your Love Wound can also impact your relationship with money. You may overspend on yourself and others. You may even end up in debt to fill the void or to gain love and approval. It can impact your relationship with your career, going into jobs or taking directions others want for you to please them, rather than what you want for yourself. You may end up working for toxic bosses, as you've learned that behaviour is normal. It impacts your relationship with success because you play small, fearing you might lose people if you become more successful. All of this is subconscious, of course. Most people do not even realise it is there.

There are many complex dynamics at play: as you grow up, there are often multiple key influences on your identity and relational blueprint. The closer a relationship is to you, the greater its impact on your sense of who you are – and the greater its influence on your heart wounds and the wall around your heart.

The majority of the deep wounds of your heart do not come from interactions with strangers. They come from people you have (or should have had) some form of close emotional connection to: parents, caregivers, grandparents, teachers, siblings, school peers. HeartHealing works with these relational blueprints and attachment patterns within and transforms them into healthier ones so that every relationship you have with yourself, others and the world around you begins to change. This can only happen when you focus on healing the relationship that caused the wound (not the experience) and the painful, buried emotions it caused. Relational wounds need relational healing. This is one of the most powerful aspects of a HeartHealing session, transforming the relational blueprint into a healthier, more positive one.

For many people, working with the mind can help, but doesn't always feel enough to heal the pain in the heart and the negative impact this has had on the relational blueprint, even more so when big trauma is involved. Research has found that 'spirituality' is a proven factor in significant post-traumatic healing and growth. This is why HeartHealing moves beyond the current 'scientific evidence base' and integrates spirituality too.

At its core, spirituality is a remembrance. It is about remembering your true, authentic self and living in alignment with who you really are. Wholeness, purpose, intuition, and the soul are all spiritual concepts. In HeartHealing, we work with mind, heart and soul using the heart as the portal to a holistic transformation.

We teach that a part of our soul fragments when we experience an emotional wound and is stored in the heart, kept safe until we are ready and equipped to rescue it, heal it and reintegrate it. This bears similarities to the concept of the inner child in psychology and of soul loss in shamanism. We work with the integration of many 'parts' or soul fragments to create a sense of wholeness and remembrance of who you really are beneath your wounds.

The Institute of HeartMath has found that your heart emanates an extremely powerful toroidal energetic field, scientifically measured to reach as far as five feet from your heart. Incredibly, they found that this energetic field is influenced by your thoughts and emotions and is not just felt by other people energetically, but transfers to others (McCraty *et al*, 1998).

We believe the energetic heart walls limit this energy field. The more we bring down those walls, and transform the wounded thoughts and feelings into more positive ones, the more powerful, magnetic and far-reaching your heart's energy field becomes. People feel your heart. They feel a change in you that cannot always be put into words, and respond to you differently because your heart field is different. You stop chasing success and become a magnet to it instead.

This powerful integration of spiritual and scientific, mind and heart and soul, makes HeartHealing a truly magical and unique experience. Whilst it is important to emphasise that HeartHealing is a complementary approach and is not a substitute or replacement for traditional psychotherapy, our clients and practitioners report results in the following areas:

Emotional and Psychological Results

More positive thoughts, speaking to self more kindly, and big shifts in levels of confidence, ability to trust themselves and make decisions. An incredible new level of self-belief that leads to huge shifts in their life and career. Deeper levels of self-worth, finally feeling lovable and enough for the first time in their life. A deep sense of inner safety and reduced symptoms of anxiety or depression.

Relational Results

Healing deeply painful wounds with parents and being able to forgive, accept and even love their parents again. Healing from the emotional impact of adoption. Feeling more connected to their children and reconnecting to older children. Marriages on the brink of divorce repaired and falling in love with their partners again. Estranged family members getting in touch 'out of the blue'. Magnetising healthier relationships and friendships with healthier people. Ability to say no to the wrong relationships. Having better boundaries and a healthier relationship with self.

Financial Results

A more positive relationship with money. Businesses growing dramatically, having their highest ever income months or years. Unexpected financial windfalls. Clearing debt. Out of the blue promotions and bonuses. Able to receive more money, start saving and build wealth too, as sabotage of it stops.

Spiritual Results

Feeling safe to be their authentic self. Reporting a greater sense of wholeness. Discovering their true purpose and having the courage to act on it. Increase in intuition and feeling connected to something beyond them. Spiritual gifts such as psychic abilities. Feeling supported and guided by a higher power.

Who Am I?

So who am I? What makes me qualified to lead this movement to heal hearts? I didn't know it then, but healing hearts was destined to be my purpose from the moment I was born. I had my heart wounded *every* way you can imagine, surviving a childhood of chronic abuse, bullying, and never feeling loved or safe. It sent me on a lifelong quest to understand myself and my wounds, why I felt so unlovable, unworthy and disconnected from others and the world.

A typical high achiever, I ticked off the psychology degree, the master's, the endless qualifications and certifications. Professionally, I innovated lifesaving initiatives, became a rapid intervention social worker and worked in many professions I would consider as being a 'hidden healer'. In 2017, I had a healing crisis after the birth of my first child and left it all behind to go all in on my true mission – to help others heal and rapidly transform their lives. I trained in the scientific mind-based 'masculine' paradigm modalities that focused on talking about my trauma and healing from experiences. I very quickly realised something was missing – in me and in my work.

Where was the heart? I didn't just need to heal from experiences. I needed to heal from people, the people who had deeply hurt me and wounded my heart. And whilst my credentials looked good on paper, my biggest teacher was the healing of the wounds of my own heart. When I focused there, everything shifted for me. My business went from being plateaued to dramatically growing to new levels of impact and income beyond my wildest dreams. I went from undercharging and struggling to hold on to money to charging my worth and becoming a cash millionaire by the age of thirty-three.

I escaped a history of abusive, toxic and narcissistic relationships (an unfortunate side effect of my own relational blueprint from childhood relationships), finding soulmate love and the safe, loving family I always dreamed of. The more I healed my heart, the more my external world and the relationships in it changed. The most important shift for me was becoming the cycle breaker for my own children and creating a life of true abundance in love, money and safety for them. Statistically, I should never have been able to become the woman I am today with the trauma I've been through. But I beat all the odds. That's how I know you can too.

When I went on this journey, I began integrating my own innovative techniques and knowledge of attachment, relational trauma and lived experience and wisdom of personally healing from every kind of trauma you can imagine (and the people who caused it) into my work. I realised I had created something new entirely. That's when my new paradigm healing modality, HeartHealing, was born.

I became widely known as an expert in healing relational wounds, and more than that, alchemising those wounds into tangible, powerful results in life, love and success for myself and others. I spent thousands of hours healing the conscious and subconscious minds and hearts of thousands of women entrepreneurs who saw more success in their businesses from our work together than from anything strategy-based. I saw time and time again how we all had the same patterns of wounding – the same Universal Receiving Wounds of the Heart uniting us through pain, instead of love.

These wounds were creating disconnection, struggle, sabotaging behaviours and a deep hole inside that no money would ever fill. It is these wounds that are stopping you from being the human, parent, leader and partner you want to be in the world, and from truly receiving the love, success and abundance you are destined for. I know this to be true: no amount of money or success will ever make you feel satisfied if you don't have wholeness, worthiness and a positive relationship with the most important person in your life – *you*. This happens when we heal our hearts. The external success happens as a side effect.

The power of this healing blew me away. It was unlike anything I had ever seen. I knew I couldn't keep it to myself. To truly help more people heal and collectively impact the world, I needed to train others in this modality.

So, since 2020, I have been training hundreds of HeartHealing Practitioners across the world – collectively healing hearts powerfully in different languages, different cultures and different audiences than I could ever reach alone. Every single one of these practitioners has gone on a deep journey of healing their own heart and beautifully merges their own wealth of expertise with HeartHealing to create their unique magic. That brings me to the authors of this book, from whom you will get to learn and heal as you read each transformational chapter.

The Magic in This Book

You are not here by accident. There is something in one of the chapters in this book that was written especially to help heal and understand your heart and the hearts of others you impact.

Equally, it is no accident that these eighteen incredible leading healers from across the globe have come together to share their expertise, story and wisdom with you. They all have in common that the heart was the missing piece for them, too, personally and professionally. Each had to heal their own heart first to become a better healer of others' hearts. I have had the honour of knowing each practitioner individually and deeply, through their in-depth training in my HeartHealing qualification and some of them before that in my signature success healing programmes like the Ultimate Uplevel Academy. Their wisdom is profound. Their gifts are unmatched. Together, we create a bigger ripple effect in this world. I could not be prouder of the healers, practitioners and leaders they have become and the impact they are having.

Each chapter teaches you insights into healing yourself and others on a deeper level, organised into the following sections:

Healing Self

Explore fascinating insights into the Heart of Identity with Marketing and Communications Expert Jane Hoareau. She shares the psychology of identity and identity wounds passed down through our ancestors, as well as her own powerful journey of stepping into her identity as a healer.

Receive wisdom and expertise on the Heart of Wholeness from scientist and healer Lynne Katz, illuminated by her journey from fragmentation to finding wholeness for herself and her disabled child. Wholeness is the key to reclaiming self-worth and living in alignment.

Discover the Heart of Self-Image with Physician and Healer Dr Judith Borger as she takes you on a journey of understanding wounded self-image and the power of transforming it into an empowered self-image that supports you to receive the life, relationships and success you desire.

Master the Heart of Reinvention with healer Susannah Robinson as she shows you how to rewrite the concept of a midlife crisis into an awakening where you reconcile your past roles, release outdated beliefs and reconnect with your authentic self.

Journey into the Heart of Healing Families with Clinical Hypnotherapist and Master Coach Rose Cleaver to break generational cycles and create healthy relationships, a flourishing family and a successful life.

Healing Limits

Discover fascinating insights about living with perfectionism with esteemed psychologist Dr Gocke Bulgan as she deep dives into the Heart of Perfectionism and how to free yourself and others from its negative impact.

Unveil your voice wounds and discover the Heart of Finding Your Voice with astrologer and healer, Kinga Kujawa. Get ready to speak authentically, reclaim your self-worth, and overcome fears that silence your voice and hinder personal and professional growth.

Learn how to identify what is truly at the Heart of Imposter thinking and start shifting it too with the incredible Sile O'Broin, coach and healer within the United Nations, as she shows you how to tap into your true worth and potential.

Join esteemed Italian Mentor and Healer Laura Ballerio in the Heart of Thriving as she teaches you about the emotional and ancestral wounding keeping you stuck in survival and how to find the golden thread that makes the difference between surviving and thriving.

Explore the Heart of Burnout with Teacher and Healer Lucy Lambert, who shares her expertise and personal journey around the emotional, physical and mental toll of burnout and the steps you can take to truly heal from it so you can live and lead differently.

Healing in Mental Health

Expand your awareness of addiction and delve into the deep connection between trauma, relational wounds and addiction in the Heart of Addiction with highly experienced trauma expert, Laura Truesdale.

Open your heart to understanding grief (both obvious and hidden) on a deeper level with our grief expert Hannah Darby, who shares her powerful H.E.A.L. model for strength and resilience in the Heart of Grief.

Join acclaimed psychotherapist Aaron Swartz, who has dedicated his chapter and his life to healing the Heart of False Masculinity by awakening the power of the heart to meet men's deepest unmet needs.

Read fascinating, unique insights into the Heart of ADHD with Psychiatric Nurse Practitioner Diane Hutcheson, who beautifully blends her personal self-discovery journey and professional expertise in this area to help you recognise and manage symptoms of ADHD in a different way.

Healing in Success and Leadership

Journey into the Heart of Self-Mastery with renowned Master Coach and Therapist Darcy Bailey as she shares her insightful five core cycles which prevent transformation from the False Self to the True Self that is needed for higher wisdom, self-mastery and success.

Discover what is truly at the Heart of Limitless Potential with Transformational Healer Donna Hicklin, as she shares her journey and expertise to help you unlock your highest potential for self-love and soulful success.

Dive into the Heart of Conscious Evolution with Sheetal Vithlani as she teaches you how to take back your power and consciously evolve and create a different way of being, living and leading that impacts the world.

Learn about the Heart of Feminine Leadership with Success Coach and former government leader Emma Mason. Her chapter takes you into a deeper understanding of how you can lead more powerfully from your feminine rhythms to create meaningful change in the world.

If you take away just one thing from this book, let it be your innate power to heal your own heart. We are all healers – of ourselves first and foremost.

In that moment we finally decide to heal our hearts, we create a ripple effect for our families, the people we impact and our future generations. Let each chapter activate your capacity to be your own healer and open your heart to the transformation and ripple effect possible for you.

It all starts with one heart. *Your* heart.

When hearts heal, families heal, the world heals.

Love Natasha

Success Mastery Coach, Creator of HeartHealing and Founder of the School of Healing Mastery

Discover your deepest Receiving Wound of the Heart here with my free online assessment:
https://schoolofhealingmastery.com/receiving-wounds-assessment/

References:

Armour J. A., (1991), *Anatomy and function of the intrathoracic neurons regulating the mammalian heart.* In: Zucker I H and Gilmore J P, eds. *Reflex Control of the Circulation.* Boca Raton, FL, CRC Press: 1-37.

Figueredo, V., *The Ancient Heart: What the Heart Meant to Our Ancestors. JACC.* 2021 Aug, 78 (9) 957–959.

McCraty, R., Atkinson, M., Tiller, W. A., Rein, G., & Watkins, A. D. (1998), *The energetics of emotion: The role of the heart as an access point to the energetic systems.* Proceedings of the Tenth International Montreux Congress on Stress, Montreux, Switzerland.

McCraty, R., Ph.D., Atkinson, M., Tomasino, D., B.A., & Tiller, W.A., Ph.D. (1998), *The Electricity of Touch: Detection and Measurement of Cardiac Energy Exchange Between People.* In: Pribram, K.H., ed. Brain; *Values: Is a Biological Science of Values Possible?* Mahwah, NJ: Lawrence Erlbaum Associates, Publishers, 1998: 359-379

ABOUT NATASHA LEIGH BRAY

Natasha Leigh Bray is the multi-award-winning founder, transformational teacher and creator of HeartHealing®, a groundbreaking subconscious healing method transforming thousands of lives across the globe. Revered by leaders, therapists, and healers alike, Natasha is devoted to helping people break generational cycles of wounding and unlock true success through the power of the heart.

As the visionary behind the School of Healing Mastery, Natasha is setting a new gold standard in the healing industry by training world-class practitioners to become safer, more confident leaders in their field. Her work beautifully bridges psychology and spirituality, blending science with soul to create lasting change.

Her mission is to heal ten million hearts and lead a new paradigm of success, one where there is more love, money and safety for all.

www.natashabray.com
www.schoolofhealingmastery.com
facebook.com/natashabraycoach
facebook.com/schoolofhealingmastery
instagram.com/natashaleighbray
instagram.com/schoolofhealingmastery

1

JANE HOAREAU

THE HEART OF IDENTITY

I never wanted to be a healer. Not even close!

Teenage me, sitting wide-eyed, watching the Indian Ocean lap the shores of one of the most popular beaches of the Seychelles, had bigger dreams. I wanted to be a commercial pilot. I saw myself soaring through the skies as I flew people on amazing adventures to discover faraway places. I had glorious dreams!

But, life? Oh, life just laughed and in its typical fickle way said "Wait, you think you're writing the story?" and decided differently.

I look back, and cannot believe how far I've come. Today I'm published in this book. I've embraced my role helping children in my country with literacy; with the magical gift of books, reading and a brighter future. I spend my days helping business owners to find their voice, much as I found mine, ensuring it comes out in their marketing. I am working on a revolutionary marketing program. I have photos and videos of myself on social media. I continuously invest in myself and my growth.

At the beginning of 2024, Natasha Leigh Bray's book, *Your Next Six Figures*, tilted my world on its axis. Since then, I've trained as a HeartHealing practitioner and received countless healing sessions. I'm now combining this powerful modality and marketing to truly enable my clients to grow abundantly. By intertwining the two disciplines, I support them to feel both confident and authentic. I have provided HeartHealing sessions that have changed people's lives.

And I proudly say, "I'm a healer."

None of this would have happened without healing the wounds in my heart - the wounds that eroded and suppressed my identity.

But that is not all.

I have bigger plans, grand ambitions, because even though I'm far from the beach of my childhood, I have learnt to dream again. And that in itself is a beautiful thing; because there was a time where I didn't see myself as a woman who could dream.

I'm now on a mission to empower the women around the world, but especially on my small island archipelago and across the African continent to celebrate their identities, take pride in themselves and recognise the gifts they have and the change they can make.

All of this, because I firmly believe that to change a woman's life for the better is to illuminate an entire community. When women can break the legacy of pain, violence, self-doubt, oppression and inferiority, they break it for future generations. For women are the nurturers, the mediators, the educators, the caregivers, the cultural stewards and the healers of communities and families around the globe.

The African continent and its island states are held up by strong resilient women. Women who are holding generations of pain, hardship and injustice. Women who want to heal, know true freedom and thrive. Women who are ready for abundance and wealth. Women who want to make a difference. All they need is a companion. One who has gone before and understands. One who believes in them, when they cannot even see themselves.

And life, again is laughing, but this time with joy and relief. It's saying to me, "This is your purpose," and I, for once, am listening.

This is the journey I'm on. This is the Heart of Identity. This is my story.

Identity is one of the core pillars of a person's psychological make-up. Broadly speaking, identity is, "a person's sense of self, established by their unique characteristics, affiliations, and social roles." (Yilmaz, 2025) It plays a central role in our psychological development and wellbeing.

There are two main branches to the study of identity, developmental and social.

In the field of developmental psychology, Erik Erikson and his followers have focused on the concept of personal identity. Here, identity is seen as a mix of an individual's choices about the things they value plus their experiences, creating a picture of who they are. (Erikson, 1968)

Social psychology looks at identity as " … the part of an individual's self-concept which derives from his membership of a social group (or groups) together with the value and emotional significance attached to that membership." (Tajfel, 1978)

However, I base my understanding of identity on the research of Crocetti et al. (2022), which blends both of these perspectives, particularly the following principles:

1. The Eriksonian thought that "identity is a life-long journey, constantly evolving over time."

2. The social psychology outlook that identity is always influenced by social connection and the experiences of individuals in a group context, rather than being formed in isolation.

This means that our identity is constantly evolving, shaped by both our internal choices and our external connections. This is an important understanding and we will come to it in detail later.

For now, let's consider how the different emotional wounds we receive throughout our lives impact our sense of identity.

Andrea Mathews, a licensed professional counsellor states it clearly: "The central damage found in any wound is in its ability to change our identity. We accept as introjection an external circumstance, another person's projection, or someone else's personality or emotions. We absorb these things and identify with them so that we now see ourselves, at least in part, as that external circumstance, or that other person's projection, personality or emotion." (Mathews, 2013)

Because identity is a central part of our psychology, *all* emotional wounds have an impact on it.

Identity wounding presents in a multitude of ways and very often, it is subtle, hidden behind the veil of something more obvious.

As a HeartHealing practitioner, I have yet to work with a client who comes to me because they recognise that they don't have a strong sense of self. Instead, I see clients who are dealing with:

1) Addiction: Whether to alcohol, work, or video games, addiction can erase parts of an individual that previously gave them a sense of self. Additionally, an individual can label themselves as an addict and see themselves as part of a community of addicts, making it harder to kick the addiction. People can employ addictive behaviours to numb emotional pain or feelings of emptiness caused by a poorly defined identity.

2) Unworthiness: A wound all HeartHealing practitioners are trained in, the Worth Wound is defined as a person's difficulty to acknowledge and embrace their value. People who have a low sense of self-worth normally have a negative, distorted view of themselves. This can weaken or alter their sense of identity, causing them to feel lost or adopt an unfavourable identity.

3) Difficulties in decision-making: These individuals aren't sure who they are, what they want or where they're going. They find it very hard to make decisions, not trusting themselves. I've encountered this in both a professional and family setting.

4) Lack of boundaries or people-pleasing: In HeartHealing, we approach this as a manifestation of a Love Wound. Many people struggle to set healthy boundaries, finding it hard to distinguish their needs and responsibilities from those of others. They may believe their needs don't matter or that they have to be useful to have value. They don't believe they are loved unconditionally. A byproduct of this is a weakly developed identity.

5) Burnout: When a person over-invests their entire selves into their career, their work defines them, overshadowing their personal identity. This is often found in high achievers. Any professional mistake can lead to them spiralling, because their definition of self correlates to work accomplishments. In these situations we normally see a lack of self-complexity. The self is defined as "professional" or "provider", with few other roles. Thus, when these main roles are threatened, the other roles are not strong enough for these individuals to fall back on.

6) Fear of visibility: As a marketer, I often meet clients struggling with visibility. Some don't like being seen or using their voices. Yet others fear speaking up in meetings/negotiations or owning the room, even when they are clearly the expert in that setting. This is all due to a fear of being seen or heard and a fear of judgement, normally based on a lack of self-worth and self-acceptance of who they really are, their skills or how they look or sound.

These are but a few examples; as we have already seen, every type of emotional wound impacts a person's sense of identity.

A poorly defined identity can lead to severe depression, constant self-sabotage, a susceptibility to manipulation and abuse, an inability to form meaningful connections, a constant feeling of inadequacy and a lifetime of chasing external validation.

Unknowingly, our younger selves often surrender the shaping of our identity to external influences. While this is normal, what is often overlooked is that our identity is not a fixed construct, and as adults, we have the ability to shape it.

HeartHealing sessions are delivered in such a way that allows us as practitioners to significantly support the exploration and development of a healthy sense of self. It's a modality that aids individuals in reshaping their identity.

French philosopher René Descartes is famous for his sentence, "I think, therefore I am," or, "I am thinking, therefore I exist." While the interpretations of the statement differ, I consider it from the viewpoint that the meaning of our lives is ours to define. Descartes (1637) goes further to say that only our thoughts are completely under our control and the essence of a person is their ability to think.

To me, this reminds us that our thoughts influence our beliefs about ourselves, our lives, other people, and how we see the world. Basically, our thoughts are the basis of our identity.

While I agree, I would argue that an important aspect is missing. One, that Descartes, as a philosopher concerned with the mind and soul, did not consider.

My experience as a HeartHealing practitioner and that of my clients show that feelings are key in the formation and manifestation of self-identity.

Childhood experiences involving strong emotions such as rejection, humiliation, love, pride or joy greatly impact our beliefs about ourselves and our place in the world.

Conversely, how we express feelings impacts how others see us, and therefore our identity. Someone who expresses empathy and joy is perceived as fun and caring, reinforcing a friendly, compassionate identity.

In this space, the heart becomes vital.

Our identity, constantly evolving and partly influenced by our external connections, is often wounded in relationships. These wounds don't simply harm our minds, they break our hearts.

And this is the Heart of Identity - the emotions that dictate how we face and interact with the world. The emotions that are impacted by the wounds resulting from our relationships with others.

HeartHealing addresses the deeper relational wounds; the very wounds that scar our sense of self. It is this unique focus that positions it as the ideal modality with which to confront identity wounds. It addresses the root of identity wounding, leading to authentic self-reclamation and identity development.

While mindset work is ideal when reprogramming how we think, it only works on thoughts. By contrast, traditional therapy works on wounds caused in the past, but hardly integrates heart-based healing to remove those deep emotional scars that dictate who we believe we are.

Another thing to consider is that there is an intergenerational aspect to HeartHealing and this is especially powerful when it comes to the Heart of Identity.

Younger generations learn about the world not only through their experience of it, but through the experience of their families. They use the stories of their parents and grandparents to interpret society and life, influencing their identity. (Bray, 2023)

Imagine a parent whose identity was severely impacted in childhood by a negative event or patterns of behaviour involving people they cared about. These changed the parent's view of the world and how they navigate it. Through their narrative, and behavioural interactions with their child, this parent gets to influence their own child's identity. (McGill, n.d.)

Years later, HeartHealing allows that child, now an adult, to heal the wounds caused by their parents through their interactions. But that is not all. HeartHealing makes it possible to energetically heal that wound in the older generations, often uprooting years of pain and confusion, and removing elements that have negatively impacted the identity of members of that family line.

"According to epigenetics…, we don't just carry our trauma imprints, we may also be genetically and energetically carrying the wounding of seven generations before us." (Bray, 2023)

When this practice is applied to identity healing, the implications are significant, as I'll illustrate when discussing my own journey later on.

And now, the question arises: what transformations can individuals experience after healing the Heart of Identity?

Let's consider three different groups of individuals and the transformations that I've witnessed:

1. Individuals with narcissistic parents, partners, siblings or acquaintances:

These individuals often endure extreme identity erosion, where their sense of self is purposefully and systematically undermined (Saeed, 2018). HeartHealing enables us to identify the ways a person's identity was eroded, encourages the client to express anger and pain towards the wounder and activates the imprint of new beliefs that affirm the desired identity. Importantly, it facilitates the creation of protective boundaries for clients who are still in contact with narcissists.

Children of narcissists struggling with clarity, decision-making and communications have:

- taken action to create and grow their own businesses.
- shown up online proudly.
- set firm boundaries with narcissistic parents.

2. People with strong Trust Wounds:

Lack of self-trust often masks a weak sense of identity. Natasha Bray tells us that while experiencing trust wounds, "you may struggle to make decisions about your life or career path and have a deep fear of getting it wrong or making mistakes." Acts of betrayal are often the cause of deep self-trust wounds, altering a person's identity at a fundamental level. Healing the relational wounds that have caused this is quite cathartic.

People experiencing it have:

- developed better relationships with their children and spouses.
- stood up for themselves at work.
- defended their business interests in negotiations.

3. Women with beauty-based trauma:

Women who have undergone body/beauty shaming and find themselves unattractive hide deep identity wounds. Clients rarely disclose this wound. Often we don't admit feeling ugly for fear of being seen as shallow. HeartHealing effectively digs through the layers and exposes it. It is harsh to look at yourself and hate all you see - "I'm ugly, I'm nothing" - leading to self-loathing and self-rejection, damaging your identity. Imagine the relief, when this is healed!

Individuals freed from this:

- start wearing makeup because they can bear to look at themselves again.
- appear on social media and feel good about it.
- dress in colourful clothes because they are not scared to stand out.

As said earlier, the road to healing was not evident for me. I was raised in a culture where mental health was often dismissed. Life was simply to be accepted. Emotional wellbeing was ignored and therapy was for the mentally ill. Though this is changing, 'Healing' is still seen as strange.

To fully understand my journey, we need to look back, not just at my own experiences, but at the legacy I inherited. My mother's story is one of profound wounds. Born out of an extra-marital relationship, she was sent away as a child, carrying the scars of rejection throughout her life. Yet, she presented a facade of independence, confidence and strength. As I learned during my HeartHealing training, she carried deep acceptance and survival wounds, a primal fear rooted in early rejection. This legacy shaped my own identity.

My early childhood, though seemingly 'normal' to me then, was in fact traumatic. I witnessed several instances of domestic violence.

Research has shown that childhood exposure to intimate partner violence (IPV) has a significant correlation to low self-esteem by age thirty (Paradis et al, 2009). The impact of this led to struggling with low self-esteem all the way into adulthood.

Research also shows that children in domestic violence situations often internalise blame and adopt a protective role, and I was no exception. Back then, I became the 'fixer', the 'saviour', a role that demanded I clean up everyone's messes. I carried it with me as a grown up, believing it was a central part of my identity.

Mum was a respected figure in our community: a maths teacher, involved in church, always helping others. She drilled into me that education was everything. "It is the one thing that can never be taken from you!" and so academic and professional success became critical. My identity was built on achievement.

As I grew up I struggled with endometriosis, dismissed by doctors for nearly twenty years as 'just period pain.' This dismissal eroded my trust in my own intuition and body. And then came society's relentless judgment about my fertility. At first, I was incomplete because I wasn't a mother. Later, I wasn't a good mum, because I didn't give my child siblings. It all added another layer of not being enough (the Enoughness Wound was the first one I ever worked on with HeartHealing), and self-doubt.

In my twenties, I moved to Europe, where I still live today. During my relocation around the continent, I consistently tried to build a career as a professional black woman in places that were not ready for me. I remember sending out my CV in Spain to get back disbelief: "You're too young to have done everything written here." Nor did they trust my boss's glowing recommendation letter. They told me my professional life was a lie and left me feeling *I* wasn't real.

I later faced an identity crisis when unforeseen circumstances compelled me to close my growing business. That loss sparked a devastating grieving process and I sought psychological help for the first time. While therapy offered some solace, it was HeartHealing that uncovered the roots of my pain and disorientation. I had fallen into the trap of investing my identity entirely in my work and when the business closed, I was lost. Did I have any value without it?

Through HeartHealing, I began to connect these seemingly disparate threads, to see how my identity was shaped by these emotional wounds. I knew I was unhappy and dealing with unresolved trauma, yet it took me time to realise the central yet hidden connection between my identity and the emotional scars I carried. This powerful modality helped me reclaim my sense of self on multiple levels:

1. Professionally and financially

Shape and claim my new professional identity. I'm working on expanding my business. I've added freelancers on my team, now feeling confident asking for help and trusting my judgement to find the right people to help me expand. I've started charging more, carrying out online events, creating new offers, showing up more as I am, pushing for new opportunities and initiating conversations that will bring me increased visibility.

2. Emotionally

I wrote therapeutic letters to forgive myself for not fitting society's mold of 'perfect' mother or 'complete' woman. I feel deep understanding, peace and love towards my parents, who did their best with the wounds they had. I addressed these through intergenerational HeartHealing. I built self-love, knowing my worth wasn't tied to others. Remarkably, I've stopped the negative self-talk! I faced shame, guilt and self-rejection head-on through HeartHealing, reclaiming my self-esteem.

3. Relationally

Targeted affirmations regularly tell me that everyone is responsible for themselves. I'm not the saviour. I never was. I set up stronger boundaries in my business, so I don't overgive, and in my personal life, so that I'm more peaceful and less resentful. It's freeing to leave others to think for themselves and make their own choices.

My transformation over this past year has been significant.

I'm no longer the woman who allows things to happen to her but the one taking action and creating change that is meaningful for others. I'm my own brand of a silly and loving island girl, mother, wife, friend, professional, and healer.

I wouldn't be anybody else!

If you wish to begin healing your Heart of Identity, start by exploring who you are. This journey of self-discovery, which lies at the core of HeartHealing, involves increasing your self-complexity because you're more than just one thing. In this way, you build a more robust and resilient sense of identity, resulting in a more integrated and authentic you.

1. Write individual letters to those who negatively impacted how you see yourself.

- Tell them what they did and how that made you feel.
- Destroy the letters once you have done step two.

2. Write positive affirmations that contradict the negative feelings identified in your letters. For example, "You made me feel stupid and ugly," becomes, "I am clever and beautiful."

- Read them to yourself daily.

3. List all the roles you play.

    - What values are important in each role?
    - What skills do you use?
    - What emotions are linked to it? Are these negative or positive?
    - Do you wish to continue this role?

4. List your values and beliefs.

    - Are they yours or have you adopted them from others?
    - Do they serve you?
    - Which ones do you want to keep?
    - Any new values you'd like to have?

5. List your passions/hobbies.

    - What do you enjoy? (don't have to excel at them.)
    - Is there anything new you would like to try?

On completing this exercise you'll have a deeper understanding of who you are and a clearer sense of your identity. With your list of affirmations, you can now take practical actions to solidify the identity that feels true to you. Remember, like me, *you* get to choose.

I send you love and healing on your journey of exploration to find who you really are.

References:

Bray, N. L. (2023), *Your next six figures: Reveal and heal your way to receiving and holding your next six-figure year, launch, or month—without the sabotage.* Bray House.

Crocetti et al. (2022), *Identities: A developmental social-psychological perspective.*

https://www.tandfonline.com/doi/full/10.1080/10463283.2022.2104987#abstract

Cheshire West and Chester Council. *Impact of Domestic abuse on children by development level* https://www.cheshirewestandchester.gov.uk/asset-library/impact-of-domestic-abuse-on-children-by-developmental-level.pdf

Descartes, R. (1637), *Discourse on the Method of Rightly Conducting One's Reason and of Seeking Truth in the Sciences*

Erikson, E. H. (1968), *Identity, youth and crisis.* W. W. Norton & Company, Inc.

Mathews, A., (2013), *Woundedness and Authenticity - how do we sort out the distinctions between the two?* https://www.psychologytoday.com/us/blog/traversing-the-inner-terrain/201311/woundedness-and-authenticity

McGill, M., (n.d.), *Healing and Support for Adult Children of Narcissistic Mothers: Empower Yourself* https://circlesup.com/blog/narcissistic-mother-support-group/

Paradis et al (2009), *Long-term impact of family arguments & physical violence on adult functioning at age 30 years: Findings from the Simmons longitudinal study.* Journal of the American Academy of Child and Adolescent Psychiatry. https://www.jaacap.org/article/S0890-8567(09)60029-0/abstract

Saeed, K. (2018), *Healing from Identity Loss After Narcissistic Abuse* https://psychcentral.com/blog/liberation/2018/08/healing-from-identity-loss-after-narcissistic-abuse

Tajfel, H. E. (1978), *Differentiation between social groups: Studies in the social psychology of intergroup relations.* Academic Press.

Yilmaz, E., M.S., Ph.D., (2025) *Identity: Definition, Types, & Examples* https://www.berkeleywellbeing.com/identity.html

ABOUT THE AUTHOR

JANE HOAREAU

Jane Hoareau is a Marketing and Communications Advisor and HeartHealing Practitioner who helps small business owners, independent consultants and freelancers to connect with their ideal audience and attract the types of clients that make them want to jump out of bed in the morning.

Before starting out as a marketing freelancer, Jane worked for over a decade in the travel industry, first in sales and marketing and later as the co-owner of a private excursion business in the Seychelles. After successfully growing an international audience online, enticing clients from around the world to visit her beautiful islands and winning several TripAdvisor awards for her business, she now advises other small business owners and freelancers on how to reach their target markets internationally through their brand identity, creating compelling marketing copy and public relations.

As a HeartHealing Practitioner, Jane helps her clients heal past wounds so they can feel proud and safe to show up as themselves, grow their business and receive success.

To unwind, Jane loves reading (a massive fantasy fan) and enjoys spending time in nature – snorkelling, hiking or hugging a tree.

Jane's available for brand messaging, marketing strategy or writing work as well as private HeartHealing® consultations.

www.janehmarketing.com/hearthealing
jane.hoareau@janehmarketing.com
facebook.com/jane.hoareau
linkedin.com/in/jane-hoareau-content-marketing-and-communications/

2

LYNNE KATZ

THE HEART OF WHOLENESS

I spent a large proportion of my life searching for wholeness. I am proud to say that today I feel whole - I am an empowered mother and woman, confident in my self-worth. I have been able to show my children they are whole too and help them live a whole fulfilling life. Especially my disabled son. Despite the challenges, heartbreaks and mountains I have faced. I've learned that I am whole, I can have a balanced life and have it all. Through healing your heart, you can feel whole and have it all – one can have a fulfilling career, and family, and leisure time, and raise my children.

It was actually my journey to helping my first child, who was born disabled, on his own journey to wholeness that highlighted the need for my own.

I discovered many things on my journey to wholeness. How our children can inspire us to find it before we can do it for ourselves. I realised wholeness isn't found in something outside you - it's found inside.

As I connected more with my own heart, through heart coherence, and deepened my intuition, many new experiences unfolded.

As a result I feel totally aligned with any decisions I make, as all parts of me are in harmony with each other: my heart, my mind, emotions and my physical being. Instead of vacillating back and forth on my decisions, I now act on them and am actually getting things done. My life has moved forward because I am taking aligned action without the struggle. I have healthy boundaries in place in both my private life and in my career.

Self-care has become paramount for me: I ensure that I protect my energy and reset my nervous system at frequent intervals. I went from pleasing others to loving myself first, choosing myself first and satisfying myself first. And this changed everything. Leading with a strong positive vision and a higher purpose; leading with heart, having the inner knowing that love makes all things possible, have led me to a life of ever-growing purpose and fulfillment. I have learned that I am whole and can experience life in its wholeness - a fulfilling career, raising children and leisure time - being all of me. My heart is so full and expansive when I witness how my children have learned how to navigate life with wholeness too.

My goal in this chapter is to share what worked for me, in the hope I can inspire you to take the first or next step on your own journey to wholeness - not just for you, but for your loved ones too.

This chapter has an important message: you are not broken. You are already whole - but life, people and experiences have made you feel differently. We are all on our own journey to wholeness. You already have all you need inside you.

What Is Wholeness?

Wholeness is the state of being complete and integrated, where all aspects of yourself—mind, body, and spirit—are aligned. It involves embracing both your strengths and flaws, acknowledging and healing past wounds without being ruled by them. Bear in mind, though, that wholeness is not perfection! Rather, it is a deep sense of inner coherence, balance, worth, and authenticity. Dan Siegal describes integration and wholeness as "the organizing principle that links the ways energy and information flow is shared (relationships), is shaped (the mechanisms of the embodied nervous system), and is regulated (the mind)." (Siegel, 2012)

The opposite of wholeness is fragmentation, a state in which different aspects of yourself remain disconnected or in conflict. It leads to inner turmoil and often manifests as feelings of emptiness, unworthiness and not feeling good enough. Without integration, without wholeness, you can struggle with knowing your worth, your purpose, and with giving and receiving love. When you lose the connection within yourself, you lose the connection to your loved ones and the world around you. You may even feel broken inside.

Here are some other ways this lack of wholeness might show up for you:

Emotionally - a yearning to feel complete, constantly looking outside of yourself for that missing piece. Second-guessing yourself, overthinking simple choices, or needing validation from others. Feeling overwhelmed or out of control with emotions, reacting intensely, or suppressing feelings entirely, feeling stuck, anxiety, depression. Self-worth and shame – "not good enough," criticising yourself, blaming yourself, taking on too much responsibility for everyone and everything.

Relationally – emotionally shut down and not able to connect fully, attracted to unavailable or unloving partners, push away a loving partner because deep down, you don't believe you deserve love. People-pleasing and overgiving – saying yes when you mean no, feeling resentful, and struggling to set boundaries.

Physically - numbing and disconnection from your body, not taking care of your physical health, eating when not hungry or not eating enough, ignoring pain.

Financially – overspending or not spending at all - living in scarcity where it feels like there is never enough, not feeling able to be financially secure.

Professionally – the fear of being seen, struggling with visibility in your career, in business or personal life, you avoid opportunities due to fear of judgment.

Spiritually - lack of purpose – feeling lost, unmotivated, or unable to commit to a path that truly excites you. Spiritual disconnection, unable to trust intuition or a higher power, struggling with all the big why questions that make life meaningful.

Maybe you recognise yourself in this? You are not alone. Awareness is the first step to changing this.

When you live a life without wholeness there is always a sense of something 'missing'. It can impact every area of your life and your relationships; it is a very lonely state. I was pushed into recognising my inner fragmentation, my own shadows and lack of wholeness by my journey to support my son's right to wholeness, but the fragmentation in me was there even before he was born. It was just that the added pressure of caring for him, and all my other responsibilities that thankfully shone a light on it. Maybe you too have found yourself in crisis and unable to ignore the inner cracks any longer, maybe the cracks have become chasms under the stress or maybe, like me, you just have a sense of something missing? Either way, finding your way back to a state of wholeness will be the greatest life-giving gift and the biggest transformation you can ever imagine.

How Do We Find Wholeness?

The founder of analytical psychology, Carl Jung, believes we achieve wholeness through a process of individuation where conscious and unconscious aspects of the self are integrated to achieve wholeness. He believed that true psychological growth requires confronting and assimilating the Shadow (the repressed or hidden parts of the psyche) and harmonizing it with the Self. This integration leads to a deeper sense of authenticity, balance, and inner completeness.

The Shadow, in Carl Jung's theory, is the unconscious part of the psyche that contains repressed thoughts, emotions, desires, and aspects of the self that one denies or rejects. It can include traits deemed unacceptable by society or one's personal identity, such as aggression, envy, or vulnerability. Confronting and integrating the Shadow is essential for personal growth and wholeness, as it allows for a more authentic and balanced self. We cannot be whole if we are denying or rejecting parts of ourselves.

In Jung's theory, wholeness means encompassing both the conscious and unconscious aspects of a person including the Shadow. Although there is no empirical evidence for his work, his theories have been hugely influential in psychotherapy and have shaped modern psychology.

Healing and Integrating Your Shadow

Each one of us has shadow parts that we hide from the world. These shadow parts are not as scary as they might sound. They are often created in childhood when we were made to feel bad about aspects of ourselves and our personalities. Maybe we fear that part of us will be rejected. Or that part of us isn't good enough. Or that part of us isn't deserving of wholeness, love or success. On my extensive journey of healing, I tried many different modalities to heal and integrate my shadows but found they mostly focused on cognitive or physical aspects leading the conversation.

I'm going to share with you a powerful 'missing piece' to wholeness I discovered on my journey. An approach that allowed me to deeply heal my inner child and integrate more shadows in a matter of months than my whole lifetime previously. Healing your heart. Without an open, engaged heart, wholeness remains fragmented, lacking the compassion, love, and vulnerability necessary for true integration. Finding wholeness doesn't have to take years when you have HeartHealing in your toolkit.

I discovered those shadow parts we reject don't just live in our minds, they live in our hearts. Stored there waiting for us to reclaim and reintegrate them again. Maybe it was the five-year-old you who felt unloved and like you didn't belong in your family. Or the ten-year-old you who felt shamed when you were punished for expressing your anger in the only way you knew how. Or maybe even the fifteen-year-old you who felt broken hearted and rejected when your first love didn't love you back. And every time, you blamed yourself. You blamed that part of you and shut it away in your heart, building metaphorical walls around it to never feel the pain, shame or blame of that part of you again. These walls don't just block your pain, they block your capacity to both give and receive love, they block self-worth and lead to a loss of connection within yourself and with others. A wounded, guarded heart can never truly feel whole.

Finding wholeness lies in healing your heart. It is the gateway to the soul, the key to a vibrant, soul-aligned whole self and life. Healing the stuck emotions and integrating the shadow parts of self from deep within your heart as well as mind is what can bring us into wholeness and a deep state of inner coherence, balance, worth and authenticity. Wholeness isn't just a feeling. It's a deeply spiritual state of being.

In Shamanism, the four chambers of the heart are thought to be linked to different aspects of the soul and each chamber has its own purpose in healing and restoring wholeness. HeartHealing combines modern psychology and many different spiritual practices, including ancient shamanism principles. It works with the heart as a whole, but also individually with each of the four chambers of the heart that all have a specific wound attached and different shadow parts, that when healed and integrated, opens the heart to wholeness.

The shamans also believed that your mind communicates what is in your heart, so a clear heart actually supports a clear mind. This is supported by modern research which has discovered the heart has its own mind or heart-brain, which can independently learn, store memories and communicate to the brain. Our heads and hearts are in constant dialogue and our hearts are leading the conversation (Armour, 1991). This means our mindset, our sense of self-worth and our relationships are significantly influenced by our hearts and the energy held in our hearts. If we are still holding emotional pain or energetic imprints of trauma in our hearts, it is going to affect our minds and the way we think. This is why how we feel is essential to our healing, as it can dramatically impact how we think.

Knowing we are whole doesn't make us feel whole. Just as knowing we are loved doesn't make us feel loved. We need to feel it in our hearts and know it in our minds. When we have the courage to journey into the shadows within our heart, to heal and reintegrate those parts of us we banished, rejected or judged - we feel whole again.

The heart of wholeness? Integrating, accepting and loving every part of you - the shadows and the light.

HeartHealing offers a profound approach to addressing any feelings of a lack of wholeness. There are five core deep-seated Receiving

Wounds which when healed facilitate a return to wholeness and break down the walls around the heart. Each HeartHealing session involves journeying into your heart, meeting your unconscious shadows, healing the wounds that led to them and integrating those forgotten or rejected parts of yourself back into you again. Each session leaves you with a profound sense of completion.

Whilst healing all of the universal wounds facilitates a return to wholeness, for me and my clients the key wound has been the Worth Wound. I believe this is because a lot of our unconscious sabotaging behaviours and rejection towards ourselves is triggered by this wound. The parts of us that feel unworthy, undeserving, are the parts we are most ashamed of.

Through this process, individuals meet parts of themselves they have rejected due to feelings of shame or unworthiness. By healing this, they reintegrate their shadow self and experience a renewed sense of self-worth, allowing them to embody their true essence without overwhelm, inner conflict and self-sabotage.

Clients who have healed their hearts with me have seen incredible results like rekindling their marriages, improving their quality of life, feeling more seen, heard and understood and living more purposefully. Their children begin to thrive too as their wholeness ripples out onto everyone around them.

Your worth and wholeness is found in your heart, and when you heal yours, your whole family benefits.

My Journey to Wholeness

My journey did not begin with wholeness. Six months after we married, my husband and I moved to a different country. I worked in a medical laboratory as a medical technologist, a very left-brained profession. During that time I realized I'd been gifted with an intuitive brain, enabling me to find even the one and only atypical cell on a 100-cell slide. That's when I began to realize a profound difference between using parts of myself versus the whole of myself.

Three years into my marriage, I gave birth to our much wanted firstborn son, who was born prematurely with a very small birth weight. I remember, just like yesterday, the doctor peering over his glasses at me looking back and forth at the large textbook he was holding and our child before he came to the diagnosis that our son suffered from an as yet unknown syndrome which included profound deafness. In one second, the delivery of this news changed the trajectory of our entire lives. The joy of becoming a first-time mother was soon clouded by many concerns about the future.

I made a decision then and there that whatever diagnosis was given, that diagnosis was not going to define my son. My credo was: I'm a powerful creator and my intention to hold the power to create is my reality. My intentions influence my experiences and results I achieve. It was pivotal for me to get consciously intent on what I wanted. I get to empower my intentions and direct the energy in the direction of what I desire. That was my moment of awakening and expansion. This credo appeared before me like a download and that's what I've been following ever since--there is a way. There is another way.

I didn't know it then, but my journey to wholeness began with helping my son on his journey to wholeness. I was determined that his life would be whole. I made the conscious decision to keep my career in addition to tending to my son's every need, since work offered me a sense of purpose and identity. But as I began searching for the best ways to assist him, running back and forth between different professionals, all the while juggling three jobs and keeping up appearances that I was coping, the extreme stress eventually took its toll on me.

I witnessed my son's wholeness and slowly I began to wonder, if we had been able to give our son all we could to have his physical and emotional needs met and witnessed his coming into wholeness, could I have this too?

My first meeting with the esoteric world was Reiki healing, which literally started healing my husband and I on mental, emotional, physical and spiritual levels. I started experiencing a sense of wholeness, where all aspects of myself--mind, body and spirit--are aligned.

Studying Reiki was the first time I allowed myself to take a vacation from work for myself for my wellbeing. This helped me and my family balance the mental, emotional, physical and spiritual stresses of our lives. Huge! I continued with all the levels of Reiki until I became a Reiki Master. Holding classes to initiate other students into this healing system gave me such meaning as I witnessed their healing results. This sense of a newfound purpose uplifted and vitalized me- and from then on, I was unstoppable!

Years later, when my daughter was born, I took a year off from work. I was constantly anxious, drained out of energy, tired of pretending everything was okay with me so as not to burden the people surrounding me. I was well rewarded for my concealment of efforts by society, gaining many accolades for my impressive coping, all the while on the inside I felt ever increasing stress and lack of work-life-parenthood balance. Then, during an occasional stroll down the street, I stumbled upon a studio offering exercise beds. After ignoring my own needs for so long, those exercises must have been the first kind thing I've done for myself in years, and they had awoken something inside of me that was numb for some time. While at the studio, I noticed miscellaneous self-help booklets that piqued my interest—they spoke of self-love and acceptance, offered positive affirmations and fostered a feeling of wholeness that touched upon what was apparently my deepest wound—the Worth Wound. There, right before me, lay the entrance to my path.

That initial information that was revealed to me in those studio booklets was further supported by the work of Dr. Karl Pribram and David Bohm on quantum physics. The world surrounding me suddenly seemed like a giant buffet of possibilities—simply express clearly and coherently what you need and desire, and you'll attract it! Following the healing work I have done, I am now in a place where I *can* have it all—advancing my career, learning new modalities and expanding my knowledge, all the while taking care of my precious son and giving him the optimal care he needs.

I started healing people with Reiki and bought a flourishing healing practice on the side. I loved my lab work and I loved my healing work. While this gave me a sense of purpose and a way to balance my now hectic life due to running back and forth between my jobs and my son's doctors' appointments. I felt depleted energetically and emotionally. I discovered that the Reiki helped me with the mental, emotional and physical aspects of keeping my personal balance. But something was still missing. I was aware that there were not enough hours in the day for me. I was divinely led to the quantum healing world. As I began using these quantum healing technologies on my clients and on myself, I witnessed their amazing transformative powers.

I was being called to connect with even more parts of myself which would lead to even more wholeness. I knew that all I had to do was just trust and take the next step. I found that the divine started working through me.

I took a look at two aspects--transformation means constant shifting of energy and integration into their lives, to cause lasting change. Then I've asked the divine, how can we have a lasting change?

First I learned by myself how to tap into and trust my own desires, and I learned that what I want can be mine now, that I can have what I want and desire now, but I have to clear, heal and resolve what shows up and gets in the way.

I had to know specifically what I wanted, needed and desired versus what others desired for me, versus what they thought I should want and versus what I needed first. At some stages I felt that I was giving my power away to these well-meaning professionals who gave us their advice. So it was a journey for me to know what I wanted for our child. Some things they suggested made sense, while others didn't resonate. I became aware of needing to take back my own power back to best support my child. There were many times when I questioned my enoughness, my worth, as a mother.

I decided not to settle and just sit back and wait for life to happen. I continued with all the necessary medical appointments, all the while utilizing the quantum healing techniques I'd acquired to heal my son, i.e., to bring him back into wholeness by making the decision to give him sign language. The divine dropped this thought into my head, my body and my soul: "When the desire is present, the way is present."

I realized that the divine wanted me to know that I was gifted my son to activate me and send me on a journey of self-discovery to wholeness, authenticity, a purpose-filled life, a life of bringing others into wholeness, and of a deep sense of inner coherence, balance and authenticity, and then I discovered that the magical combination of the healing methods I use, together with the coaching, is what creates long-lasting change. Today I have more than enough energy to support our son who is doing so well; even with his limitations, he feels so whole and has a healthy sense of identity and purpose in life. My spiritual journey led me to trust my intuition and trust my choices and decisions.

A mother's love was my catalyst for finding wholeness. I was determined that my son would have a whole and fulfilling life and I am proud to say that we achieved that goal. And of course, the Universe surprised me and not for the first time, by introducing me to Natasha Bray's HeartHealing Certification - the heart was the missing piece and I knew that it was healing my heart that would bring me the same depth of wholeness that I witnessed in my son. And it was.

My son is now an adult and he is my greatest joy and achievement - he experiences wholeness in his life every day. His birth led me on my own journey of healing and to the discovery of what wholeness truly is. Now it is my passion, my soul purpose, and my deepest desire to help others to know what wholeness is too.

I asked myself: What if I truly believed that I could have, be, and do anything I desire—regardless of my past or present circumstances? What if I become the conscious creator of my life by releasing and healing painful patterns? For me, HeartHealing has been a life-changing journey. It has taught me that we are not broken to be fixed; we are inherently whole and it's about remembering our wholeness through healing. It brought those fragmented and shadow parts back and integrated these parts of myself into one whole self, enabling me to feel whole again. I now stand in my worth, empowered to continue my path of healing—both for myself and for others. My calling is clear: to heal fragmentation which is intrinsically connected to the wounds of the heart, and to guide others toward their own sense of wholeness.

Healing is a continuous journey, and as one heals one's own heart, one becomes a catalyst for others to do the same, stepping into the role of a true Healed Healer, healed and whole.

Please take this bit of advice with you: You are not your challenges!

Your challenges and limitations are only a part of your life journey and do not define your identity or self-worth. See them as an opportunity for self-growth and self-acceptance. Keep focussing on the positives, practice self-care, because your resilience and compassion do make a difference in this world!

I invite you now to ask yourself *'What if I truly believed that I could have, be, and do anything I desire regardless of my past or present circumstances?'*

Imagine yourself five years from now, who fully believed in that truth, living from a place of wholeness and write a letter from your future self.

In the letter, describe:

- What your life looks like now that you've stepped into your desires.
- How it feels to live in wholeness and free of limitations.
- What you had to let go of to get here.
- What you now know to be true about yourself.

Read the letter aloud to yourself as you embrace this truth.

References:

Armour, J. A. (1991), *Anatomy and function of the intrathoracic neurons regulating the mammalian heart.* In: Zucker I H and Gilmore J P, eds. *Reflex Control of the Circulation.* Boca Raton, FL, CRC Press: 1-37.

Siegel, D. J. (2012), *The Developing Mind: How Relationships and the Brain Interact to Shape Who We Are.* 2nd edn. New York: Guilford Press.

ABOUT THE AUTHOR

LYNNE KATZ

Lynne Katz is a HeartHealing Practitioner and Transformational Coach for high achievers, specializing in deep HeartHealing work to help entrepreneurs and business leaders create inner freedom in their businesses and lives.

Lynne has developed **The Conscious Creators Code**™, a transformative process that clears the root causes of success blocks—such as trust wounds, worthiness struggles, and fear of visibility—so her clients can align fully with their purpose and unlock greater wealth and impact.

Her signature approach blends mindset shifts, a heart and soul-aligned strategy and a touch of alchemy to create lasting transformation.

Before launching her own practice, Lynne was a successful professional in the healthcare industry for thirty years. She now helps high achievers have it all by reclaiming their innate power.

Lynne is available for private consultations with her Conscious Creators Code Method™ and for guest speaking on podcasts. She enjoys collaborations with like-minded entrepreneurs, healers and professionals in the wellness industry internationally.

lynnekatz.com
Lynne@Lynnekatz.com
instagram.com/lynnekatzcoach

3

DR. JUDITH BORGER

THE HEART OF SELF IMAGE

The world of self-image is that universe of self that we disappear into inside our minds. It is a universe of worlds relating to the different aspects of our personality, of history, of situations, of beliefs we have about our abilities and of judgements about ourselves - good and bad.

Each person inside of them has a vast and colorful universe of their self-image, of valleys and seas, of mountains and caves. Depending on what you believe about yourself, this universe gets colored in rich shades or drab monotony. It may house fields of blossoms and abundance, overflowing with trees laden with rich fruit, and in other areas may be uninhabitable craters or deserts too hot to sustain any life.

When I look inside my internal world of self-image, I see a world of richness, one of nuances, one of possibilities, of self-love and fierce self-compassion. My self-image – that mental internal representation or view I have of myself – is positive and healed.

I believe that I am worthy of love, worthy of success, and through continued healing I am resetting the eternally swinging balances of work and rest, and my relationships with all the other humans in the world. I am setting boundaries and am a fierce advocate of myself. I prioritize my wellness, my wellbeing, my sleep – because I believe I am worthy.

In business and life, I know that everything is figure-out-able.

I have an innate belief in my abilities to overcome, to adapt and to grow. Through healing, I have transformed this universe into the beautiful one it is, and I have gotten to know it, and myself. Through subconscious HeartHealing as well as through meditation, I journey through my inner world of self-image like an explorer sailing the seas, mapping these universes and reaching and illuminating the crevices.

Self-image is an individual's mental representation of themselves, their internal world so to say, and to a certain extent, their external appearance as it relates to the self and how they view it. Self-image, this internal world, is created by everything we believe about ourselves, including all the stories about who we are, woven into an internal world of considerable complexity, texture and depth, a mental internal tapestry of self.

Our internal world of self-image gets constructed and modified over life through our experiences, as threads get constantly added to this tapestry. Experiences with intense emotion, such as joy and fear and embarrassment and love weave more threads than others. We know through experience and research how pervasive the threads of trauma can be, and how seemingly permanently they can get stored.

Our self-image expands into worlds of possibilities of ourselves, worlds of color, like a beautiful, luscious garden in a dream world. A garden that is watered by positive self-affirmations, by feeling loved and by those parts of ourselves that are flourishing and healthy.

When we are wounded or not feeling enough, that internal view includes us believing we are not enough, or that we are not worthy of love, or success. It is almost as if that part of our self-image and our internal world goes grey and becomes barren lands of thorns devoid of color.

The heart is truly at the heart of self-image, coloring our beliefs about ourselves. It is from the heart that beliefs and emotions and stories flow to both brain and body. Any wounds inflicted on the heart leave our self-image dark. Once wounded, we carry negative beliefs such as not being enough or not being worthy, and wounds relating to trust and love into any relationships and actions in the external world.

This shows up in a variety of patterns. The wounded self is a barren and uncomfortable place. Often, people try to seek external ways to compensate for their internal feelings. This may include an over-attachment to achievements, such as hiding behind professional status and degrees, and defining our worth by our profession, by one's roles and titles. In private life, we may define ourselves by what we do instead of simply by who we are just by being us. We may not be able to rest or relax or be quiet as we have to constantly prove to our wounded self that we are worthy and achieving something to "prove our worth."

Similarly, our wounded self that feels unworthy or not enough may crave constant eternal validation and need the external world to tell us we are worthy. This may include needing to look and act a certain way (that is deemed desirable by society) and relying on status symbols.

One can think of this as creating an artificial safe exterior to compensate for internal feelings of being not enough or not worthy of love so that society may deem us enough and worthy of love. This may manifest as over-obsession with being at the "perfect" weight, with designer clothes and purses, a fancy car, having had plastic surgery to look perfect, and fitting into all the right societal circles. In our current world of social media, we may be obsessed with curating the "perfect" social media image of ourselves, maybe even to include reliance on filters to make pictures of ourselves appear more flawless, or needing a certain number of likes and views of our social media channels as external validation.

A wounded self-image may also limit us to and trap us in relationships and situations that we deem we deserve based on the wounds of the heart. Childhood patterns of trust wounds with a narcissistic parent may be repeated in a current partner who is unpredictable, unsupportive and emotionally cold. Wounds of confidence may limit the job position someone applies to and explain a job plateau where this person does not believe they can achieve more despite the people around them clearly seeing their potential. Wounds of perfectionism may cause an individual ongoing frustration and a series of job resignations or breakups over seemingly minor issues, or the inability to be an effective manager or leader. Wounds of love may have consequences that expand like endless tentacles through every aspect of someone's life, including their relationship to every other human in their life, from their parents to their children, from their lovers to their friends.

The single most important relationship, the one that is at the core of self-image, is the relationship to self. Any wounds of the heart deeply impact our relationship to ourselves. As our internal world is the mental representation of self, what we believe about ourselves will determine how we treat ourselves. Positive beliefs that we have about ourselves, where we truly feel that we are worthy, we are lovable, we are enough just for being us without doing anything are those beautiful parts of our internal world that are the sunshine, the warmth, the blossoming flowers in rich colors, the clear skies with butterflies and peaceful, abundant nature.

This positive relationship to self leads to positive internal self-talk and lots of self-compassion for the parts of us that may experience failure and pain. Examples of this are self-soothing and taking care of ourselves in emotional and physical ways that replenish us.

When our heart is wounded, the beliefs we hold about ourselves become negative and result in negative self-talk, where the internal voice becomes that of self-blame, self-criticism and often shame. Self-compassion is absent, and our internal world of self-image is dark and jarring and unpleasant.

The heart is the central hub of self-image, as from there the strongest energetic frequencies originate, flowing through the entire body, including the subconscious and conscious minds. The heart is the creator of the universe of self-image. The heart's incredible range of energetic frequencies gives birth to the colors and flavors and shades and subtleties of the internal world. Given the depth of emotion and wisdom stored within the heart, healing the heart is the way to heal the wounds that affect self-image.

So much of our self-image lives in corners of the internal world the conscious mind has never explored or has access to. Conscious thought encompasses the awareness we have of our thoughts, feelings, and environment at any given moment. It's the deliberate, intentional aspect of our cognition.

In contrast, subconscious (or unconscious) processing operates below the level of conscious awareness, influencing behavior and thought patterns without explicit recognition. Science has shown that the majority of our thoughts are subconscious, and that the conscious mind can only access a fraction of all that is happening (Budson, 2022). Imagine the universes of self-image and conscious thought being only one world or even part thereof, certain valleys and rivers and forests with familiar patterns of birdsong. And then, there is everything else; the subconscious, the heart, wondrous worlds of exotic shapes and sounds and adventures - and also wounds and hauntings we don't perceive consciously, but that nevertheless are the deadly, hideous creatures hiding in the shadows that influence all we do.

Attachment theory posits that the patterns established in early caregiver-child relationships form internal working models, which shape a child's expectations and interactions in future relationships (Cassidy, 2013). The effects of early attachments extend into adulthood, influencing emotional regulation, social relationships, and mental health.

Depending on the exact relationship pattern experienced, we can see this show up as wounds of the heart: mother wounds, father wounds, wounds of trust or not enoughness. These are all imprinted throughout childhood and will affect someone's entire life. The complex moon craters devoid of life within the universe of self-image, the thorny bushes and the driest deserts. HeartHealing is a unique modality able to dive into the subconscious, unravel the layers of wounding and heal the wounds of the heart rapidly and with lasting change.

HeartHealing utilizes a psychological concept called the inner child to heal existing childhood wounds. The inner child refers to the subconscious part of ourselves that retains the emotions, memories and experiences from childhood. During HeartHealing, we connect with our inner child within the safety of the heart. We give our inner child the voice it never had during childhood, as well as giving our inner child the love and validation her or she needed. We heal the wounds our inner child still carries within us. Doing so heals the wounds our adult version carries concurrently as these two versions of us (past and present) share one heart, one memory, and one concept of self.

Central to our relationship to ourself is our inner voice, our narrator, the thoughts that are constant companions to our day. When the self and our self-image are wounded, our inner voice can become full of self-criticism, self-blame and self-shame. A screeching chorus of negativity. The wounds of the heart of not enough, not worthy, not confident can cause our inner voice to echo the voices and phrases we heard from those who hurt us in the first place.

By healing the heart and giving the inner heart child the love he or she always wanted and needed, the inner voice transforms into one of self-love and self-compassion. Valleys within our inner universe that were formerly flooded or inaccessible to us can grow beautiful vines, trees and flowers, becoming a habitat for loving kindness, and self-compassion. With self-compassion, we take a benevolent and supportive attitude towards ourselves rather than condemning ourselves coldly (Neff, 2023) We acknowledge our shortcomings while caring for ourselves regardless. We practice self-acceptance and self-kindness. When we respond to ourselves with warmth, we feel validated, supported, and encouraged, in a similar manner to how we feel when we receive kindness from another.

Transformations through HeartHealing are magnificent, especially as self-compassion rises within us. Self-compassion can take a tender, nurturing form, especially when it is aimed at self-acceptance or soothing distressing emotions. We are able to give ourselves everything we emotionally need from within us. However, self-compassion can also take a fierce, powerful, agentic form, especially when it is aimed at self-protection, meeting our important needs or motivating change (Neff, 2023). We become better advocates for ourselves and set boundaries that protect us. The results may be huge successes vocationally, financially and also emotionally by protecting our sacred life force energy.

By healing wounds of love, trust and worth, our self-image in those corresponding worlds changes, and we see ourselves worthy of healthy relationships with others. The internal trees of life and love blossom, bloom and bear fruit. We no longer act from a place of perceived brokenness and repeat unhealthy relationship patterns from childhood. We embrace wholeness and love and our existential divine right to peace and love and belonging.

I grew up with a very poor self-image due to my own wounded heart. Not once throughout my entire childhood did I hear, "I love you" from my parents. What is burned in my memory though, is a family member telling me that I was worth, "less than the dirt of the earth". I also believed my grandmother who told me how much I did not belong.

Any positive recognition I received was for achievements, and my siblings and I competed for our mother's attention and praise, and also against each other, while my youngest sibling was the golden child. The golden child in family dynamics and psychology refers to a child who, in a dysfunctional family relationship, is favored over other siblings. As the "problem child" in this family dynamic myself, I was criticized, and punished, which led to my low self-esteem and also to a degree of independence and rebellion.

This upbringing led me to believe that I was not worthy of love. I had wounds of the heart of trust, and love and enoughness. As a teenager I was a rebel and put myself in a lot of danger.

I moved to another continent and built my own life - the only way I knew how: by working incredibly hard and by achieving. Functioning by having a coat of armor made of steel that hid and locked away the parts of my self-image that were worlds of destruction and darkness and trauma. I got a medical degree, my top choice residency and a prestigious fellowship, while working. I chose Emergency medicine, a field of medicine that was tough and raw and full of trauma, as it felt the most real and the most familiar to me.

My romantic relationships were where the wounds of my heart showed up the most: a series of intimate relationships with physical, emotional, sexual or financial abuse. Partners that cheated. Partners that put me down. Partners that reinforced that I was not worthy of love. Partners that reflected my wounded self-image back to me. That part of me and my inner world that felt like a war zone of destruction and unworthiness and brokenness. That part of my world where no beauty of flowers grew, so utterly devoid of innocence.

After years and years of cognitive behavioral therapy and other forms of counseling and coaching, the deep wounds of the heart remained. There were certainly changes in parts of me, like new snow caps on the mountains of self-image. However the heart was still not healed, and with it the deep wounds remained, sending their frequencies throughout all areas of my self-image like waves of sounds or light. It was not until I found HeartHealing that I was able to truly heal and become whole. That those vast lands of apocalyptic destruction were able to grow life, and luscious fields emerged full of grass and flowers and wildlife. That rivers sprang and forests appeared filled with wonder and safety and magic.

There were obvious wounds of the heart to heal: those of not enoughness, of being not worthy of love. Wounds of trust, love and worth.

Every layer of healing brought wholeness to a different part of my self-image, of my relationship to self, and illuminated caves and crevices of universes so full of magnificence and wonder and beauty. The healing of every wound of this and of past lives has transformed me. The shift in my self-image has been fundamental.

I no longer feel that I have to 'do' to be worthy. I am no longer seeking external validation from my achievements, or level of income, or the recognition and praise from others. I am my biggest advocate, my biggest defender and the one that keeps my heart and soul sacred. Through HeartHealing, I was able to give my inner heart child all the love and safety she ever needed. I was able to give her unconditional love and acceptance. I have the ability to repeatedly give myself every bit of reassurance and love and compassion I need at any given moment in time.

My self-image has transformed into one of wholeness and of being worthy, which has profoundly affected everything else in life. My inner voice has shifted to one of self-love and self-compassion. With loving kindness, I see how in my past, I attracted romantic partners that were reinforcing my own broken self-image. Healed, from a place of wholeness, I can form healthy relationships that are based on mutual respect and self-agency, support autonomy and allow for authenticity and vulnerability. The entire universe of my self-image has changed. It is flourishing in every dimension. No inner world remains untouched.

When our self-image is whole, we can truly fall in love with all that we are, and exhibit high levels of self-acceptance and self-compassion. Common patterns that I have observed when the heart is healed is that people are able to embrace themselves just as they are. They are able to see their common humanity. Healed, they release the negative thoughts and self-talk that reflect the voices of those that hurt them and instead shift towards the voice of a loving, supportive friend.

The Heart becomes whole. Self-image becomes assured, abundant with goodness and a beautiful rainforest teaming with interesting inner life. As the wounds of the heart are healed and our self-image is healed, everything in our life changes.

We believe in our wholeness, trust our intuition and set boundaries that protect our energy. Because we feel enough and worthy, we engage in meaningful relationships with other individuals that reflect our worth. We are able to receive their affection and kindness. We no longer accept being treated less than in jobs or relationships, as it no longer reflects our worthy self-image. When we are healed and feel whole, we no longer need status symbols or excessive praise or are dependent on social media likes and views to tell us that we are indeed loved and accepted. Because we feel that we are accepted and whole and we love and trust on the inside. We no longer have to achieve or constantly do, instead we can just be Us. In our humanness. In our wholeness, in our healedness. With our self-image that unfolds into beautiful worlds of riches, of wonders, of magic.

It is from our self-image; all the beliefs and thoughts that we have of ourselves, all the mental images, all the remembrance in our gifts and traditions that we hold, that we make every decision in life. Our entire construct of self lives in this wondrous internal world, made up from emotions, memories, subconscious and conscious thought, fueled by the frequencies of the heart. When we are healed and our self-image is healed, every decision comes from wholeness, from healedness. And that is a most beautiful place.

In order to start shifting your self-image, I invite you to start practicing mindfulness to become increasingly aware of all the things you believe about yourself as well as the tone of your inner voice as separate from your essence. Mindfulness is a type of balanced awareness that neither avoids nor exaggerates the discomfort of our present-moment experience (Shapiro, 2006). Because we need a certain degree of perspective, mindfulness is the pillar on which self-compassion rests. Simply observe the internal judgements you have about yourself. Let them come and take note. Please avoid judging yourself for your inner voice. Just collect information.

As a next step, practice mindful self-compassion. Try speaking to yourself kindly in times of struggle, like you would speak to your best friend or your child. (*"I know this is hard. I see you trying your best. It's OK to feel disappointed. I'm proud of you for…."*)

Research has shown that informal mindfulness practices can be just as impactful in learning self-compassion as formal meditation practice (Neff, 2023).

A second practice I would invite you to try is to write a HeartHealing based letter to your inner child. This will allow connection, validation, nurturing, love, compassion and healing to flow from you to your inner child.

To do so, create a safe and loving space. Close your eyes, take a few deep breaths, and imagine your younger self at an age when they needed love and protection and reassurance.

Start by writing a warm greeting, imagining your inner child as someone you care about deeply. ("*Dearest [name] - I love you. I see you and it is so great to connect with you.*") As you continue to write the letter, acknowledge your inner child's feelings and experiences based on your past. (Example: *"I know how hard it was for you to keep trying to feel loved and no-one did." "I see how absolutely terrified you were when X happened.")*

Offer him or her comfort, reassurance and love while empowering and reparenting your inner child. What were the words you, as a child, needed to hear and never did? ("*You are enough just as you are." "What happened was never your fault and I am so sorry you had to experience that." "I love you unconditionally.")*. End the letter with more love and a commitment to your inner child. ("*I am so proud of you and I am always here for you, to protect you.")*

Allow this outpouring of love and compassion to flow from your heart to the rest of you. Allow it to nourish and emotionally soothe yourself. Imagine that universe of self inside you, receiving warmth and sunshine and high vibrational energy. You are on the path to healing your self-image. It is a wonderful and wondrous journey into the heart of self-image that awaits, with rewards that will surprise and delight you.

References:

Budson, A.E., Richman, K.A., Kensinger, E.A. *Consciousness as a Memory System.* Cogn Behav Neurol. 2022 Dec 1;35(4):263-297. doi: 10.1097/WNN.0000000000000319. PMID: 36178498; PMCID: PMC9708083.

Cassidy, J., Jones, J.D., Shaver, P.R. *Contributions of attachment theory and research: a framework for future research, translation, and policy.* Dev Psychopathol. 2013 Nov;25(4 Pt 2):1415-34. doi: 10.1017/S0954579413000692. PMID: 24342848; PMCID: PMC4085672

Neff, K.D. *Self-Compassion: Theory, Method, Research, and Intervention.* Annu Rev Psychol. 2023 Jan 18;74:193-218. doi: 10.1146/annurev-psych-032420-031047. Epub 2022 Aug 12. PMID: 35961039.

Shapiro, S.L., Carlson, L.E., Astin, J.A., Freedman, B. *Mechanisms of mindfulness.* J Clin Psychol. 2006 Mar;62(3):373-86. doi: 10.1002/jclp.20237. PMID: 16385481.

ABOUT THE AUTHOR
DR JUDITH BORGER

Dr Judith Borger helps high-achieving women create their most authentic and beautiful lives, to include their self-image and relationship to self, relationships with others and their businesses.

She believes healing is the ultimate luxury and the key to personal happiness and financial success.

Dr Borger is a mom of three, wife, board-certified physician, HeartHealer, and successful business owner of Concierge Medical Arts and JB Coaching LLC.

Concierge Medical Arts is a concierge medical aesthetics and wellness practice located in Fayetteville, NC, offering full-spectrum non-surgical medical aesthetics and wellness services centered on the patient's experience and goals.

Dr Borger's coaching brand encompasses the top 5% global podcast "The Aesthetic Doctor" as well as Luxury Retreats, HeartHealing, Life and Business Coaching. Her zone of genius is in seeing infinite possibilities. Dr Borger is an experienced public speaker and teacher who has hosted workshops throughout the US and Canada. She is available for speaking, coaching and teaching engagements as well as private consultations.

In her spare time, Dr Borger enjoys Reformer Pilates and traveling.

www.judithborger.com
borgercoaching@gmail.com
instagram.com/doctorborger
facebook.com/conciergemedicalarts
Podcast: https://podcasts.apple.com/us/podcast/the-aesthetic-doctor/id1611578378

4

SUSANNAH ROBINSON

THE HEART OF REINVENTION

Midlife is nature's call to dig deep into our souls and bring forth the Elysian harvest of this lifetime. It's a coming of age. And with this realization, we can chafe at the prospect of living the rest of our lives pretending and projecting personas that no longer align with who we truly are.

There is work to do here in the middle passage of life and opportunity as well. A reconciliation of self and a heart of reinvention in which unwanted roles and expired dreams fall away leaving space to create from the truth of our being. It is our time to shift from the busyness of roles to the sacredness of soul.

While midlife doesn't have to be a crisis, it can be a wakeup call. An imperative to finally own all of who you really are for the rest of your life. As Dr. Brené Brown, American academic and author, said, "Midlife: when the Universe grabs your shoulders and tells you 'I'm not f-ing around, use the gifts you were given.'"

We all live from a cast of internal characters without stopping to consider if their stories are wholly honoring who we are and our heart's desire. Some originate from default roles like daughter/

son or sister/brother or chosen roles like mother/father, wife/husband, employee/entrepreneur. Other unwelcome parts arise from past trauma or parentification, a childhood shouldering of adult responsibilities at great emotional cost. Rather than a role's origin, it's the beliefs, strategies, and stories about who and how we think we have to be in any role which diminishes our free expression.

Midlife is often a pivot point of perspective. We've lived enough life to differentiate between dealbreakers and desires, dead ends and divine direction. The heart's call for reinvention grows insistent. Of course, change is constant, yet the middle years are an enlightening era on the pilgrimage home to yourself.

I used to think of middle age as old. The reality is the world average life expectancy is seventy-six for women and around seventy for men, making midlife thirty-eight and thirty-five respectively (Worldometers, n.d.). More of us are in the second half of life than we thought.

Well beyond halfway, I've experienced the seismic upheaval of shifting roles moving from childcare to parent care, from chasing career paths to creating a calling, from living a lifespan to optimizing a healthspan.

This is how I arrived at HeartHealing, asking myself if I was spellbound by the stories of my life or if there was any room left for new beginnings. The definitive answer was yes. There was the possibility of revitalization not through a single healing moment but rather a sacred journey of breath and being.

HeartHealing not only helped create a grand sequel in the story that is my life, it also gave me power to rewrite my prologue as well with ancestral and past life healing. Today I embody my innate gifts as a safe and gracious space, healing myself and others as we grow hope through life, loss, and renewal.

The blessings of reconnecting my inner and outer lives have become the alchemical 'wonderfuel' of reinvention. No longer am I like Cinderella's stepsister trying to fit into someone else's shoes. I walk with my own soul, holding the truth of my heart's calling in the world.

Reinvention challenges the borders of our being, starting with our innerwise compass. For many, yearning for reinvention begins when you see yourself in others. The recognition of a quality or trait redirecting you back to who you remember yourself to be. Something speaks to your heart's longing producing an 'Ah Ha!' recognition. This is where my journey with HeartHealing began, suddenly seeing all the pieces and paths of my life come together with the singularity of divine direction.

To be clear, the journey of transformation is not about throwing out the past and being someone you're not. Rather, it's inventing yourself anew, a refinement of your authentic self, because of or despite, a lifetime of experiences, choices, and the resulting beliefs and patterns leading you to this place in time.

Some of those beliefs and patterns have worked for you and some haven't. It's the dissonance of unworkability which most often attracts seekers of an authentic, aligned life to HeartHealing.

Many clients arrive with a feeling of suffering or being lost, and it has many faces including sadness, fear, grief, anger, despair, judgement, insecurity, anxiety, and disappointment. The quagmire of being stuck in an ill-fitting life is a strong motivator for change.

Steeped in the holy trinity of regrets: should've, would've, and could've, suffering and feeling lost are poisons of disillusionment in the well of life. They give us the illusion of one day, someday possibilities, but really, they are 'stopabilities' bringing hope of an authentically lived life to a full inactionable stop.

Many have built moats around the interior castle of their vulnerability. Even the most outwardly appearing successful individuals can have areas of distress. Some feel they can't show the outside world they feel less than. Others never leave space for contemplative rest, allowing perfect to become the enemy of good enough.

Rather than viewing suffering and regret as the cause of life's problems, consider them to be emotional signposts signaling you've strayed from the answers within you. The good news is by expanding your awareness, there's a way back to your true light. Reinvention is a journey beyond self-imposed limitations and beliefs. You're not lost; you're simply rerouting.

As the great Sufi mystic Rumi said, "If your heart is your guide, you will find your way home." You're closer than you think. You couldn't have the awareness of suffering or regret without a deep inner knowing you're not meant to live that way, and you have the power to do something about it.

Yet when clients reach out, upset and suffering are stifling their experience of wholeness and joy. The reward of reinvention then is to harvest a new experience of life. The process brings forth the beauty and wonder unequivocally defining who you are using your heartfelt truth to bridge your life's experience with your soul's substance.

Using a bespoke blend of HeartHealing and breathwork, my clients change the frame of their lives without losing the picture. It is a Hope Journey™ from remembering and reconnecting to recalibrating and rejoicing.

Achieving heart harmony and transformation need not be hard. Sometimes the simplest shifts in being, like gratitude, can produce the greatest gifts. Just as the body cannot exist without breath, the soul needs an aligned heart to optimize the human experience. With renewed hope and sense of direction, the beauty of reinvention is that the more healed your heart, the more your life is balanced with soulful purpose.

Your power lies within. You'll find, as author Jo Coudert said, "Of all the people you will know in a lifetime, you are the only one you will never leave or lose. To the question of your life, you are the only answer. To the problems of your life, you are the only solution." Your heart is the key.

There was a time I needed that reminder. I found myself in the early sunrise hours of a cool Hawaiian morning turning the last pages of a self-help book.

I was in paradise, but not peaceful. Finally, I had time to breathe and look at life. I was dissatisfied with my assessment. I owned a nearly half million-dollar business I wanted to escape. One son had left for college while two others were quickly approaching the same milestone. I was missing precious time with them, and devastatingly, I was also ignoring my heart's desire. I felt I didn't even know what it was anymore. I had lost my way, myself, my heart.

Certainly, the need for change was at hand, but there was also a deeper stirring. The need for course correction back to what was important to me. To listen to the whispers of my heart.

I was hearing nothing, but then how could I overcome my internal chaos? My wish was clearly present as evidenced by the book on my lap about finding my north star. But it was just a wish, and it wasn't enough. Wishes left me in the same place, unfulfilled and dissatisfied. They left me blind to what was already there including the purple majesty and miracle of a new day unfolding before me.

Hot tears of frustration began to roll. As I slid toward the depths of despair, a sudden noise shocked me from my sucky, stuck state. I could hear and feel the thump of his shoes on the walkway before I saw him. My heart was pounding, but then so was his.

A lone soldier running, creating, and aligning with his own being. With every stride, a word. Every dozen paces, a mantra. "I AM 100% RESPONSIBLE FOR MY EXPERIENCES IN THIS LIFE."

Like CPR, it was the shock I needed. He didn't say circumstances. He didn't say wishes. In that moment, he reminded me what I feel in all moments shows me how I'm choosing to experience life. And that was a seed of hope.

Hope, unlike wishes, requires action. As Jane Fonda, activist and actress, said in a 2024 interview, "Hope is a muscle like the heart. You have to activate it to feel it."

Many of us don't go beyond the why's and how's of the mind and wishes never bloom in the garden of hope. To grow, reinvention requires integration of heart, mind, and spirit. It builds resilience, and it creates breathing space for rediscovering joy and living from a new narrative.

Healing the heart doesn't mean life stops presenting challenges. For me, the promise of 2025 began with great hope for business expansion.

Because of my own HeartHealing work, I felt this despite 2024's wave of big life events including becoming an empty nester, health concerns, becoming a grandma-to-be, and multiple parental stressors from hospitalizations to hospice, and a sad but beautiful passing just before Christmas.

The year 2024 was not an easy year, and yet the practice of staying true to what matters would provide the needed strength for the first days of 2025. While out for a training run my husband of thirty-six years was hit by a car.

The miracle is he survived, but life as we knew it drastically changed. In the beginning were all the feels: shock, confusion, anger, fear, and devastation. We averted death's doorway, and even as life continued, it wasn't the same.

Resilience built from a daily self-practice of breathwork and the support of my own HeartHealers, provided an opening to ask, "What am I feeling in this moment?" And then feel it. "What are the blessings here?" And then welcome them into my grateful heart. "What learnings can be gathered?" And then grow from them.

A favorite Carl Jung quote has always been about the richness of looking inward, yet most leave off the most important landmark on the map of reinvention. He said, "Your vision will become clear only when you look into your heart. Who looks outside, dreams; who looks inside, awakens."

The heart of reinvention gets to the soul of what matters. It's hope in action. If you're masterful at 'what ifs,' isn't it time to make those 'what ifs' masterpieces of the heart?

Creating your wholehearted self necessitates addressing emotional, psychological, and spiritual healing to navigate transitions with clarity and intent. On your Hope Journey™, holistic shifts in identity, roles, and stories, create openings for profound personal growth and transformation in all areas of life.

It's not unusual for clients wanting to address an issue in one area of life to discover that the restrictive belief was rooted in another. Like spokes on a wheel, one area out of integrity impacts the whole wheel of life.

Time and again, those wanting to embrace their entrepreneurial spirit discovered the constriction was not their abilities but rather the origins of childhood beliefs about worthiness, safety, or money. Others wanting to be free of relationships found what they no longer liked in their partner or friend was a shadow aspect of themselves being overly protective and needing to break free.

Sometimes personas or parts no longer supporting you were created as a childhood protection. Studies show more than half of U.S. adults have faced adverse childhood experiences (ACEs), from abuse to family dysfunction, which are significantly associated with lower psychological and social well-being as well as diminished life satisfaction (Mosley-Johnson et al, 2019).

Freeing yourself of limiting beliefs created by ACEs is a powerful start on the path of reinvention. Time is your most precious capital, and healing work not only impacts your timeline but also others' too.

Randy Jirtle, Ph.D. is an innovative researcher in epigenetics studying the inheritable changes in gene function, or basically the familial on-off switches. His research, which he describes as "the science of hope," reveals the impact of early life experiences, especially ACEs, on midlife health and beyond. Equally exciting, he has found epigenetic changes are possibly alterable, offering an optimistic avenue for disease prevention (Jirtle, 2022).

Additional research focused on heart rate variability, hypnosis, and epigenetics suggest heart-centered practices are powerful approaches to healing. In a study of mind-body therapies impacting cancer and the immune system, author Maria Michalopoulos noted the potency of shifting our focus inward, "We are only beginning to conceptualize how the mind/body psychotechnologies truly promote healing…[and] the human body's God-given ability to heal and the power of the unconscious mind" (Michalopoulos, 2018).

The new frontier of gene studies suggests accelerated healing modalities such as HeartHealing and breathwork support epigenetic modulation. Embracing reinvention by healing your heart can restore wholeness and health for yourself and future generations.

Once your soul seeker's truth has been revealed through processes of remembering, releasing, and resourcing yourself, the suffering of an unfulfilled life immediately loosens its grip in all areas of life. Reconciling early life relationships opens the doorway of reconnection within yourself and with others. I've witnessed fractured families, reconnect through healthy communications and boundaries.

I've also walked with clients who are entangled in grief having lost loved ones or themselves through loss of relationship, job, or dreams. In my own experience, there was nothing like the death of a child. The human cracks. The mother of all endings nearly became the end of this mother. My heart seemingly shattered, and my breath, for a time, became a betrayal, necessary but unwanted.

Rebuilding with breathwork and HeartHealing, I became a "yes" to life again. From utter destruction to indomitable renewal, life flourished once more. Having this transformative experience is a gift I pay forward as clients reconcile loss with life and realize there is grace to be felt in every moment, even the hard ones.

Clients with life-altering diagnoses find joy in living the story which is theirs to create and in letting go of the stories and roles that no longer serve them. And for others, compassion and understanding create openings of forgiveness, not for the inexcusable, but for their little selves whom, once upon a time, they harshly judged as not enough.

In all circumstances, unbound through HeartHealing and breathwork, love is once again present, liberating life while restoring a sense of wonder and soul purpose. An incomparable reinvention of the heart.

Healers often connect because of our common soul path. One such explorer felt drained and lost in her expression of healing contribution. On her Hope Journey™, using HeartHealing and breathwork, she was able to reconnect with her deeper resolve once again. It was as if her future self was saying, 'I came back to give you thirty more years of joy.' She remembered there's a difference between connection and oneness. Oneness is not bathing in the light. It's being the light.

Sometimes in life, there just aren't words. But there's always breath. If your soul is the destination, and your body is the vehicle, then your heart is the driver and your breath is the fuel necessary to move you from one destination to another, both physically and ontologically.

ACE imprints from early stages of life can maintain their presence in somatic tissues. Left unaddressed, they can impact personal health, physiologically and psychologically, and epigenetically influence future generations. Children learn what they live, and they live what they learn. Clients with the courage to say, "It stops here" break the cycles of familial patterns.

Self-regulated breathing is a beautiful beginning to the reinvention process. After all, each breath is an invitation to refresh and begin anew.

Breathing is one of the most accessible autonomic physical functions which can also be consciously controlled. Slow, controlled breathing techniques like the Conscious Connected Breath enhance autonomic plasticity by improving your heart rate variability and promoting altered states for healing (Zaccaro et al 2018).

Breath is a powerful tool of emotional attunement facilitating the body's natural unraveling of what the mind cannot always do through language alone. You can't breathe deeply and worry at the same time.

In a dance of hope and healing, breathwork facilitates the release of grief, pain, and trauma stored in the body without the need for language. HeartHealing breaks the grip of past beliefs, freeing the present, and giving voice to your truth and future possibilities.

Reinvention is about building a life of resonance. A daily practice of breathwork and HeartHealing imprints is like starting each dawn with a love note from spirit. And with that blessed hope comes the difference between living your life fully aligned and leaving your life unlived.

Growing up in a transient home due to my father's military career, I often found myself trying to fit in or fly under radar, both of which made me a master of roleplay. The older I got, the harder it got. Then again, in some ways it got easier, because I became more practiced at my mesmerizing. Painfully shy in high school and faced with yet another midyear move was the first time I realized I could consciously create a different me. After all, no one at the new place would know the old me. Of course, the gregarious role didn't really fit me any better than the shy persona.

Moving through life, expanding, contracting, and adapting, there were micro changes and mega moments of devastation to life as I knew it. In those moments, I felt spiritually orphaned from myself and experienced life from a belief that things just don't work out. There was someplace, anyplace, to be other than me.

Reinvention is a result of seeking our wholeness, through necessity or desire. The first was when reality gobsmacked me and the second was when I reached into the heart of what mattered to choose. It's at this intersection of chaos and creation that reinvention begins. Where I could move beyond creating change out of necessity and into the realm of generating a transformative opportunity to return to my tenderhearted self.

My journey home began. Like Michaelangelo's David, I had to release all that wasn't me. First, I had to see those unwelcomed roles and honor them, for they too were a part of my journey.

With an explorer's spirit, I found myself following my heart and went on to learn interpersonal hypnotherapy, the depth work of Jungian coaching, grief guidance with David Kessler, and the power of Conscious Connected Breathwork for somatic release.

And so, having arrived at HeartHealing, I was ready to welcome my newly discovered self and yet not quite sure how to integrate it all into my life, my spiritual being, and my business. HeartHealing pulled it all together with the love of a carefully crafted yet exquisitely beautiful heirloom quilt. It freed the last vestiges of my past, while grounding me in my gifts for a future of unlimited possibility.

On my HeartHealing journey I discovered I've always been a healer, yet I didn't trust myself to be it. My secret belief was I felt too broken to ever help anyone if I needed help myself. It was this linchpin which required liberation. The time had come. I was done living by default.

Determined, I was ready to dissolve what was in the unseen in order to be seen. Having done a lot of healing work, a phrase many clients say to me, there were still substantial beliefs to heal and shift from my rolework of go-to patterns, to my soulwork, an authentic alliance of hope and heart guidance.

Much had been neatly tucked away by behaviors and beliefs driven by survival. From a healed perspective, I can see now there was much trauma. I had good reason not to trust and therefore tightly control my experiences. The world had seemingly taken much from me: my sense of belonging anywhere, a feeling of stability and safety.

It didn't occur as trauma at the time. It just was what it was, and the primary strategies of my life became about trust and control so I could be perceived as "enough." It gave me toughness and determination, yet it also left me wary, in a constant state of high alert. Resourcefulness became an artform and a military-like defensive maneuver. Being helpful was a way to be loved and gave me, as writer Anne Lamott describes, "the sunny side of control." The roles I took on were: be smart, be strong, be stealthy.

Born from this is what Natasha calls the Hidden Healer. I'd use my gifts, but only for the fortunate few who found me. I kept training to ensure I was always more than enough as an abundant resource of wisdom and compassion. The conflicting roles of overdelivering and doing it all myself had me spinning out in analysis paralysis. Like a rocking chair, I had a whole lot of movement without going anywhere.

Healing the Receiving Wounds, especially those of Trust and Enoughness, liberated me. Continuing to receive revitalizing gifts through ancestral timelines, I more deeply stepped into my soulwork. Releasing the need for projection, which is after all a protection against disappointment and the pain of potential failure, it felt as if the fear and grip of negative beliefs and familial patterns simply fell away.

In the dawn of my self-reclamation, I became more than enough. The inner sage could experience the miracle that was me all along. And with it came clarity, hope, and purpose. As James Hollis, Jungian psychologist, said "To ask, every day, 'What matters in the end?' is to create the possibility of differentiated choice, the potential to overthrow the tyranny of our history, so is to honor something in us that has always been there, waiting for our courage."

Here my heart has blossomed. As a new story unfolds, I've reinvented the rest of this life in the smallest yet biggest of ways by listening for my truth and following my heart.

Hope is a journey of grace, and my heart is the portal uniting my inner and outer lives. Guided by the soulforce within, I know I'm exactly where I need to be, exactly who I need to be. There is truth here and surrender, beauty and love reconciling the pieces of this life with the wholeness of peace. And it is always more than enough.

And now, in the spirit of reinvention at midlife, or NOW, which is always the best time, what are your heart and soul asking of you?

Journey to Your Heart's Desire

Begin with three deep, nurturing breaths.
Attune to your heart with gratitude, promising to listen.
Think of an everyday belief or role inhibiting you. Likely found in an area of life that feels dissatisfying.

Interview yourself about that belief, trusting your first impressions.

Is it really true?
Is it still necessary?
What does it provide you?
What does living from it cost you?

Take three more deep, cleansing breaths and ask yourself:

What would life feel like lived as a heart-designed masterpiece?
What's possible in a life of that creation?
What's the next small step toward your heart of reinvention?

References:

Jirtle, R.L. (2022),. *The Science of Hope: An Interview with Randy Jirtle.* Epigenomics, 14(6), 299-302. https://doi.org/10.2217/epi-2022-0048

https://www.tandfonline.com/doi/10.2217/epi-2022-0048?url_ver=Z39.88-2003&rfr_id=ori:rid:crossref.org&rfr_dat=cr_pub%20%200pubmed

Michalopoulos, M. N., *"Mind/Body Healing: Hypnotherapy, Functional/Integrated Medicine, Epigenetics, Cancer & the Immune System."* Journal of Heart Centered Therapies, vol. 21, no. 1, spring 2018, pp. 69+. Gale Academic OneFile, link.gale.com/apps/doc/A539922312/AONE?u=tamp44898&sid=bookmark-AONE&x-id=92bf146a

Mosley-Johnson, E., Garacci, E., Wagner, N. et al., (2019), *Assessing the relationship between adverse childhood experiences and life satisfaction, psychological well-being, and social well-being: United States Longitudinal Cohort 1995–2014.* Qual Life Res 28, 907–914 (2019).

https://link.springer.com/article/10.1007/s11136-018-2054-6

https://doi.org/10.1007/s11136-018-2054-6

Zaccaro, A., Piarulli, A., Laurino, M., Garbella, E., Menicucci, D., Neri, B., & Gemignani, A. (2018),. *How Breath-Control Can Change Your Life: A Systematic Review on Psycho-Physiological Correlates of Slow Breathing.* Frontiers in human neuroscience, 12, 353. https://doi.org/10.3389/fnhum.2018.00353

https://www.worldometers.info/demographics/life-expectancy/

ABOUT THE AUTHOR
SUSANNAH ROBINSON

Susannah Robinson is a Hope Healer and guide for soul seekers and life adventurists ready to flourish from their heart and soul wisdom.

Before expanding into transformational healing, Susannah worked as a freelance writer, business owner, and corporate coach. Steeped in the practice of creating anew, Susannah shifted to the intimate side of what truly matters to the heart, focusing on aligning life for soul-versed living. Susannah now works with those navigating life's transitions using the gentle, yet powerful, generative work of HeartHealing, Conscious Connected Breathwork, and Jungian Life Coaching.

Susannah's passions include rowing, nature walks, and snuggling with her goldendoodle pups.

Available for Hope Journeys™, Susannah works with individuals, small groups, and B2B partnerships interested in deepening their coaching programs with certified adjunct healing modalities.

www.sacredaire.com
myheart@sacredaire.com
facebook.com/sacredaire
instagram.com/sacredaire

5

ROSE ISABEL CLEAVER

THE HEART OF HEALING FAMILIES

The Journey From The Outcast to The Exemplar™

Gratitude comes when you are finally able to take off the mask and with a healed heart, reveal your true self; inner confidence to lead by example...rebuilding relationships and families, setting healthy boundaries, or building your own flourishing family. Knowing you have the power to start again.

Change the story. Break the cycle. From performing a role you didn't know you were given, to accepting yourself and others deeply; confidently leading from within.

This is the inner confidence of a healed heart. This is the journey to becoming *The Exemplar™ (one who leads by example, from the heart).*

This has been my personal journey; a twenty-five-year career beginning with teaching theatre; outer confidence and public speaking, becoming a Clinical Hypnotherapist... finally healing inside to release the inner confidence that was always there.

This inner confidence has allowed me to look with gratitude at my loving partner, amazing thirteen-year-old son and enjoy the process of blending a new family; feeling safe in a relationship for the first time. I live close to my parents and enjoy spending time with all the family. I have a thriving business where I guide leaders to heal so they can release true inner confidence and receive more (more joyful relationships, family, love, wealth, health, success), becoming *The Exemplar*™ of confident authenticity.

This is my wish for your heart too.

Why?

Belonging…
Somewhere…
To someone.
Something every human being at our deepest core needs.

But…

The Outcast

What if you feel like an outsider at school and at home… what if those places are unstable, volatile, harmful, toxic, abusive? What then? Are you safe?

Maybe you try to hide and become invisible… or do the opposite; reject everything and everyone first. Perhaps it won't hurt as much. Brand yourself a "free thinker", "proud outcast"... choose flamboyance, fear and freakin' ATTITUDE… in place of what you really need to have it all. It is there for *all* of us if we know how to choose it. For a long time I didn't.

Fear based relationships and scarcity mindset resulting in abusive relationships with those unavailable to love…maybe they are suicidal or absent… married… abusive… or narcissistic. Maybe you're trying to finish a story from your childhood because somehow, just maybe, you can find someone who mirrors the person who wounded you and create a different ending. You can unconsciously prove it wasn't your fault.

You know the irony? *IT WASN'T YOUR FAULT.* Those invisible wounds you carry? They were created by others, probably carrying wounds of their own.

Imagine a beautiful hand carved driftwood sculpture, created to float down a diamond stream, catching the sunlight. There's just one problem. This beautiful sculpture is caught under a rock. It can't see the surface, can't float along its natural path. You see, the rock has been there since the beginning, so it doesn't understand why others float along the surface; something invisible prevents it reaching up there.

The Wounded Heart and the Confidence Cover Up...

Your relational wounding ripples throughout your lives; until you pay attention inside (rather than fixing what's visible), something will always be missing.

Perhaps you ran from your family, thinking it's better in a new one. Or ran into someone's arms thinking you'd found "The One", only to find the same patterns and wounds playing out again. A broken family (again) or broken marriage. Worse still, wounded children of your own. You don't understand. You worked so hard to create an amazing career, give your kids what your parents couldn't give you, have a relationship with someone so different... only to wind up wounded again. *Why?*

Healing your heart is the secret to dropping the mask. The confidence of a healed heart releases old roles you carried from birth and old wounds... it sets healthy boundaries and builds lasting relationships so you become *The Exemplar*™ for you and your dear ones.

Belonging

Most of us simply want to belong; what better place than within our family?

The core of "stable family" (apparently), is a partnership of radiant smiles, perfect peace; a model home for angelic, neurotypical, undemanding children with space for flourishing adult romance, all feeling loved as their needs are met. There are no financial stresses. Everyone is in perfect balance with perfect health and perfect teeth. Did you grow up in this family? Nope? Me neither!

The "perfect" family is made up of imperfect adults, each carrying wounds from childhood, triggered in relationships, overcorrecting or repeating dysfunction they've experienced. This perpetuates generationally. You may leave, yet your wounding travels with you.

Sound familiar? But there is another way. Once in a while a very special person comes along and breaks the cycle.

Hint: if you're reading this it's YOU!

Sometimes, wounding includes narcissistic patterns of abuse, neglect, mental, physical or emotional harm. More often, it is invisible harm caused by well meaning people, carrying wounds of their own.

It's unsurprising you grow up believing you a) don't deserve, b) don't know how to create a flourishing family, because you haven't experienced what it looks and feels like.

Unless you heal your heart and release your inner confidence from under that rock, you never will.

Oh, the roles we play!

Virginia Satir, a pioneer in family therapy, defined some family roles as; *The Sick One, The Carer, The Perfect One, The Rebel.* Remember, *the role someone plays is not who they are*. Although therapeutic work is now more trauma informed than when Satir was writing, the unconscious roles she identified are still relevant. My further work explores *"The Rulers Who Raise Us™"*.

Roles may change during your life, but they create imbalance. Where there is imbalance (or abuse/trauma), there is a wound of the heart, invisibly keeping you stuck in cycles of hurt.

This prevents you from shining with inner confidence to create authentic relationships both at home and in business.

The Ruler™

Recognised as "Head" of the house, their word is law. Those who question are punished.

The Secret Ruler™ (uses their "weakness" to control others)

Has perceived physical, emotional, mental needs and requires support from family members. In dysfunctional families the sickness (or need for attention) is used to manipulate the family into putting one person's needs first in an effort to "prove" / "earn" their love, causing others to be ignored, shoved aside, (even abused). Remember: *this isn't about whether they have a need; this is about whether it is used to seek attention, or control/manipulate others.*

The Ruler's Right Hand™

This person needs to be needed and rushes around *The Secret Ruler™*. Phrases like... "my mother won't visit if I don't..." are sure signs of a person who supports another's controlling or manipulative behaviour.

In dysfunctional families, there's an adult who knows there's addiction/abuse, but doesn't confront it, or pretends the abused child is "acting out".

The Absent Ruler™

They have abandoned their post and is physically or emotionally unavailable, yet expects the house to run a certain way. *The Ruler's Right Hand*™ dictates what s/he thinks they would want, in case they ever return. So far from heart-led leadership of *The Exemplar*™.

The Guilty Ruler™

The post-divorce guilt-based "yes" parent (usually with lesser custody), sometimes inadvertently creates roles for their child. There maybe *Parentification* (role reversal; child instructing parent) *Emotional Incest* (overcommunication emotionally replacing partner with child), leading to *The Mini Parent*™, where a child/teen is emotionally treated as another adult. There are few if any house rules, or boundaries around conversations they are involved in. Parenting is based on the fear of loss, creating a fear of discipline and boundary setting, meaning the child doesn't have consistency to know which behaviours are ok and safe.

The Narcissistic Ruler™

Worse still, some rule to feed their desires, wants and ego. The family provides their supply and is abused or dispensed with when no longer feeding their image. Their love is highly conditional.

Without radical self awareness and healing, the cycle continues generationally, harming future generations.

The Ruler's Children™

The Scapegoat/Outcast believes they are a "problem" or are "not normal" due to the way the Ruler(s) have branded them. Sometimes suffers physical, mental, emotional or sexual abuse.

The Invisible Child hides / is ignored whilst the drama unfolds.

The Mini Parent™ role harms a son or daughter's relationships. For example, during teenage years they may be vulnerable to inappropriately older partners "spoiling" them; parent figures. They may hold unrealistic relationship expectations and be poor at setting or respecting boundaries, mirroring their experience at home, but now within a sexual relationship; leading to heartbreak and possibly abuse. This contrasts with healthier, more equal peer relationships of those whose parents set healthy boundaries.

The Perfect One™ (*Golden Child* where narcissism exists). A child raised by *The Ruler™* with expectations they are "special". The role is comparative. This pedestal creates enormous pressure. Because they have a lot to lose, they please *The Ruler™*(s), studying hard, often following their career and lifestyle. This creates jealousy between siblings. Their role of feeling "special" only survives if other siblings are made to seem worse or absent. They unconsciously believe being loved is only attainable by being "better". They feel unable to share family (especially parents) feeling their attention diminished if others (siblings, or divorced parent's partner) are present. This perpetuates control issues and unrealistic expectations of partners when forming romantic relationships later.

It is unsurprising that most of us approach relationships somewhat wounded. Attachment styles within romantic relationships are hugely impacted by your childhood wounds!

Finally, *The Outcast* (*the Scapegoat* where narcissism exists). They have been brought up by wounded *Ruler* parent(s) with negative comparisons to *The Perfect One™*. They may hear, "why can't you be more like your sibling?" They feel they can never live up to or be loved like the favoured child; and can never please *The Ruler*™. The family see them as the "problem" child, easy to point at and likely to act out, especially during teenage years, often ending up in abusive relationships where they're trying to "rescue" the abuser. Appearing outwardly confident, yet inside wounded, isolated and unsafe. If later they are accepted by family, *The Perfect One*™ will likely struggle with this. Sometimes *the Outcast* has undiagnosed neurodiversity, making it easy for neurotypical siblings to be *The Perfect One*™, pushing them further into *The Outcast* role. They believe they are "wrong" as often shamed by the family.

If this is you, there's good news! Despite being raised to think you caused the family's dysfunction, *you* are actually the cycle breaker. Feeling "different" causes a search for healing. Through HeartHealing you release your inner confidence, find forgiveness, closure or boundaries with others and finally create healthy relationships yourself. This healing and awareness releases your true inner confidence, so that instead of becoming *The Ruler*™, you can consciously become *The Exemplar*™; you lead by heart-led example.

The Exemplar™ leads by maintaining lovingly appropriate boundaries, gently releasing the child from roles, re-affirming them as son/ daughter. *The Exemplar*™ is empowered to provide healthier family dynamics and have their own needs met! The child forms healthy relationships modelling the parent(s). In business, *The Exemplar*™ leads from the heart, maintaining appropriate boundaries to creating thriving businesses, empowering themselves and others to shine.

Sounds like something that would take years? It's quicker than you think!

First, let's understand *The Exemplar*™ and why heart-led leadership from within is more empowering than *The Ruler*™ and notice how many of the dynamics of each are currently within us.

The Ruler™	The Exemplar™
Never say sorry. Blame others for negative outcomes. Take credit for positive.	Self responsibility. Own actions; able to apologise, forgive, celebrate as appropriate.
Do as I say, not as I do!	Peaceful inner confidence living consistently by own values, modelled to family.
Decrees with severe consequences for non compliance. Questions assumed disrespectful of authority. Always say yes to The Perfect One™, be much tougher on others. My way or the Highway!	Create win/win situations. Firm, fair consistent boundaries. Plans are made first with partner, yet consider everyone. Say "no" (with love) to children and remain firm. Treat all children equally whilst acknowledging their uniqueness.
Children; seen and not heard. Partners exist to agree/serve me. Trigger at perceived criticism if partner questions my methods. No compromise.	Seek first to understand. Active listening: Open mind to new possibilities. Discuss with partner as equals. A united team towards children. Acknowledge children's thoughts and guide with wisdom and experience.
Make partner / outcast child do chores whilst pampering The Perfect One™/Mini-Parent™. Different kid? different rules! Create resentment/ comparison/ jealousy in the family.	Synergise; everyone in the family contributes (eg chores, helpfulness encouraged) to make an effective team. Everyone feels valued. Children learn to be productive, proud team players.

Ignore wins unless yours or The Perfect One's™. Physically or emotionally absent (or abusive). Berate others' mistakes.	Encourage everyone's strengths, celebrate everyone's small wins as individuals within the team (family).
The problem is always others. Tell them so, forcefully.	Work on self improvement, never "arrive". *Active Healing, release inner confidence.*
Lead by instruction, physical control, manipulation, guilt trips, abuse or abandonment (absence of leadership).	Lead by Example. Model healthy relationships/values you want kids to have. Model healing, Inspire the change you want in your family - *be the Exemplar*™.

> *"When you change the way you look at things, the things you look at change."*
>
> — *Dr Wayne Dyer*

Following my journey towards *The Exemplar*™, I have reverse engineered key ingredients of how to release invisibly damaging roles, becoming a loving *Exemplar*™ within your relationships and business; knowing that a healed heart is crucial to receiving more in ALL areas of life (money, love, health, success)!

The journey begins with understanding your story in a safe environment "Story in Safety™", next receiving HeartHealing™ to release your Inner Confidence allowing you to receive more. From this healed heart you uncover your Soul Purpose™ and Navigate Neurocreatively™, according to how your unique brain works best. Finally, you learn techniques for becoming a heart-led leader in business *and* at home, alongside skills of public speaking and presentation, empowering your inner and outer worlds to SHINE™ with true confidence, joy and love. You become The Exemplar™. This journey's purpose is to uplevel ALL areas of life, releasing your unique gifts to SHINE™ both in your relationships and business simultaneously.

SHINEmethod™

S tory in Safety™
H eartHealing™
I nner Confidence
N avigate NeuroCreatively™
The **E** xemplar™

Here I will share some healing stories, based on a combination of some leaders I have supported on their journey to The Exemplar™. Please note that for client safeguarding, no story is based on any one individual and all personal details have been changed.

During your imprint period (ages 0-7) your logical critical faculty is undeveloped. You store everything emotionally, unconsciously carrying it into adulthood. Even without abuse, your imprint carries wounds you are unaware of... invisible triggers: you unconsciously self sabotage the good, or embrace the toxic. You try to rewrite stories of your childhood - write a happier ending. The good news is, with HeartHealing these people did.

Family Journeys to The Exemplar™

Tom had been in the services, now corporate. Publicly he had everything; a successful public image, wife, kids, health. There was one problem; Tom's media image hid a lonely reality. His unconscious abandonment of anyone close; including his wife Judy and three children (one older daughter who was the reason for Judy's first marriage and young twins). She had her own struggles. Scapegoated as a child, she became *"The Ruler™"*. Judy became aware of her need to develop empathy. She was the first to come for healing. She blamed Tom; his absence, his coldness. Judy was planning to leave Tom.

As a former military wife, her coping mechanism was controlling the home with military precision and a mask of perfection. Her children's material needs were met, yet her young twins from her marriage to Tom became *"The Perfect Ones™"*, and daughter *"The Outcast"* (whom she blamed as her reason for entering her first abusive marriage). During our HeartHealing sessions, her whole physicality shifted. Light returned to her face, tears of healing allowing a soft beauty to return. A huge weight was lifted. She began to realise the part her own wounding played.

Judy's healed heart empowered her to become *The Exemplar™*. She reconnected with her daughter Sophia, reached out to Tom for marriage counselling, and set boundaries to treat the children equally. Her impact was transformational.

Three months later, I had a call from Tom *(The Absent Ruler™)*. For the first time, he voiced feelings of being "not enough" for his family. Being super successful financially was his cover, not believing he could enjoy a flourishing family simultaneously. During his HeartHealing session, Tom dissolved the walls he had built to protect himself, allowing Judy fully into his heart, to nurture rather than control. He talked bravely with the children, releasing his inner confidence and stepping up as *the Exemplar™*. The effect on his loved ones was palpable. His setting of loving boundaries brought them closer; they appreciated his interest and presence *and* Tom's media career became even more successful as he became more authentic on camera and client demand increased.

A week later Sophia (aged nineteen), came for HeartHealing. Badly hurt by her parents' wounding, not feeling like a "proper" family member since her mum's second marriage, she got into a pattern of abusive relationships with unavailable men. She was also suffering with OCD (indicating a root cause with control). We worked through the five Receiving Wounds of the heart and she began journaling her behaviour changes. She ended a destructive relationship with a married man twenty-four years older. Sophia bravely stepped away from toxic people in her life, having inner confidence to create space for something better. Becoming *The Exemplar*™, she built healthier relationships with both parents. She recently contacted me to say she's dating a lovely single man her age. She feels enough with or without another person, for the first time. She has just begun a new job which is far more aligned to her soul purpose and finally understands that *it wasn't her fault!*

Not all relationships heal by re-uniting; sometimes healing brings inner confidence to step away or create space (as with Sophia and her relationship), but for this family, becoming *the Exemplar*™ one by one brought them back together. Tom's career is still thriving… and so is his family.

From Invisibility to Front Page News!

Stacey came to me because of narcissistic business relationships. She'd spent years doing 'self help', but something was missing. Tolerating abusive behaviour in the workplace was affecting her marriage to Colin and confidence in raising her stepchildren. She no longer expressed opinions in case she was "wrong", avoiding confrontation (*the invisible one*). If discussions became heated she clammed up. During her HeartHealing, she realised *The Narcissist* in historical romantic relationships had caused her to fear visibility. She had been *The Invisible One* and this was playing out at work and home, despite her awareness. After our HeartHealing on visibility, her inner confidence began to shine. She informed *The Narcissist* she would find an alternative supplier. The emotional blackmail, threats and manipulative behaviour failed to weaken her resolve; she upheld her boundaries, cutting off this toxicity.

As she became *the Exemplar*™ almost immediately a new supplier appeared. The very next week, by chance, a reporter visited. Stacey's business was featured on national TV. Her social media following tripled as did her business. But that's not all: this inner confidence and ability to be *the Exemplar*™ showed up at home too. Her partner opened up about a work situation and she was able to support him. Her confidence in setting healthy boundaries and loving her stepchildren grew too. She told me recently, "I'm getting twice as much done, working less hours and my income is higher than ever. I can finally afford to see a health specialist and love having more time for my children. I am planning a holiday surprise for my husband because I can finally afford it. My visibility fears are definitely behind me."

My Journey From Outcast to The Exemplar™

It took seventeen years Theatre Directing. I had "outer confidence": public speaking, performance, directing shows, teaching teens (drawn to empower those outcast or bullied). Simultaneously, I trained business leaders, actors, teenagers, teachers and directors to create extraordinary visible success, yet behind the scenes, romantic and family relationships crumbled. I spent the next fifteen years training professionals in presentation skills, interview techniques, communication, certifying Master Practitioners in NLP, Timeline Therapy™, Coaching and Clinical Hypnotherapy. Despite my clients and I enjoying outward success, something was preventing success with relationships and family. With a social media image, it's sometimes easy to assume all is well "backstage". Just like my clients, my outer life looked successful but was privately falling apart.

Simply put, the outer confidence and inner confidence didn't match. Something was missing. But *what*?

There were hints during my Root Cause Clinical Hypnotherapy sessions. My clients accessed different brainwave states to discover their subconscious triggers and heal them. We would gain significant insight. Big shifts. But it wasn't enough. The jigsaw still had one piece missing.

Twenty-six years earlier...

"Missing you already!"

It was a warm scented Summer day, that day he walked through the airport gate. He waved. We stared. Neither of us moved for what felt like a very long time.

Eventually the lady at security distracted me. She had a job to do and being in limbo with geographically challenged couples wasn't it.

Our eyes met from the other side of security in one last connected moment. There seemed so much to say, but his ear was far enough I'd have to shout. The words stuck in my throat. I was too embarrassed. Scared of what others would think. I tried to look cool. Like I could handle anything. Turns out I couldn't.

"It's not like you'll never see him again!" she said. She was wrong. Five days later he committed suicide.

That was the moment I finally acknowledged that even before, I had felt alone. Despite the outer confidence, I felt like an outsider. Like I didn't really belong in my immediate family. And as it turns out, not in the relationships I tried either. Different people. Different situations. They all failed.

The only common denominator was me. It would be another ten years before I realised what was missing. And many more years to find it.

Hopefully, if you're reading this, it won't take you as long.

Before that...

At home, we learned to be compliant. We moved house three times and I had five schools in five years (three for my sister). An easy target for school bullies. For me, the outcast became the rebel. From a teenager, I ended up in a string of abusive and toxic relationships that lasted decades.

By adding HeartHealing to decades of theatrical, therapeutic, and business expertise, as well as spirituality, I have created an empowering methodology to ensure you will heal a lot quicker than I did. It is based on my journey from *Outcast to Exemplar™: from Invisible to Inner Confidence™.*

Here is a little exercise to begin your healing journey towards becoming The Exemplar™.

A Story in Safety™ exercise from my signature SHINEmethod™:

> Find a quiet space, notebook and pen.
> Thinking over your life, what roles did you accept in childhood?
> How old were you?
> Have you consciously stopped playing that role, or are there triggers that have you play it even now?
> What are they?
>
> Close your eyes and imagine "little you" standing in front of you now. They are holding a mask with a role written on it. What does it say?
> Imagine adult you walking over to them.

> What would you say to them now about the role(s) they were handed?
> What do they need to hear to drop that mask?
> What words can bring healing to that little you right now?
>
> Write a letter to that younger you, explaining the roles s/he accepted were never their fault.
> For example:
> Reassure them; they are beautiful; worth hearing, worth being visible, worth being loved *just as they are.*
> Tell them how much you love them, you will keep them safe to be authentic, reassure them that they have the choice to leave the mask behind now and you are committed to doing what it takes to release true inner confidence to become *the Exemplar*™ for them.
> Tell them the amazing life that is waiting and that you believe in their ability to SHINE.
> Tell them the impact their transformation will have on their happiness, relationships, money, success and loved ones
> Tell them you will help them become *The Exemplar*™.

Read the letter aloud.

Decide: one action towards this (e.g. I will decide my boundaries around conversations. If a conversation crosses my boundaries, I will politely say "I would prefer to talk about something else" and change the topic or walk away).

Say: "I release the role of (name the old role). This role has no power over me. I am (your name). I choose to be *The Exemplar*™.

Discovering HeartHealing and incorporating it into my *SHINEmethod*™ has allowed the "front of house" and "backstage" balance. No roles required.

Releasing inner confidence has allowed me to forgive myself and others, realising that those who wound can also become *The Exemplar*™. This inner confidence of *The Exemplar*™ has allowed me to receive more: more work/life balance, better love relationship and happier family life. Though imperfect, I choose to step up in leadership to become *The Exemplar*™.

After all, how great can your success feel if you have no one to celebrate with and nowhere to belong?

Is it time to release that beautiful driftwood sculpture from under that rock and watch it float gracefully along its diamond stream?

Your FREE SHINEmethod™ gift will further support your healing journey to *The Exemplar*™: www.rosecleaver.com/shinemethod-freebie

HeartHealing A personal HeartHealing card reading *plus* understanding your attachment style and releasing toxic roles in love.

Inner Confidence A thirty-second energy reset.

Navigate (NeuroCreatively™ First steps to a more "on purpose" life.

The Exemplar™ Eleven ways to lead from the heart.

References:

Jung C. "The Electra complex". and Secunda V "Women and their Fathers; the sexual and romantic impact of the first man in your life"

Lavine A. and Heller R. "Attached: the new science of adult attachment and how it can help you find-and keep-love"

ABOUT THE AUTHOR

ROSE ISABEL CLEAVER

Rose Isabel Cleaver is a Healer, Clinical Hypnotherapist and Master Coach with over twenty-five years' experience. She specialises in releasing the inner confidence of independent professionals, freeing them to enjoy fearless love and flourishing family whilst thriving in a life they are proud of.

She pioneered the SHINEmethod™, her bespoke programme to release inner confidence, heal the heart (incorporating Natasha Bray's HeartHealing) and combine this with the ability to become an excellent communicator, both in people's public and personal lives. Rose enjoys skiing, renovating old buildings, and being in the ocean at all times of year. Rose is available for Speaking,

Interviews and private consultations with individuals and families to release your inner confidence and communication in your public and private life.

www.rosecleaver.com
happyhealthyrose@gmail.com
rose@rosecleaver.com
facebook: Rose Isabel Cleaver
linkedin.com/in/rosecleaver

6

DR. GÖKÇE BULGAN

THE HEART OF PERFECTIONISM

When I was preparing for my predoctoral internship interviews as a Ph.D. student in counseling psychology, I remember perfectionism being shared as an example of a quality to highlight when discussing our weaknesses as a high achiever while also emphasizing the positive aspects of the trait, such as being conscientious in our work and having the determination to reach our goals. Like many things, perfectionism is not entirely good or bad. Ample evidence demonstrates the functional benefits (Stoeber & Otto, 2006), alongside the associated psychopathology. (Frost et al, 1990) Perfectionism may serve you well in certain areas of your life but can also lead to detrimental health issues if not acknowledged and addressed.

Let me be transparent from the start: I am a perfectionist. So are most of the clients I work with in therapy. Perhaps you are a perfectionist yourself or know someone who is. If so, this chapter will help you better understand perfectionism and recognize HeartHealing as a helpful approach to addressing perfectionistic tendencies without sacrificing your health, as I once did. Addressing perfectionism starts by recognizing it within ourselves and acknowledging it not as an issue to overcome but as a personality trait to live with.

As perfectionists, we might unknowingly choose to live by struggling and making life difficult for ourselves, or we can become aware of our tendencies, accept ourselves for who we are, and find ways that work for us. At this stage, I fully accept myself as a perfectionist, embracing it with all the benefits and painful challenges. After all the work I have done, I can now easily see my perfectionist tendencies kicking in when I have too much on my plate, show myself the compassion I need in difficult times, allow myself to feel all the feels, and use practical tools to regulate my emotions, think clearly, and then act from a place of presence and inner peace. This was not always the case.

Looking back, there were times I called myself a "recovering perfectionist," as if perfectionism was something one could recover from. I also told myself I was "perfectly imperfect," which felt alienating, as I did not like the idea of being imperfect. You may have had similar experiences. Do not get me wrong. I am not here to tell you what to do or how to feel. We are all unique in our ways, having a different combination of certain personality traits and tendencies. My goal in this chapter is to share what worked for me and my perfectionist clients, hoping that it could inspire you to understand yourself better and find the tools that could work for you. The underlying message is this: There is nothing inherently wrong with you. You do not need to change who you are to thrive in business, life, and relationships as a perfectionist. I will show you how.

Perfectionism is a complex personality trait involving setting high personal standards, striving for flawlessness, and critical self-evaluation. Although there is no agreed-upon definition, perfectionism is accepted as a multidimensional construct. To explain the concept better, I will share two empirically validated models tested for over thirty years by several researchers.

The first model conceptualizes perfectionism in three dimensions: a) self-oriented perfectionism, b) other-oriented perfectionism, and c) socially prescribed perfectionism (Hewitt & Flett, 1991). Self-oriented perfectionism refers to individuals requiring perfection from themselves, such as setting high-performance standards and striving to achieve them. Other-oriented perfectionism is concerned with the perfectionist individual requiring perfection from people around them, such as their partners, family members, coworkers, and friends. Socially prescribed perfectionism is related to the belief that other people expect perfection of the individual, as in believing that one needs to be perfect for one's parents to love them or for one's friends to accept them. Therefore, being loved, accepted, and valued is attached to the need to be perfect rather than for who we are.

In the second model, perfectionism is comprised of a) high personal standards, b) excessive worry over making mistakes, c) questioning the quality of one's actions, d) a preference for order and organization, e) perception of high parental expectations, and f) perception of high parental criticism. In this model, you can easily see setting high personal standards bringing along anxiety, self-doubt, the need to control, and perceiving parents to have high expectations of the individual and criticizing them when their expectations are not met.

I want to underline the word perceiving/perception here. As perfectionists, our parents might not verbally criticize or tell us they will only love us when we meet their high expectations. However, based on our inferences of our parents' attitudes, facial expressions, and behaviors amplified by our inner critic, we perceive them to do so. As psychologists, we are not focused on getting the facts right. It is more about understanding an individual's perception of their lived experience, how it made them feel, and the meaning they attached to it we are interested in.

Would you like to know a common misconception about perfectionists? Perfectionists do not want everything to be perfect; they seek perfection in what is relevant and important to them. In a sense, perfectionism is fundamentally about control. It centers on the desire to manage our lives and environment. Perfectionism intensifies when we cannot control what goes wrong in our lives or when things in the outside world do not go as planned, leading to even greater inner chaos. To work with perfectionism, we must understand its origins and the need behind it, identify when it is primarily activated, and discover ways to cultivate a healthier relationship with it.

A combination of genetic and environmental factors plays a role in its origins. Twin studies indicate genetic factors partially determine perfectionist traits. On the other hand, environmental factors could result from parental influences, adverse childhood experiences, or the role of culture. For example, parental expectations of high academic performance can develop perfectionist tendencies in children by creating a sense of conditional parental love and approval. More specifically, children could fear not being loved or accepted by their parents if they fail in school and strive to be perfect. Most likely, perfectionist parents have children genetically prone to perfectionism and raise them in a family environment that encourages their perfectionistic tendencies. What gets reinforced early in life amplifies in time. Adverse childhood experiences such as experiencing emotional neglect, trauma, or a dysfunctional family environment can contribute to perfectionism. These experiences often create a strong need for control, which could emerge as perfectionism. In a way, perfectionism acts as a self-protection mechanism from the outside world. Lastly, perfectionism could stem from a family or school culture where high achievement and academic success are highly valued, and competitive environments with intense pressure are normalized. For instance, having teachers who are critical of us or having peer pressure to be the most successful in class could contribute to perfectionism.

Imagine an individual exposed to all these factors at an early age. How would their life be? Most likely, they would do their best as a kid and try hard to succeed at school. They would probably see their friends doing the same and start an unspoken competition with their peers. When they come in as second or third in class on any given topic, they might believe they have failed, feel ashamed, beat themselves up for it, and continue to strive even more.

Imagine this continuing throughout their childhood and adolescence. How would they end up in life? They most likely would have low-stress tolerance, develop anxiety, and have a loud inner critic as their closest companion, further feeding their already low self-confidence. The inner critic would do its job perfectly by reminding the person they are not working hard enough and ultimately make them believe they are not enough as they are.

As you can imagine, this scenario is the recipe for mental health issues in adulthood. Research findings indicate perfectionism could lead to increased levels of stress and anxiety; procrastination; lower self-esteem, self-acceptance, and self-worth; a greater risk for depression and burnout; a tendency toward eating disorders and obsessive-compulsive disorder; as well as an elevated risk of suicidal ideation (Frost et al, 1990; Hewitt & Flett, 1991; Limburg et al, 2017; Lunn et al, 2023; Smith et al 2022).

Considering the mental and physical health risks, perfectionism must be acknowledged and addressed to prevent people from unknowingly looping in this vicious cycle.

By now, you probably want to know how to break this vicious cycle. Based on my story and over twenty years of experience working with clients, the only way out is through. Journeying through ourselves by getting to know ourselves better, strengthening our relationships with ourselves, letting go of parts that do not align with us as we evolve, and living as our authentic selves are different steps of the transformation process.

A wealth of evidence-based approaches is available for addressing perfectionism, including cognitive behavioral therapy, psychodynamic therapy, interpersonal therapy, mindfulness and compassion-based therapy, and acceptance and commitment therapy. In this chapter, I will focus on HeartHealing, as it has been the approach that has created the most significant shift for me and my clients. Being a therapist and a university professor, I acknowledge HeartHealing as a modality, currently in its early stages and not having the research evidence to support it at the time of publishing. I am happy to share that we are working on conducting research studies to test the effectiveness therapists using the approach are already experiencing in their sessions.

As perfectionists, setting high personal and performance standards, working on achieving them, doubting ourselves along the way, being afraid of judgment by others, and thus criticizing ourselves more harshly than anyone else can create a sense of not feeling safe and needing to protect ourselves. We naturally close ourselves off when we feel unsafe in the world. In HeartHealing, this is represented as building a wall around your heart. Think of the times you doubted yourself and felt not enough; you most likely did not want anyone else to see that and did your best to hide it by protecting yourself. This protection may have led to further loneliness, the feeling no one gets you, and the fear that someone might hurt you. The more you closed yourself off, the lonelier and more isolated you felt inside. This is the heart of perfectionism. That is why learning to accept ourselves as much as possible is important in working with perfectionism. Both the parts we like but do not appreciate much and the parts we do not like.

That being said, we could tell ourselves we love and accept ourselves all day long, and it would not work unless we felt it and believed in it. HeartHealing helps us to embrace ourselves fully and genuinely believe we deserve love, appreciation, and belonging. What I love about HeartHealing the most is that it allows you to gently yet drastically open your heart and powerfully shift your whole relationship with yourself. It is like self-compassion with a turbo engine. I can confidently say this as I have experienced its immense power in my journey.

The best way I could explain how it works differently than other modalities is this: Imagine yourself closing off your heart further with each hurtful experience, thinking it was the safest way to protect yourself. Getting laughed at in front of class in elementary school and feeling like we made a fool of ourselves, thinking there is something wrong with us because we are in a way different than other people around us, being bullied for our looks, having a heartbreak, feeling like a failure, and so on. I could give a million examples of experiences that made us close ourselves off, but you get the point. HeartHealing tears down the wall around the heart of perfectionism all at once, taking the excruciating pain away created by thousands of accumulated experiences in our lifetime.

Imagine having several HeartHealing sessions addressing a different part of you getting hurt along the way. We address issues of not feeling enough, not trusting our wisdom, not loving and accepting ourselves for who we are, not feeling worthy without achieving, subconsciously choosing to make life difficult for ourselves by getting in our way and needing to be perfect as we move along and evolve through the process. My clients have experienced significant life changes, such as feeling free of the heavy burden of childhood abuse and neglect, recovering from grief, overcoming fears of public speaking, recovering from burnout with a newfound sense of joy and motivation, showing the courage to follow their heart's desire, transforming their marriages to happier, fulfilling, and supportive ones, allowing themselves to have romantic relationships, and finding their voice to express themselves in high stake situations powerfully.

I have experienced self-acceptance, self-trust, and self-worth as the biggest needle movers in addressing perfectionism. When we learn to accept all the parts we like and do not like about ourselves, we feel liberated and, in a way, start to breathe easier. It is a whole new ball game when we learn to trust the emotions we experience as valuable data points of what we want and do not like, learn to trust our decisions and gut feelings, and let go of defining our worth based on achievements. We feel authentically powerful. We acknowledge what we want to say is worth saying and thus find our genuine voice. We stop judging ourselves and start to stand up for ourselves instead. We allow ourselves to experience happier and more deeply satisfying relationships. We begin to live. Imagine how different our lives could be then. Much easier. More fulfilling. A lot more joyful and purposeful. That is the power of HeartHealing.

To illustrate my point, let me invite you to snippets from my own story. My earliest memories of being a perfectionist date back to when I was two years old. I remember reorganizing my toys as I saw my mom doing it after I was done playing—classic social learning. My dad also told me the story of me crying after falling in the playground and getting hurt. I did not cry because I was hurt. I cried because my outfit got dirty as I fell and did not look neat and clean anymore. You cannot make this up. I equated being loved and accepted with looking well put together in my two-year-old mind. At what age did the heart of perfectionism begin to develop for you?

Perfectionism dates back to early in life and is strengthened by each experience. Every little experience shapes the lens through which we see the world. Things got worse for me at age five when we moved from Türkiye to the U.S. due to my dad's job. I started Kindergarten and did not speak a word of English. I felt like an alien. All the kids were playing and talking to each other in a language I did not understand. I felt anxious, as if there was something wrong with me. Fast forward a couple of months, kids being kids and very open to new information, I quickly learned the language and performed well in school. As I performed well, I liked the feeling of accomplishment and kept up with it. This went on my whole life. In time, I became an overachiever and was never satisfied with how much I had accomplished. The sky was the limit.

Basing our identity on achievement without even noticing it early on in childhood sets us up for dissatisfaction and the downward spiral of overthinking and experiencing difficult emotions. At least it did for me. This continued into my college years when I experienced painful headaches daily and was diagnosed with gastritis due to high levels of stress. I learned to eat healthily for the gastritis and pulled through the stress. Even though I was taking multiple psychology classes at the time, I did not get help for the stress I was experiencing. Why would I? I could cope with it on my own, or so I thought. Having had the experience of feeling alone in the world, I learned to be self-sufficient early on. Most likely, I had unknowingly developed a trauma response. This sense of self-sufficiency prevented me from asking for help when I needed it the most, which is also true for my clients.

Not asking for help in times of need could have a damaging impact on one's health. It did for me. As a perfectionist overachiever, I have experienced multiple health issues throughout my life, such as stress and anxiety, painful migraines, gastritis, duodenitis, chronic fatigue, and finally, burnout. In my mid-thirties, my hands used to tremble so severely under stressful situations such as presenting at a conference or joining a television program (i.e., basically anything that put me at risk of being criticized or judged by others) that one physician suspected an early onset of Parkinson's Disease and asked for a brain scan. I remember going to the hospital before sunrise as I had the day's first appointment. It was a scary wait. Thankfully, the scan results came out clean. After a series of tests and several doctor's appointments, the diagnosis was an essential tremor, a neurological condition causing the hands and voice to shake due to an unknown reason. Looking back, I can easily share that my condition at the time was due to high levels of stress. My daily stress was more than I could handle and was exacerbated by my job environment.

After my body cried out for help, I decided to take my health seriously and made significant lifestyle changes. That was when I began meditating daily, listening closely to my body, resigning from my job that did not support my mental health, and seeking ways to maintain a healthy lifestyle. I was determined to ensure I would never go through a similar experience again. I told myself nothing was more important than my health. I truly meant it. To this day, I have never regretted my decision to prioritize myself and care for my needs, even if it meant leaving behind a career I loved. It was not always like this. I have had plenty of moments of ignoring and minimizing my situation, acting as if everything was fine, and just pushing through. Nothing worked. Why would it? We cannot escape from reality. Unfortunately, sometimes we remain unaware of our reality, especially when we are on autopilot mode.

The first step for me was accepting my struggles and acknowledging I was a perfectionist prone to anxiety who needed help. I started to slow down and listen to my body to give me clues of what I needed. I returned to daily meditation and integrated mindfulness practices I had learned during my doctoral studies. As the saying goes, the teacher appeared when the student was ready. Everything I learned years before suddenly took a different meaning for me. I finally began to see what had been in front of me the whole time. I started practicing healthy habits, which helped me recover from burnout and significantly reduce anxiety. Mindfulness and compassion-based practices were a lifesaver for me before HeartHealing. So, I was learning to celebrate my accomplishments, acknowledge what I love and appreciate about myself, and not buy into what my inner critic had to say.

As I quit my full-time job at the university, I had more time to focus on my business and develop myself personally and professionally. Roughly around the same time, I ran into Natasha Leigh Bray's work and invested time and energy to learn more. After experiencing the benefits, I started offering HeartHealing to my clients who were open to it. As a side note, I primarily work with highly analytical individuals who feel comfortable with evidence-based approaches and like questioning things out of their comfort zone before trying them out. They loved it. It was gentle yet powerful. Most importantly, it worked. The transformation they experienced was remarkable.

HeartHealing has helped me process my early childhood experiences, let go of feeling unsafe in the world, and trust myself more than ever. My stress levels have decreased significantly, and the tremors have completely stopped. I attribute this change to addressing the stress and anxiety that have accumulated over the years in a way that felt safe to me and finally feeling free of that heavy baggage. How does this reflect in my daily life? To give a practical example, I wrote this chapter in two sittings over a weekend. I had guests on the second day, so I worked on the chapter for the first half of the day. I collected my thoughts, meditated, and started typing on both days. Before? It would have taken me weeks, if not months, going back and forth while struggling to write a word.

Is it the perfect chapter? Of course not. Does this bother me? No. When perfectionism took over, I focused on myself and my performance, buying into my loud inner critic. After shifting my relationship with perfectionism, I can focus on who could benefit from reading this chapter and how it might inspire them. It is no longer about me. I suggest you also look at things from this perspective. So, perfectionism is still there, but it does not bother me as much as it used to, and I choose not to give it the power to get in my way.

As for my clients, all have different stories, and it is not mine to tell, only theirs. HeartHealing has strengthened our work by enabling them to experience transformations they could not have imagined. Their whole lives, from their businesses and careers to their romantic relationships and mental and physical health, have been transformed. The significant shifts they went through bring immense joy and fulfillment to my heart.

As for you, try it out for yourself. Come experience the power of HeartHealing by booking an individual session with me or one of my fellow practitioners, as we would all love to support you. For an immediate action step, I suggest a three-part healing task. First, ask yourself when the heart of perfectionism began to form in you. Let's say it was at age two, as it was for me. Second, list five different ways perfectionism shows up in your life. Third, tune into your heart space as you go through each item on your list and ask yourself: "What does my two-year-old inner child need to hear from me in this case?" Tell yourself what they need to hear while staying connected to your heart. Check in with your heart space to see how it feels in your body to acknowledge your inner child by telling them what they need to hear from you. Keep repeating this practice each time perfectionism gets activated for you.

Finally, if my clients and I could have stopped getting in our way by transforming our relationship with perfectionism and allowing ourselves to live the lives we desire, so could you. My wish for humankind is that we all love, live, and lead from our authentic presence with an open heart. Thank you for being part of the movement.

References:

Frost, R. O., Marten, P., Lahart, C., & Rosenblate, R. (1990). *The dimensions of perfectionism. Cognitive Therapy and Research,*14(5), 449–468. https://doi.org/10.1007/bf01172967

Hewitt, P. L., & Flett, G. L. (1991). *Perfectionism in the self and social contexts: Conceptualization, assessment, and association with psychopathology*. Journal of Personality and Social Psychology, 60(3), 456–470. https://doi.org/10.1037/0022-3514.60.3.456

Limburg, K., Watson, H., Hagger, M., & Egan, S. (2017). *The relationship between perfectionism and psychopathology: A meta-analysis*. Journal of Clinical Psychology, 73(10), 1301–1326. https://doi.org/10.1002/jclp.22435

Lunn, J., Greene, D., Callaghan, T., & Egan, S. J. (2023). *Associations between perfectionism and symptoms of anxiety, obsessive-compulsive disorder and depression in young people: A meta-analysis*. Cognitive Behaviour Therapy, 52(5), 460–487. https://doi.org/10.1080/16506073.2023.2211736

Smith, M. M., Sherry, S. B., Ge, S. Y. J., Hewitt, P. L., Flett, G. L., & Baggley, D. L. (2022). *Multidimensional perfectionism turns 30: A review of known knowns and known unknowns*. Canadian Psychology / Psychologie canadienne, 63(1), 16–31. https://doi.org/10.1037/cap0000288

Stoeber, J., & Otto, K. (2006*). Positive conceptions of perfectionism: Approaches, evidence, challenges.* Personality and Social Psychology Review, 10(4), 295–319. https://doi.org/10.1207/s15327957pspr1004_2

ABOUT THE AUTHOR

DR. GÖKÇE BULGAN

Dr. Gökçe Bulgan is a full professor of psychology at Istanbul Rumeli University, an executive therapist, and a leadership mental health consultant in private practice. She specializes in helping leaders struggling with anxiety, perfectionism, burnout, trauma, and career or business-related challenges to improve their mental health and emotional well-being so they can live and lead confidently.

Gökçe earned her Ph.D. in counselling psychology from Purdue University and has over twenty years of experience working with clients worldwide. She offers a unique blend of psychotherapy, HeartHealing and mindfulness-based practices, and facilitates mindfulness-based group programmes to enhance leadership mental health.

She has authored multiple scientific publications on psychological well-being and work-life issues, and she co-authored the book Happiness 2.0 (in Turkish), which offers evidence-based practices for cultivating mental and emotional well-being.

Gökçe enjoys being in nature, playing golf, dance and daily meditation.

She is available for therapy, coaching, leadership consultations and guest expert workshops.

www.gokcebulgan.com
gokce@gokcebulgan.com
linkedin.com/in/gokcebulgan
facebook.com/gokce.bulgan

7

KINGA KUJAWA

THE HEART OF RECLAIMING YOUR VOICE

I never thought I would ever reach the place where I am now. I am an established and highly respected astrologer and healer, known for my unique approach that combines astrology with HeartHealing and human design, which I call Astro Healing. I've built a reputation for my deep insights and transformative methods, helping people navigate their spiritual and emotional journeys. My work resonates with many, leading to widespread recognition, including appearances on television to share my wisdom with a larger audience.

For years, I struggled with an invisible barrier. I had valuable knowledge of astrology to offer, yet I couldn't shake the feeling of being an imposter. Every new reading, every piece of advice I gave, felt as though someone would expose me for what I thought I was—a fraud. It was a relentless voice inside me, echoing doubts that chipped away at my self-worth.

But it wasn't just the imposter syndrome that held me back. There was a deeper wound, one that had been with me ever since I could remember. I grew up in rural Poland, "where kids and fish had no voice." My words were dismissed, ignored, or even ridiculed. Over the years, this created a deep wound in my soul, spirit, blocking not only my ability to speak but also to write with confidence. I was terrified of being misunderstood, or worse, ridiculed or silenced, and eventually of being seen.

I developed a coping mechanism: fake it till you make it. I looked confident and sounded confident, but deep down I was anything but. I second-guessed myself and was afraid of being recognised as an expert. I was so afraid of speaking my truth that I played safe in every area of my work.

Through various spiritual practices, including energy healing and working with my own chart, I began to heal the wound in my voice. I started to embrace my unique astrological voice and used my knowledge of the stars to guide me in my transformation. I worked with the energy of the planets to rebalance my communication channels, allowing myself to speak more freely and openly.

But the breakthrough came when I discovered HeartHealing. I realised that for my voice to truly heal, I needed to connect it with my heart. By doing so, I could speak from a place of authenticity and love, rather than from fear. The heart would guide me, infusing my words with compassion and truth.

Healing my heart not only healed my fear of being seen and heard but transformed my life on many levels. It led to significant growth in my business, reaching a milestone of 1.5 million in revenue in 2024, and more importantly, it improved my relationship with my partner and my four children.

Eventually, I developed Astro Healing. It allowed people not only to understand their astrological charts and human design charts but to use HeartHealing to heal deep emotional wounds. I began to attract clients drawn not only to my knowledge but to the transformative energy I embodied. People started referring to me as an established astrologer who had found a new way to integrate healing and astrology.

Looking back, I see how far I've come. No longer held back by Voice Wound or the fear of speaking my truth, I've stepped into my power. My voice, once wounded, now sings with authenticity. The stars no longer just guide me—they've helped me heal, but the missing piece was found through HeartHealing. Now, through my method, I can help others do the same, allowing their hearts and voices to shine as brightly as the stars themselves.

I suffered with a Voice Wound until my forties. Since I healed that side of me, not only have I grown online but I have appeared on TV as an expert in my field and have now been asked to take part in a TED Talk to discuss this topic.

Most importantly, I have worked with women to help them heal their Voice Wounds. I work with women entrepreneurs who are afraid of sharing their opinion, hiding behind other people's work, too afraid to show what they can do and share their knowledge and experiences. About 80% of these women were too afraid to write an ebook 'as they did not have enough to share' or relied on assistants to create their posts online as they thought they didn't have 'the way with words' without realising it was actually their words that were helping them grow their businesses. As a spiritual business mentor, I work with women who also want to grow a spiritual business but are too scared of what people will say and are afraid that their words will be ridiculed.

Let me explain what the Voice Wound is. The Voice Wound is not only what you say but the voice inside and outside. It is a belief that comes from within and, like many other wounds, is very much shaped through experiences and feelings that your voice does not matter. It can come from a feeling that somehow it is unsafe to express your opinion, or that what you say and how you say it is fundamentally flawed and as such is not valid. It usually happens when a person repeatedly encounters environments where their words are dismissed, ridiculed, ignored or punished.

It can happen through various situations like subtle social conditioning, prolonged criticism, rejection, or even internal self-censorship developed to avoid threats you might be subject to if you spoke up. For example, I came from a background where I was told that, "children and fish had no voice" and as such my words could be ignored. When anyone complained about anything I did or said, not once has anyone asked me for my side of the story. My side was never taken into consideration at home or at school: in the nineties, kids either followed the crowd or fell out.

The Voice Wound is so much more than the words that come out of your mouth (verbal expression) — it is about the way you see yourself, how you perceive your right to take up space in world and in conversations; it affects how you show yourself in the world or internet, how you share ideas or express emotions, and how you stand out in the world.

Sometimes it can be so deeply ingrained that it affects both spoken and unspoken communication. Rooted inside that, it influences a person's sense of self-worth, confidence, and capacity for meaningful connection.

How the Voice Wound Manifests

The effects of the Voice Wound are complex and far-reaching, and influence both internal experiences and feelings and external behaviours. While it may manifest differently in each person, common patterns include:

1. Fear of Speaking Up:

A person with a Voice Wound may hesitate to share their thoughts in conversations, meetings or relationships. You might notice this at home but also in a work environment. You might second-guess yourself, waiting for the 'right moment' to speak, which rarely arrives. You might fear being judged, misunderstood, dismissed, or having someone invalidate your opinion, make a laughing stock of you, or put you in the corner.

2. Over-Explaining or Apologising for Speaking:

You might feel the need to over-explain your ideas, your reasoning behind your decisions, even seeking external validation before expressing yourself to double check that you are right or starting your statements with phrases like, "Sorry, but..." or, "This might not make sense, but..." or even, "I might be wrong but..." as if apologising for existing or speaking up.

3. Suppression of True Feelings and Needs:

Such a person develops a deep fear of rejection or conflict that leads to self-censorship. You might avoid saying what you truly mean, as it is best not to express yourself. You can develop a need to people please and/or communicate passively, agreeing to things you do not want to do. Over time, your resentment builds up due to unspoken needs.

4. Difficulty Making Decisions:

Because the Voice Wound undermines your trust in your own thoughts, abilities and personal strength, you may struggle with decision-making, fearing you will make the wrong choice or that your judgment is inadequate and others will ridicule you.

I see it a lot in my practice as an astrologer. Many people rely excessively on guidance from stars, tarot or therapists, reinforcing their sense of powerlessness.

5. Performance Over Authenticity:

To compensate for your fear of being unheard, you may develop a persona that is designed to be acceptable or impressive to others, so what others see is not what is actually within you. You may start wearing a mask.

You may say what you think people want to hear, adopt a role you believe will gain approval, or push yourself to be 'perfect' in communication to avoid criticism. This can even lead to people being so afraid of sharing their opinions that they copy other people's work due to being afraid of showing their own. They might be afraid of telling the naked truth about their path or story because they don't believe it is as impactful as the story of someone else who lived through extreme hardship.

6. Inner Criticism and Self-Silencing:

Inner criticism can be a result of experiences where your voice has been suppressed by others. When those external circumstances are no longer present, you can internalise the rejection you have experienced. A harsh inner critic may belittle your thoughts before they are even expressed, leading to a self-perpetuating cycle of silence and self-doubt. We all have moments of self-criticism. However, imagine that your inner critic becomes the one and only voice in your head, and it keeps you from verbalising your needs and boundaries.

7. Physical Manifestations:

The suppression of voice can also have physiological and physical effects. Tightness in the throat, frequent throat infections, difficulty breathing when trying to express oneself, or even habitual throat clearing can be physical signs of a Voice Wound. Even tumours on vocal cords can show up, or vocal cord issues, as I myself have experienced. I struggled with a constant sore throat and almost lost my voice at the end of 2021. As I continued to work with my Voice Wound, I felt my throat chakra open up and the tension became much easier.

The Negative Effects of the Voice Wound

The Voice Wound does not only affect a person's ability to communicate—it shapes their entire experience of life. It limits personal freedom, relationships and creative potential, often creating patterns of suffering that go unnoticed for years, especially when a person is 'outspoken'. The Voice Wound might not make a person silent: on the contrary, it can make a person extremely outspoken and loud. The loudest ones are often the most wounded. The silent ones might suffer because of the Voice Wound, but also those who say a lot.

1. Isolation and Disconnection:

Communication is the foundation of connection. When you hold back your voice, you struggle to form meaningful professional and personal relationships. How to show love if you can't truly be yourself? You feel unknown or unseen by others, which leads to loneliness, frustration and a sense of alienation.

2. Lack of Fulfilment and Unmet Potential:

Being inauthentic in how you voice yourself can lead you to feel that you do not matter or only matter if you are like someone else. As a result, you tend to self-criticise and are less likely to pursue opportunities that require you to advocate for yourself.

You can be afraid of moving forward, and you stay in unfulfilling situations—whether in work, relationships or personal projects—because speaking up feels too risky and unsafe. Over time, this can create deep regret.

3. Powerlessness and Victimhood:

This is a biggie. A Voice Wound can create a belief that you have no control over your circumstances. If speaking up feels futile, you may resign yourself to a passive role in life, waiting for things to change rather than actively shaping your reality, and I often see that in my work with people. This can lead to patterns of being overlooked, underappreciated or mistreated without protest, and an inability to set boundaries in relationships.

4. Repressed Emotions and Anxiety:

Unspoken thoughts and emotions do not disappear; they fester. Suppressed feelings can turn into chronic anxiety, stress or even depression. A person with a Voice Wound may experience an inner turmoil that manifests as persistent restlessness or dissatisfaction without fully understanding the reason behind it.

5. A Cycle of Generational or Social Repetition:

Many people with a Voice Wound unconsciously pass it on to others. Whether as a parent, mentor or friend, if you learned to silence yourself, you may inadvertently reinforce the same suppression in others. As you grow, though, so will they. Without awareness, the cycle continues, affecting future generations.

Breaking Free from the Voice Wound

Recognising the Voice Wound is the first step toward healing. Reclaiming one's voice is not simply about speaking louder or more often—it is about restoring a deep internal trust in the validity of one's thoughts, feelings and right to expression.

Most people have, at some point, felt unheard or afraid to express their truth. The ability to reclaim your voice and connect your heart to healing in order to do so is an act of courage, liberation and self-acceptance. In learning to reconnect your heart with your voice, you not only reclaim your personal power but contribute to a world where all voices are honoured and heard.

The Heart: The Missing Piece of the Puzzle in Healing

The heart is the organ that pumps blood, but its significance extends far beyond physiology. In many cultures, the heart symbolises emotion, intuition, and the essence of our being; this is where feeling starts and ends.

When we discuss healing, it's easy to focus on physical ailments, psychological issues or lifestyle changes. However, the heart is the missing piece of the puzzle—an integral component that links our emotional, mental, spiritual and physical health as well as our soul.

The importance of HeartHealing can be conveyed through an exploration of its multifaceted role in our lives. It is not just about the ability to sustain life; it is about the quality of that life.

The heart is the portal to your soul. It holds all the emotions and memories you have lived through, and the experiences that have built your life. Who you are today has its foundation within your heart. For instance, stress and unresolved emotional trauma can contribute to heart disease, while a strong emotional state can significantly improve heart health.

To truly heal, you can address the root causes of many ailments rather than merely treating the symptoms. This is not to say that other modalities are ineffective; rather, HeartHealing can serve as a unifying thread that enhances their impact.

Through HeartHealing combined with astrology analysis and human design, I have witnessed powerful transformations in people. Common patterns emerge, regardless of their backgrounds. I have incorporated healing of the voice as my main line of work as

I have experienced it for years. It has changed me and my ability to build a happy relationship with my partner and my kids, while allowing me to set boundaries where needed.

In my observation, people have not only developed a stronger sense of self but started online businesses, spoken up within family environments and even rebuilt their marriages, as they finally dared to speak up and be honest about their needs. A mother stopped judging herself and stopped following other people's opinions on how to raise her children as a result of healing her Voice Wound through HeartHealing. She not only healed her own self-critic but reconnected with her mother and made a more spiritual environment for her own daughter to grow in.

The heart holds the capacity to not only heal your emotions and your past, but also holds the hope for a better future. With a healed heart, you can build the life you always wanted.

The heart is indeed the missing piece of the puzzle in holistic healing. By recognising its significance, we can foster a deeper understanding of the interconnectedness of emotional, mental, spiritual and physical health.

As I witness transformations in people who embrace heart-centred approaches, it becomes clear that this work is accessible to all. The journey toward healing the heart can lead to profound changes—improved relationships, enhanced physical health, and a renewed sense of purpose. By prioritising HeartHealing alongside other modalities, we create a more comprehensive and effective approach to overall well-being, ultimately leading to richer, more fulfilling lives.

My HeartHealing Transformation

In the tapestry of life, each thread is woven with stories—some vibrant, some muted, but all essential to the overall picture.

My own journey toward HeartHealing transformation began in a space filled with silence, a silence I had constructed around my own voice. For years, I was a chatterbox, effortlessly discussing the lives and experiences of others, yet crippled by an unshakeable fear when it came to sharing my own.

My words were like butterflies trapped in a jar, beautiful but unable to soar to their rightful place in the world. This fear of exposure, of "showing off" my work and my truth, held me captive. I was building a business but I was afraid to call myself a healer, an astrologer. I was always told that what I have to share is less important and less valid than what other people have to say. I was told from a very early age that as a woman, I would have to be more obedient to my future partner.

No-one would ever have thought that I struggled with my voice. I was an outspoken woman who was witty, funny, but never showed her full potential, as I feared that what I had to share would be mocked. I suffered with throat infections over and over again and in 2021, I was diagnosed with tumours on my vocal cords. I almost lost my voice in January 2022. I was terrified. I knew something had to be done, otherwise I would be muted for life. It felt like a life sentence. I slowly worked through the process of healing my heart and reconnecting with my voice.

I remember vividly the moment I was sharing my experiences on Instagram and I couldn't finish writing the post. I felt that the way I had written and how I described my experience was not as inspiring as the way others would put it. I craved sharing my story, to let my people know that more people were dealing with this issue than they thought, yet I found myself retreating into the shadows of self-doubt. What would they think of me? Would my story be worthy of their attention? These questions plagued my thoughts, creating a rift between my inner self and the world around me.

The first step on my path to healing was recognising this pattern—the tendency to hide my light under a bushel. It was a slow realisation, one that crept up on me during quiet moments of reflection. I had spent so much time trying to fit into the mould of what I thought was acceptable that I had lost touch with my authentic self. I needed to break free from the chains of fear and step into my power as a storyteller.

I began the journey of HeartHealing with Natasha and fell in love with it. Writing became my sanctuary. I started journaling, pouring my thoughts and feelings onto the pages without fear of judgment. Initially, it was a struggle. The inner critic loomed large, whispering doubts about the value of my experiences. But with time and a lot of healing, I learned to silence that voice, embrace the messiness of my emotions, and celebrate my journey.

Alongside writing, I explored teaching as a medium of expression. I created a programme for aspiring astrologers, allowing my knowledge and view of astrology to represent my feelings and stories. Each class became a cathartic release, a way to communicate the inexpressible. In those moments, I discovered the beauty of vulnerability—how it could transform pain into art and isolation into connection.

I also sought out community. I built a strong audience across social media and was invited to talk on national TV several times. I discovered that vulnerability is not a weakness; it is a bridge that can lead to profound healing. As I shared my journey, I noticed the shift within me. The more I opened up, the more I felt the weight of my fears lift.

My transformation was not instantaneous; it was a gradual unfolding. As I began to share my truths, I found that others resonated with my experiences. I was not alone in my struggles. This sparked a fire within me—a desire to continue sharing, to inspire others who might be trapped in their own silenced narratives, to heal those who struggled the same way I did.

The results of my healing were profound. I began to see myself as a vessel for stories—not just my own, but the stories of others as well. I felt empowered to call myself a specialist, a healer, and an astrologer who knows stuff. I witnessed a shift in my relationships, too. As I opened up, I found deeper connections with those around me, my partner and my four children. Conversations became more meaningful, filled with authenticity and understanding.

I also noticed the ripple effect of this transformation. My kids are learning to speak their truths and I support them in their path.

As I reflect on this journey, I recognise the universal patterns of transformation. Healing often begins with a willingness to confront our fears, to peel back the layers of self-doubt, and to embrace our authentic selves: the authenticity part is extremely important in this process. It is a process of discovery—unearthing the stories that have shaped us and finding strength in sharing your story with others so they can learn through your mistakes and experiences.

I encourage you to take a moment to reflect on your own narrative. What fears are holding you back from sharing your truth? What stories are waiting to be told? Start small—perhaps through journalling or art, or even by speaking your truth in a safe space. Heal slowly… but *heal*, connect with your heart and use HeartHealing as a way to break free.

This advice has served me well during my healing journey:

Embrace vulnerability as your superpower.

The act of sharing your story is a brave step towards healing, not just for yourself, but for those who will find solace in your words. You have the power to inspire others, to create connections, and to foster a community of healing.

Take a moment today to express yourself—whether through writing, art or conversation. Allow your heart to guide you. You may be surprised at the transformation that awaits you on the other side of fear. Your story matters. It deserves to be heard, and in sharing it, you may ignite a spark of healing within yourself and others.

As you embark on this journey of heart-healing transformation, remember that you are not alone. Each step you take is a testament to your courage, and the world is waiting to hear your unique story. Embrace it, celebrate it, and let it soar.

ABOUT THE AUTHOR

KINGA KUJAWA

Kinga Kujawa is a Spiritual Business Mentor who helps people build successful six-figure spiritual and healing businesses online by helping them find their true voice.

Before starting a writing business, Kinga spent ten years as an Astrologer and Tarot Reader. She has built a very large audience and has appeared on National TV, providing guidelines on astrology.

After building a successful career online, Kinga now helps others build a business to help hundreds of other people internationally.

Kinga enjoys trying new sports (shooting and CrossFit) and learning new skills.

She is available for marketing and writing projects, as well as private consultations.

www.kingaoliwiakujawa.com
kingaoliwiakujawa@gmail.com
facebook.com/kinga.oliwia.fredah
instagram.com/kingaoliwiakujawa

8

SILE O'BROIN

THE HEART OF IMPOSTER THINKING

Having doubts every so often is normal, especially when approaching a new task. You might feel a bit anxious when you've never tried something before. Nothing wrong with that. But imposter thinking is that persistent whisper that you are a fraud, that you are not good enough, that someone will find out and sack you. You may have these thoughts even if you are good at your job. Sometimes, that's when the whispers turn the volume up.

As a result, you may have constant low-grade anxiety and frequently second-guess yourself. You may have taken a myriad of courses and certifications so you could feel good enough. That didn't work, did it? Then you may have turned to conventional therapy, meditation and (fill in the blank). My guess is that nothing has really worked to get rid of the voices, right? You think it's your shameful secret, and you are doomed to live with it. That is not true. It is possible to overcome, master, tame and even quieten these thoughts.

I now know I am enough, exactly as I am. I trust myself. I know I am worthy of everything that comes my way. I know that the game of life is about committing to the rollercoaster adventure of expanding oneself to be, have and do more.

I no longer freeze in meetings or turn bright red with my heart pounding, terrified to speak lest I say something everyone considers stupid. I don't fear other people's judgment or get sudden panic attacks at the thought of someone finding out that I am not qualified for the job and should be fired. I don't hide anymore behind a pile of half-written speeches, articles and social media posts to avoid going to social and networking gatherings for the same reason.

My head no longer feels like a pressure cooker that explodes into migraines by Friday afternoon. I no longer spend my weekends in bed in complete darkness, sometimes fearing, other times dramatically wishing for death to end the pain. My weekends now are filled with fun and adventure – unthinkable a few years ago.

I don't live in fear, shame or guilt. I don't second-guess myself, which frees up my energy. I cannot believe how far I've come. I am beyond proud of myself for saying yes to sharing my journey through imposter thinking in this book collaboration and to being able to help others as a result. Perhaps having had crippling imposter thinking, it's easy for me now to spot it in others and gently coax them to have hope that there is light at the end of the dark tunnel. Everything really did happen *for* me for a reason.

That light is my coaching programme. I feel blessed to be able to help bright, talented women all over the world break free from the shackles of imposter thinking. Some of my coaching clients fly to me, some fly me to them so I can coach their staff, and others meet me on Zoom. I work in three languages: English, Italian and Spanish.

I usually work with successful, corporate women with several things in common: they are intelligent, sensitive, creative, kind... and without fail, they all think they are not good enough, unworthy and they don't trust themselves. In other words, they have imposter thinking.

Many give it more importance than it deserves by calling it imposter syndrome. I call it imposter *thinking* and here's why.

Imposter thinking is a closed thinking loop of: I am not enough, I am not worthy, I do not trust myself and I am a fraud. In essence, it is a psychological pattern whereby the individual doubts their abilities, feels like a fraud, and believes they don't deserve their accomplishments, despite all the evidence to the contrary. In my opinion, it is *not* a syndrome, because a syndrome is a set of medical signs and symptoms often associated with a particular disease or disorder. The bad news is that it's faulty thinking. The good news is that it can be changed easily, if you know how.

Even successful individuals, people you would never suspect, have bouts of imposter thinking. Studies of employees have found that 84% suffer from imposter thinking at some point. They secretly fear being "found out" or exposed as incompetent, even though they are objectively highly skilled and successful. They are constantly anxious, looking over their shoulders and wondering when someone will realise they are faking it and send them away. When asked, they often attribute their success to luck, timing or other factors rather than acknowledging their skills or effort. They downplay their achievements, believing they're not truly qualified or capable and they just "got lucky".

In the workplace, someone experiencing imposter thinking often feels anxiety to their core. They constantly doubt their performance and ideas, causing them to censor themselves in meetings, only to find that others then offer the same idea to a receptive audience.

Common thought loops and feelings:

Thoughts: "I don't belong here," "I'm not as qualified as people think I am," "It was just luck," "I'll never be able to maintain this," "Someone will find out I don't really know what I'm doing and I'm faking it."

Feelings: These thoughts lead to persistent feelings of anxiety, shame, guilt and fear, sometimes even bordering on paranoia (i.e. does this person realise I am a fraud? Will they expose me?). Very often, there's a deep sense of inadequacy, despite tangible proof of competence or accomplishments.

Left unchecked, imposter thinking can undermine your long-term personal growth, professional advancement, and overall well-being. It can take an emotional toll on your life and lead to emotional exhaustion. It can reduce your self-confidence, and stress becomes second nature. It may cause you to procrastinate, avoid promotions, or miss out on opportunities due to the fear of failing or being judged. The negative effects of this mindset are far-reaching, often leading those who have it to feel permanently stuck, anxious, and disconnected from their true potential.

This avoidance of opportunities and promotions for fear of being "found out" as inadequate commonly leads to career stagnation. A person may feel that any success they do achieve is due to luck, and therefore they don't deserve to advance. They often remain in roles that don't challenge them or allow for growth; they feel stuck, and rightly so.

Another common pattern is the tendency to overcompensate by working excessively hard. People with imposter thoughts often believe their value lies in how hard they work, not in their natural abilities or skills, and push themselves to their limits. The pressure to constantly prove themselves can lead to physical, mental and emotional burnout. They might find themselves exhausted, overwhelmed, even resentful of their workload, but still feel unable to stop or slow down for fear of failing or being exposed as incompetent.

On an emotional level, imposter thinking can cause deep anxiety, guilt, second-guessing and shame. These feelings often stem from the internal narrative that they're not good enough, not trustworthy, or that their accomplishments aren't truly deserved. This ongoing sense of deep inadequacy can lead to chronic self-doubt, even when there's external evidence of success. It also creates an unrelenting inner critic that makes it difficult to acknowledge achievements or accept praise and makes the person constantly self-censor. As a result, the person may feel disconnected from their own success and unable to enjoy or take pride in their accomplishments.

People who experience imposter thinking frequently struggle with low self-confidence. They are often terrified of making mistakes, as they equate any error with exposing their "fraudulence". This fear of failure can paralyse them, leading to procrastination or avoidance of difficult tasks. They may also be hesitant to share their ideas or seek help when needed, as they worry that others will judge them as unqualified.

Have you ever compared yourself with others and felt you never measured up? Imposter thinking is closely tied to this kind of negative comparison. You might look at others around you—colleagues, peers, or even people on social media—and think, "They've got it all figured out, and I'm just pretending." This constant comparison reinforces feelings of inadequacy, as you feel you don't measure up to others who seem more capable or confident. The truth is, everyone has their insecurities. You are human, and comparing yourself to others leads to self-doubt and frustration.

Imposter thinking can also be a barrier to meaningful, authentic relationships. When you feel like you don't belong or are undeserving of certain relationships, you may struggle to connect with others on a deeper level. You may withdraw socially or avoid seeking mentorship or support. Why? Because you believe you are unworthy of help or that others will discover your "secrets". This can lead to isolation, feelings of loneliness, and further self-doubt.

The longer a person's imposter thinking goes unaddressed, the more ingrained it becomes. The cycle of self-sabotage continues: the individual avoids challenges, second-guesses themselves, overworks to compensate, and experiences anxiety and shame, only to reinforce their belief that they aren't capable or good enough. Over time, this cycle can become so automatic that it becomes part of the person's identity, so much so that they would think while reading this, "others may have imposter thinking, but I really *am* an imposter."

If you have imposter thinking, it is holding you back from stepping into your true power. It is causing you to doubt your worth, isolate yourself, and remain stuck in limiting beliefs. When you recognise these patterns and address them through self-awareness, mindset shifts and heart healing support, you can begin to challenge everything that keeps you from fully embracing your potential.

Test Yourself: Do You Do This?

Perfectionism: Do you often set impossibly high standards for yourself and fear making mistakes? Do you perhaps believe that anything less than perfect performance will reveal your inadequacy?

Overwork: Do you compensate for your perceived lack of competence? Do you overwork, hoping to prove your worth to your supervisor and colleagues?

Avoiding challenges: Do you avoid new opportunities or challenges for fear of failing and "exposing" yourself?

Avoiding asking for help: Do you avoid asking for assistance from colleagues lest anyone "finds out" you are a fraud?

Avoiding visibility: Do you shy away from speaking up in meetings? Do you get panic attacks or nausea at the thought of having the spotlight on you?

Attribution errors: Do you downplay your abilities, attributing success to external factors like luck or other people's support, rather than recognising your role in it.

Imposter thinking has crept insidiously into the lives of many high-achieving and sensitive individuals. It doesn't announce itself in grand gestures but quietly weaves itself into the fabric of our thoughts and feelings, creating a subtle but significant internal conflict. It is a nagging voice in the back of the mind that whispers, "You don't belong here; you're not enough." It tells you that your wins aren't yours to claim, that you're one mistake away from being "found out", that you're not as capable as others think and that it is only a matter of time before someone finds out and kicks you out.

What's at the heart of this thinking, and why does it hold such power over us?

Through my work with clients over the years, I've observed that imposter thinking often has its roots in deep emotional wounds—especially wounds of the heart. Many of us experience early-life experiences that shape how we see ourselves.

Early Childhood Experiences

Growing up in environments where validation was scarce or inconsistent can create deep insecurity. If you were praised for your achievements but not for who you were, you might have internalised the message that your value is tied to what you do, not who you are. This can lead to a constant striving to prove your worth, even if you don't consciously realise that's what you're doing. To make this harder, it can also lead you to second-guess your every move or thought.

Criticism and High Expectations

Some individuals who experience imposter thinking were raised in environments where high expectations were placed on them. Parents, teachers, or other authority figures may have emphasised achievement and success as the means of gaining love or approval. If a parent or authority figure remarked on anything less than perfect marks, as a child you internalised it as you not being good enough. In other words, love was conditional. The constant drive for perfection and fear of disappointing others can cause you to question your value, especially when you're unable to meet those lofty standards.

Trauma or Emotional Neglect

Trauma, whether emotional, physical or psychological, can leave deep scars that influence how you see yourself. If you grew up in an environment where your needs weren't fully met or where you were subjected to criticism or neglect, it's easy to start questioning your worth. The deeper this wound goes, the more difficult it becomes to shake off the belief that you're not enough.

These experiences lay the foundation for the thought loops that fuel imposter thinking. The loop of "I'm not good enough," "I'll be found out," and "I don't deserve this," becomes ingrained, and the heart—our emotional centre—becomes locked in a state of fear and self-doubt.

Healing Imposter Thinking

In my experience as a coach offering a blend of coaching with HeartHealing and NLP sessions, the heart plays a crucial role in healing imposter thinking. When we experience emotional wounds, these are emotional blockages in the heart space—deep-seated beliefs of unworthiness, self-doubt, feeling not enough, compounded with a fear of rejection and shame. These emotional blockages are usually subconscious. Mostly, they defy logic and hide from our conscious mind. Left to fester, they can distort how we perceive our abilities and success, keeping us perpetually trapped in a vicious cycle of stress.

At the heart of imposter thinking are three wounds: feeling not enough, not trusting yourself and feeling unworthiness. When you don't feel enough, you feel unworthy of love, success, or recognition, you question your value. This manifests in thoughts like, "I don't deserve to be here," or, "I don't belong in this space." You don't trust your decisions, you sabotage yourself. When wounded by past experiences, your heart creates a lens through which you see the world, one that distorts reality and keeps you from fully accepting yourself.

When you heal this not enough and Worth Wounds, you start to shift your perception and everything changes. You begin to see that you *are* enough and you *are* worthy—not because of what you do, but because of who you are. The heart has the incredible ability to release these old emotional blockages, when you heal your Trust Wound as well, you start to step into your true power.

Healing imposter thinking is not about eliminating self-doubt entirely once and for all (that's an unrealistic expectation), but about shifting your relationship with it. It is about learning to recognise imposter thoughts as they arise, understanding that they are not the truth about you, and shifting out of them to more empowering and forward-thinking thoughts and actions. Healing the heart of imposter thinking involves a process of vulnerability, self-acceptance, self-compassion and recognising your inherent worth.

When my clients begin this healing process, the transformations are nothing short of remarkable. They begin to:

1. **Embrace Their True Power**: Instead of feeling not good enough, unworthy and a fraud, they start to recognise and honour their abilities, achievements, and strengths. They begin to trust themselves and their inner wisdom, relying less and less on external validation.
2. **Cultivate Self-Compassion**: They learn to treat themselves with kindness when they make mistakes, understanding that perfection is an illusion. They begin to see mistakes as opportunities for growth, not evidence of their inadequacy.
3. **Foster Authentic Connections**: As they heal their emotional wounds, they start to form deeper, more authentic relationships. No longer afraid of being "found out", they embrace vulnerability and connection with others, knowing that they are enough as they are.
4. **Expand Their Toolbox:** When imposter thoughts arise, they no longer feel trapped by them. They have cultivated a variety of strategies and tools to shift their thinking to more positive and empowering thoughts. They no longer feel helpless or ashamed, or get overwhelmed for long. They know they can access these tools anytime to realign with their true selves, regain confidence, and shift their mindset.

5. **Take Bold Action:** Once the weight of imposter thinking lifts, they feel free to step into new opportunities without fear of failure or judgment. What used to be insurmountable risks are now challenges they welcome; they get promoted and generally go after what they truly want in life.

When clients heal imposter thinking, they are not just transforming their own life—they're impacting everyone around them. By stepping into their full potential and embracing their worth, they become a beacon of possibility for others. This means that they create space for others to heal, too, by showing them that it's possible to let go of self-doubt and step into a life of authenticity, confidence and empowerment.

Changing Your Life

Healing imposter thinking changes everything. It changes the way you see yourself, the way you approach challenges, and the way you connect with others. It allows you to embrace the fullness of who you are, to celebrate your successes, and to trust that you are worthy of all that you've achieved.

The process of healing is not a destination—it's a journey of self-discovery, self-love, and self-empowerment. But when you embark on this journey, you will begin to experience life in a way that feels authentic, fulfilling, and aligned with your true self.

You have always been enough. It's time to embrace that truth and let go of the imposter thinking that's been holding you back. When you heal your heart, you heal your life. And when you heal your life, you heal the world.

This chapter almost didn't get written. For days, I couldn't bring myself to sit at a computer, let alone write. I told myself I was busy (and I was), promising myself that I would get to it. So I set a time to sit down to write. When that time finally came, I had a shocking revelation that came in the form of poisonous whispers. They were swirling around, barely noticeable, saying, "Who do you think you are writing a chapter of this book? Why would anyone listen to you? How can you write about imposter thinking? Look at you, you haven't started so you haven't got it sorted out at all: you're a fraud. You're going to get found out." I caught myself in that moment and started laughing. I sat down, chuckled to myself and started to write.

You see, the thing about healing from imposter thinking is *not* that you will never have these thoughts ever again; you will. I sometimes do, especially when starting a new project like this one. The transformation happens in the fact that they will *never* hold you back again. They will never hold your life and your potential hostage again. You can laugh about it when these thoughts resurface. You can chuckle at their familiar voices and then get on with creating your best life.

Here's how I know. Throughout my school years, college and master's degrees, I suffered from constant bouts of imposter thinking. Thinking that I could not write (later years I became a writer for different organisations), that everyone else was better than me, not trusting myself when it came to going for opportunities only to see them go to colleagues whose only difference to me was that they believed in themselves and they trusted themselves.

My imposter thinking led me to change jobs, countries and careers every two years. I cringed at meetings, praying I would not have to speak in public and feeling nauseous at the thought. When presenting, I stuttered and my face turned bright red, compounding my already inflamed shame.

Second-guessing myself led to a series of failed relationships, including one that never should have started. I ignored the loud warnings from my gut, which was practically screaming for me to run the other way. Because I couldn't trust myself or my own judgment, I began to shut down my intuition. It stopped sending me signals, and instead, I found myself relying on the advice and opinions of others—many of whom didn't have my best interests at heart. When the internal stress of feeling unworthy became too much to bear, it manifested physically, often in the form of a migraine that knocked me out over the weekend.

It felt like constant low-grade anxiety, one that showed up in the compulsive picking at my cuticles or biting my nails. I was ashamed of these habits, believing I lacked the willpower to stop. The shame felt as unrelenting as my migraines. Socially, I'd make plans to go out with friends to a nightclub, pub, or dance event, but more often than not, I'd back out at the last minute. The anxiety would hit as soon as I reached the door, quickly escalating into a migraine. I'd offer a quick excuse, retreat to my bed, and curl up, hiding from the world.

My journey to today has been long and ragged. After a ton of personal development, NLP, coaching, psychology books, good nutrition and supplements and lifestyle changes, I got better at masquerading my unworthiness to seem 'normal'. I also was able to tame most of my bouts of migraine. While I still avoided speaking in meetings and in public as much as possible, my face would not go as red if I did speak up.

It was only when I went through HeartHealing that I was able to get to the root of my feelings of not being good enough, unworthiness, self-doubt and shame and heal them so that I had no more migraines, I stopped compulsively biting my nails, I trusted my decisions, and I listened and acted upon my intuition. Who would have thought that I now enjoy speaking in public?

I have made it my mission to liberate one million people from the prison of imposter thinking. If I can get rid of imposter thinking, so can you!

If you know you currently have imposter thinking, help is at hand. I invite you first to calm your nervous system in your body while releasing all the stuck, repeating patterns in your head. How, I hear you ask. Start with a journal with three columns. Note what you say to yourself that goes largely unnoticed. Sit in a quiet place, concentrate on regulating your breathing if you have to and listen to your internal 'radio'. What are your current beliefs, fears, attitudes and behaviours?

Split them into two columns: helpful and unhelpful, and in the third column write what feelings, emotions and reactions come up as a result. Don't censor, judge or dismiss what comes up; trust that what comes up is ready to be cleared. This first exercise will give you a good overview of the emotional and physical patterns in your life.

Once you have identified this, it's time to clear the emotional charge that holds these patterns in place. Releasing the charge with total acceptance and forgiveness will have you break free from its shackles. You are replacing these negative subliminal thoughts with positive ones and your internal radio becomes your cheerleader instead of your worst enemy.

If you want to go deeper into understanding how imposter syndrome shows up for you, head over to my website www.heartshipcoach.com to schedule a five-day Masterclass where we go into more depth into the different kinds of imposter thinking and how they show up. You'll also receive a thirty-minute strategy session where you will understand how imposter thinking is holding you back and leave with a customised plan on how you can master your imposter thinking.

References:

Clance, P. R., & Imes, S. A. (1978). *The Impostor Phenomenon in High Achieving Women: Dynamics and Therapeutic Intervention. Psychotherapy: Theory, Research & Practice,* 15(3), 241–247.

Young, Dr. V. *The Secret Thoughts of Successful Women: Why Capable People Suffer from the Impostor Syndrome and How to Thrive in Spite of It* (2011).

ABOUT THE AUTHOR

SILE O'BROIN

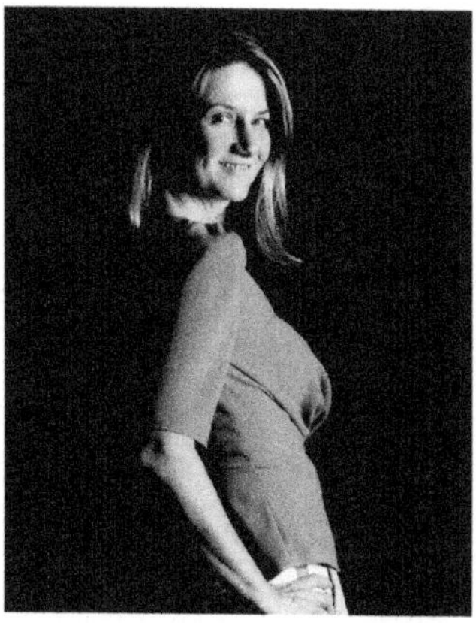

Sile O'Broin is a highly intuitive and results-driven transformational coach dedicated to helping talented women—both young and young at heart—banish imposter thinking and step fully into their power. Drawing from two decades of experience in communication, coaching, and training across twenty-four countries, she blends transformational coaching, NLP, and HeartHealing modalities to create rapid, lasting shifts in confidence, success and self-belief.

Having spent her childhood between Europe and Asia, Sile has a deep appreciation for different cultures and perspectives. Fluent in five languages—English, Italian, Irish, French, and Spanish—with rusty Chinese—her multicultural background allows her to connect deeply with women from diverse walks of life. A business nomad with a passion for adventure and making a positive impact, she has worked in high-stakes environments, including leadership roles at the United Nations.

Her coaching stands out for its depth, speed, and effectiveness—achieving in months what traditional methods might take years to accomplish.

Beyond coaching, Sile brings her passion for life into everything she does—dancing tango, dabbling in theatre, and, whenever possible, bareback horse riding.

www.heartshipcoach.com
hello@heartshipcoaching.com

9

LAURA ANNA BALLERIO

THE HEART OF THRIVING

Healing my heart has profoundly transformed the way I move through the world. It has changed how I relate to myself, to others, to my work, and to my spiritual path.

I still remember the words of one of my teachers during an intensive seminar: *"I don't know if you'll ever fully experience love."* Those words hit me like a slap in the face. And yet, the opening of my heart led me exactly there — to live the opposite.

Today, I carry within me a core of inner safety that allows me to walk through life with trust and openness, aligned with who I truly am and guided by my intuition. I am free from the pressure to do more and prove more for years in order to feel loved and seen. I am free from the vision of success that long dictated my steps, urging me to work harder and earn more. Most importantly, I have opened my heart to love.

In 2024, I had to slow down my work due to health and family issues. During that period, despite the challenges, I felt a deep trust in life and in the transition I was moving through. That inner sense of safety and perceived abundance sustained me as I rebirthed a new version of myself with a renewed outlook on life.

Today, I feel love — for myself, for others, for the Divine. I feel much more compassion and acceptance — for myself and for others — and a sense of wholeness I have never experienced before, one that expands each day. My relationship with my teenage son has transformed: I've released the need for control, and where once was conflict and opposition is now dialogue and trust. My relationship with my partner has become deeper and more intimate since I dropped the "strong woman" mask and allowed my vulnerability to be seen. Connection with others feels much more authentic.

Today, I feel free to express myself — even in my vulnerability. I feel open to trying new things, even the ones that challenge me the most. I've let go of the fear of failure, and I recognise that every experience can bring gifts. I no longer compare myself to others, because I trust myself, my path, and the path of everyone who walks this Earth.

Today, I am a recognised healer and mentor — appreciated, chosen and re-chosen. I've built a relationship of trust with my clients and audience: a trust that remained solid even when I had to slow down and show up less on social media.

This is the space from which I move in my work — a work rooted in inner safety, freedom and love.

I love guiding women to recognise and embody their power and gifts. I support them to free themselves from what holds them back from fully expressing who they are, in their relationships, lives and work. I help them cultivate deep inner safety, so they can thrive and create a life that reflects who they are, emotionally, relationally, financially and spiritually. As they rise, they lift those around them — their families, their communities and the generations to come.

Chances are you too feel a strong call to thrive — to live a life rich with meaning, with fulfilment, with relationships that nourish you, a life that honours who you are and the unique path you are here to walk, whatever that means for you.

Maybe you've only just heard this call. Maybe you've walked this path for a long time. You've chosen, built, transformed, and now, something feels stuck. You're no longer flowing, no longer expanding.

Thriving is not a linear journey. It includes beginnings, pauses, slowdowns — even steps backwards. It's made up of expansions and contractions, just like the breath, just like nature teaches us. Being in contraction is hard, I know. You were taught to do, to produce, to perform. To be strong. To do things well.

But this is exactly when a doorway opens. Because contraction — even if it doesn't seem like it — is still movement. It's a space where you can pause, listen without pushing, tend to what is asking to be healed, and then continue your journey.

To move through this space, you are called to welcome your shadows, to hold trust, and look through a lens that is as non-judgmental as possible — one that sees how every experience carries teachings and gifts.

From here, you can transform what you're living through into new wisdom that will guide your choices and actions, in alignment with who you are now.

But what is the key to thriving?

After years of personal experience and walking alongside my clients I've seen a golden thread that runs through every story: the lack of safety. This heart wound, the Safety Wound, is not always visible, yet it weaves through all the others.

This insight aligns with several foundational theories. Attachment theory teaches that a secure base allows a child to explore the world, learn and take risks (Bowlby, 1969). The same is true for us as adults.

Polyvagal theory shows that when the nervous system *feels safe,* we are more open to thriving (Porges, 2011).

Expansion requires letting go of the old and stepping into the unknown. When you feel safe you can walk your path with freedom, flowing instead of fighting. Feeling safe gives you strong roots to grow, to dare, to receive and to blossom after being shaken by life's challenges. It allows you to trust, even when things don't go as planned.

On the other hand, when you don't feel safe, you close off to exploration and opportunity. Your system goes into survival mode. All your energy is spent defending against fear — not creating from love. Consciously, you may feel the pull to thrive but deep within, there's often an unseen part of you that holds you back, afraid you'll fail or end up alone.

You may have lived experiences that made it hard for you to *feel* safe. These don't need to be big traumas. It can be any moment that left you feeling rejected, betrayed, unloved or alone (Bray, 2023). Maybe you won a competition, rushed to your best friend to share the joy — and she downplayed it.

As we grow, we forget or minimise these moments, but the heart remembers. It builds energetic walls to protect you from feeling that pain again. They served you back then, but today, they may be keeping you from thriving.

Not all of this, however, begins with your personal story. Recent research in neuroscience and systemic constellations shows that insecurity can be inherited, passed down through generations.

Healing on this level can make a powerful difference in your capacity to thrive (Wolynn, 2016; School of Healing Mastery, 2023).

Sometimes, the feeling of not being safe isn't immediately obvious. Your life, from the outside, may look "fine". But inside, something feels off. You know you can't keep going this way. Part of you senses you're not truly living.

Signs That the Safety Wound Is Asking for Healing

Internal (Emotional, Mental, Physical) Signs:

- Anxiety, hypervigilance
- Low mood
- Frequent anger or irritability
- Overthinking and mental looping
- Confusion
- Boredom, dissatisfaction or frustration
- Feeling overwhelmed
- Everything feels like a struggle
- Fear of scarcity or of losing what you have
- Fear of success and its responsibilities
- Harsh self-criticism
- Need to control everything
- Fear of rejection, judgment or loss
- Disconnection from yourself or others
- Guilt or shame
- Resentment
- Fear of being alone
- Feeling isolated
- Feeling unsafe having "more" than others (talents, success, money)

Behavioural Signs:

- Compulsive hoarding or over-accumulating
- Neglecting your own care
- Abuse of alcohol or other substances
- Overworking

Relational Signs:

- Overprotectiveness of children or loved ones
- People-pleasing, placing others before yourself
- Feeling like your needs don't deserve attention
- Difficulty saying "no" or setting boundaries
- Staying in unhealthy or unfulfilling relationships
- Avoiding authenticity out of fear of being seen
- Difficulty trusting or opening up
- Hiding who you are, your gifts, needs or opinions
- Withdrawing or isolating yourself

Work / Financial Signs:

- Feeling done with your work and wanting to give it all up
- Feeling creatively blocked
- Constantly second-guessing your decisions
- Avoiding visibility, communication or taking initiative
- Taking action from a place of fear or scarcity rather than alignment
- Avoiding change — even when you know it's what you need
- Turning down promotions or opportunities
- Failing to take action on your dreams
- Slowing down your own success because of fear
- Anxiety when seeing your bank balance drop or fear of financial loss
- Hitting an income ceiling you can't seem to break through

If you recognise yourself in even one of these signs, please know this: you are not broken. You are simply in a phase of contraction. Every one of these signs can become a portal to your next expansion. The keys to moving through this are the heart, its healing, and the freedom that rises from it.

Healing the heart brings you home to yourself. From that place, you can choose, create — and thrive.

Over nearly thirty years of personal healing, I have explored psychotherapy, family constellations, past life regression, bodywork, energy healing and more. Each path offered me something valuable, yet a piece of the puzzle still felt missing, until I discovered the transformative power of the heart.

I witness it every day in my work with clients: the heart — and HeartHealing — accelerates healing in remarkable ways. It does so gently, powerfully, and with deep respect for each person's rhythm.

Unlike many methods that stop at awareness or take a long time to bring about tangible change, this powerful technique facilitates deeply felt embodied transformation, often in a surprisingly short time. Nor does it stop with you: healing of the heart naturally ripples out into your relationships.

The heart is the master integrator between mind, body and soul. When you dissolve the energetic walls you've built around it, you begin to feel, think, act, and relate in entirely new ways. You open yourself to receiving on every level, including the spiritual.

The heart is the first organ to function in an embryo, as early as the twenty-first day of prenatal life. Recent scientific research has shown that the heart contains its own "little brain", composed of 40,000 neurons capable of processing information independently and storing memories and emotions that influence our emotional and relational state (Armour, 1999).

They also found that the heart communicates with the brain through multiple pathways: biophysical, neurological, electromagnetic and biochemical. This communication flows primarily from the heart to the brain — not the other way around — shaping the nervous system, decision-making and emotional responses (McCraty et al, 2009).

When the heart is at peace, calm and in harmony, the entire mind-body system receives signals of safety: the key to thriving.

I see this in every session I lead, whether in 1:1 programmes or group work.

My clients are mostly visionary women (and men too), many of whom have already done deep inner work and built a lot in their lives. They feel a strong call to freedom — to bring their gifts into the world through their art, services or incredible products. Others are employees seeking more love, more freedom to be themselves, and greater fulfilment.

When we begin working together, they are often in a state of contraction. It is sometimes subtle, sometimes intense. Some feel anxious and mentally overwhelmed. Others feel numb or blocked.

Many are navigating family dynamics with parents, partners or children that pull them out of their centre. They struggle to set boundaries and, when they do, often feel guilt or anger. They hold back from expressing their truth. They've internalised the push to perform, to always do things well. And this very impulse to "never give up" often leads them to lose themselves. They're caught in effort, exhaustion and self-judgment.

Many experienced emotional or physical abandonment in childhood or didn't feel protected by their parents. Often, they had to take on responsibilities too big for their age. They learned that love was conditional: to receive it, they had to hide who they really were and deny their own needs. Some experienced a prenatal life where they didn't feel safe or weren't wanted. This can deeply wound the sense of right to exist, holding them back from fully taking their place in the world (Verny & Kelly, 1981).

I guide them through transformation across five levels with my Flourishing Method:

1. **Mind Healing:** we identify conscious and subconscious beliefs that block thriving, opening the door to deeper healing (School of Healing Mastery, 2021).
2. **HeartHealing:** we heal emotional and relational wounds — personal, ancestral or karmic.
3. **Energetic and Somatic Integration:** we cultivate grounding and calm through body-centred awareness and energy work, restoring the balance between doing, rest and pleasure.
4. **Aligned Action:** we turn transformation into action with practical guidance on making empowered choices, taking aligned steps.
5. **Financial Safety:** we create a conscious relationship with money, where income is not only received but sustained and managed with care, building the base for long-term expansion.

I've found that Ancestral HeartHealing — an advanced form of HeartHealing that works epigenetically to heal the hearts of our ancestors, ourselves, future generations and the collective — is especially effective in cases of apathy, loss of vitality, or after destabilising life events. Clients often describe the change as cellular.

Working at this level anchors a deeper sense of safety that comes from the roots.

I'm integrating it more and more into my programmes to allow people to thrive, with clients reporting results in many areas:

Emotional

They begin to feel alive again – peaceful, connected to their purpose. They release the need for hyper-control and begin trusting themselves and life. From this new grounded presence, they make different choices, prioritising their well-being and letting go of the urge to constantly do and give. They reclaim their worth and their creativity flows. Their empowerment extends naturally into every part of life.

Financial / Professional

They position their business with greater clarity and freedom, and create, launch and sell new offers or products. They receive professional recognition, new job contracts and collaboration requests, even from prestigious organisations. They raise their prices and attract clients who are ready to invest. They optimise their work, earning more while working with greater ease.

Depending on their starting point and the nature of the professional path, some step into a new phase of growth, some have reported doubling their revenue, and others boldly step into a new level of expansion. Money is no longer just something to receive but something to hold and steward. They can manage it with awareness, creating a secure foundation from which to expand with confidence.

Relational

They redefine what types of relationships and behaviours they are willing to accept. Their relationships shift and become lighter. Conflicts with parents soften or are managed with less guilt. Partnerships become more intimate and collaborative. Relationships with children improve. They begin to choose and nurture more nourishing connections.

Spiritual

They reactivate or amplify their connection with intuition and their spiritual guides. This allows them to move quickly and in deep alignment. Ancestral healing brings with it a sense of being supported by their roots and by the Divine. Even in moments of uncertainty, they feel held.

When the heart opens, everything changes. Expansion takes the place of contraction. I know this path intimately. Every fall becomes a gateway into deeper, wiser power, opening the way to a new season of thriving.

At fifteen, I was reading books about teenagers dealing with addiction, dreaming of one day working in therapeutic communities to help them. I didn't know it, but my true desire was to save my father. He died in a car accident when I was two and a half years old, one month before my younger brother was born. For a long time, I lived with only part of the truth.

When I was thirty, I discovered by chance that my father had attempted suicide twice while I was still in the womb. My sense of not feeling safe began there.

After his death, I experienced the emotional absence of my mother, who was navigating overwhelming grief. My grandmother cared for me and my brother. Over time, I learned to love her, but as a child, I was terrified by her rigidity. I was afraid my mother would die too and leave me alone with her.

I learned that the world was not a safe place and that love could disappear in an instant. I grew up feeling different, as though I didn't belong here. I asked myself many questions, seeking to understand myself, others and the world.

That's why I chose to study philosophy. It marked the beginning of my conscious search for meaning.

During university, I lived a double life. I moved through environments where drug and alcohol use were normalised without fully falling into those patterns, while at the same time excelling academically. I graduated and built a career as vice president and press officer for a professional theatre company.

In my personal life, though, I struggled to set boundaries. I often felt overwhelmed by others' needs and energies. It was as if I had no filter — everything came in. The only way I knew to cope was to retreat into isolation.

In love, I kept people at a distance. I pushed away those who showed up with too much presence. Eventually, I fell in love with my partner.

When our son was born, wounds I thought I had healed came to the surface, amplified by medical negligence and obstetric violence during childbirth. Everything collapsed: I experienced deep postpartum depression.

Motherhood cost me my job. I became financially dependent on my partner. I no longer recognised myself.

Our relationship was filled with conflict and tension. Financial strain following the collapse of a business he was involved in made everything worse. We had savings, but using them made me feel like the ground was crumbling beneath me. I remember the anxiety of that period tightening around my throat.

Through psychotherapy, I began to rebuild. I reclaimed my power, returned to work, and redefined my relationship with my partner. Together, we rebuilt harmony and began to grow again.

At a certain point, I felt a strong call to align my outer life with what my soul was asking for. I trained as a counsellor, a perinatal educator, and took part in multiple training programmes. I became a Reiki Master; Reiki sparked a deep desire to stop playing small and take myself seriously.

Between 2019 and 2020, I invested in marketing and personal branding to launch my business. At the same time, I studied financial literacy, learning how to invest wisely and build my own economic foundation.

The business grew, but it was hard to scale. Despite my efforts, the results weren't satisfying. I felt invisible to my audience, like a wall separated me from them. I kept repeating to myself, "*No one sees me.*" I focused entirely on doing, believing that working harder would lead me to success. Instead, it led me to burnout.

That's when I discovered HeartHealing and I understood that beyond doing, I had to make space for being. Healing came in layers, and with each step, a new level of expansion became possible.

I began by working on myself through the Ultimate Uplevel Academy, led by Natasha Leigh Bray. I fell in love with the HeartHealing technique and overcame my fear of language barriers to train in it. I completed Level 1 and 2 certifications and introduced HeartHealing in Italy. Later, I pursued Level 3, training in Ancestral HeartHealing.

Emotionally, I became more compassionate with myself. I learned how to navigate my emotional waves. I opened my heart to love. I now feel secure and grounded in trust in myself and in life.

Professionally, I experienced an immediate up-level. I let go of marketing models that diluted my voice and resumed writing with joy and clarity. My energy and message shifted and I began to stand out. People saw me and chose to work with me. I went from having very few clients to a full calendar. I left my part-time job, took more risks, and allowed myself to shine my own way.

As a HeartHealing practitioner, I positioned myself more clearly in the marketplace. I created powerful group programmes, many of which sold out before launch. I now work with returning clients who come back when they are ready for the next layer of healing.

I released my fear of scarcity and loss. I stopped hiding, ended unhealthy relationships, and deepened those that nourished me. I rebalanced the responsibilities in my household, offering my son a new model of womanhood — one I hope to help normalise in my country: a woman who is not burdened with *all* the caregiving; a woman who explores, creates and provides for her family with confidence and joy while still saving money.

Spiritually, I reawakened my intuition. I had shut it down in childhood, because my feelings (especially about my father) were constantly dismissed. But something deeper happened: I began to feel the Divine. I felt safe again. This sense of safety has allowed me to navigate contraction with trust. I now bring everything life has taught me into my work to spark powerful, real transformation.

This is what happened with Maria. She had been a professional for years, but was afraid to show her gifts fully. She was working hard but avoiding the very opportunities that would elevate her in both the quality of her work and her income. In her private life, unresolved family tensions drained her energy.

Through our work, she set healthy boundaries and healed core family wounds. She found peace and forgiveness. She structured her business more effectively, healed her relationship with money, and began to experience financial flow. Today she spends, saves and invests with joy. She finally feels she can trust her path and has made major life decisions.

Alina, a business owner, had lost her peace. She was working constantly and had no life beyond work. Despite her efforts, she couldn't reach the next level and it was draining her. Through our work, she reclaimed peace and excitement. She made space for her most important relationships. Feeling safe and guided by her intuition, she began climbing toward her next level of success and radiated a magnetic presence.

Eleonora worked constantly, yet was deeply bored with what she did. She earned plenty but struggled to keep it. She reconnected with her inner guidance, rediscovered joy and creativity, and began organising transformational events. She attracted high-level collaborations, released her fear of scarcity, brought peace to her family relationships and started tending to her finances with care.

These kinds of transformations don't happen through effort alone. They happen when the heart feels safe.

You can begin here, without forcing anything:

Journaling Prompt

Place one hand on your heart and take a few deep breaths.
Then ask yourself:
"How would my experience shift if I felt even a little more safe — in my body, in my work, in my relationships?"

Let the answer arise without trying to analyse or control it. Repeat this practice often — it gently moves you from where you are toward where you're meant to be.

If you feel ready to hold more — to open to a deeper shift — ask:
"How would my life, my work or my relationships change if I felt deeply safe?"

Welcome whatever comes, without judgment. Compassion is the key. From here, your freedom begins.

References:

Armour, J.A. (1999), *Neurocardiology: Anatomical and functional principles*. In: Berntson, R. M. and Cacioppo, J. T. eds. Advances in Psychophysiology, Vol. 3. London: Jessica Kingsley Publishers, pp. 65–114

Bray, N.L.(2023), *Your next six figures: Reveal and heal your way to receiving and holding your next six-figure year, launch, or month—without the sabotage.*

Bowlby, J. (1969), *Attachment and Loss: Volume 1. Attachment.* New York: Basic Books.

McCraty, R., Atkinson, M. and Tomasino, D., (2009), *The coherent heart: Heart-brain interactions, psychophysiological coherence, and the emergence of system-wide order. Integral Review*, 5(2), pp.10–115.

Porges, S.W. (2011), *The Polyvagal Theory: Neurophysiological Foundations of Emotions, Attachment, Communication, Self-Regulation*. New York: W.W. Norton & Company.

School of Healing Mastery (2021).

School of Healing Mastery (2023).

Verny, T. and Kelly, J. (1981), *The Secret Life of the Unborn Child.* New York: Dell Publishing.

Wolynn, M. (2016), *It Didn't Start With You: How Inherited Family Trauma Shapes Who We Are and How to End the Cycle.* New York: Penguin Books.

ABOUT THE AUTHOR

LAURA ANNA BALLERIO

Laura Anna Ballerio is a Healer and Mentor who guides visionary women to thrive emotionally, relationally, financially and spiritually.

Before starting her business, she worked as a Process and Audit Manager at a nationally recognised association supporting individuals with Down syndrome. She applied her organisational skills to optimise processes, and her counselling and philosophical expertise to manage interpersonal dynamics, collaborating closely with a multidisciplinary team of psychotherapists, educators, pedagogists, doctors and psychiatrists.

Today, she guides women through a unique blend of mentoring and sacred healing journeys, helping them heal deep emotional blocks, reconnect with their inner wisdom, transform their relationship with money, and take aligned action as they walk along their unique path.

Laura loves walking in nature, especially near water, and dancing.

Laura is available for private and group packages.

www.lauraballerio.it
info@lauraballerio.it
facebook.com/laura.ballerio.5
linkedin.com/in/laura-anna-ballerio-3a353522

10

LUCY LAMBERT

THE HEART OF BURNOUT

Being excited about the future again has been a huge turning point for me.

It didn't happen overnight; in fact, it took a lot longer than I imagined, but I was determined and I have made it. I can finally appreciate my life, see the positivity in every day, and look forward to everything I still have to experience and achieve. I have finally allowed myself to relax.

I was gripped by anxiety for many years. I worked as a primary school teacher and managed the needs of my own three children, two of whom have disabilities; at times, I thought the mental and physical load would break me. With so much cortisol in my body, I was ready to fight a lion at any given moment, and I developed chronic fatigue and struggled to get out of bed.

I can now see the lesson in everything I have been through. Indeed, I am grateful for it, and for the huge gift it is to share these teachings with others, preventing other women from sacrificing themselves the same way or at least halting it before they burn out completely.

I have forgiven myself for being imperfect and have found compassion for my needs, which has led to enormous shifts in my mindset and my physical body. My recognition of my 'big T' and 'little t' trauma, some of which I had filed away and hoped never to visit again, has resulted in finally healing the physical and emotional burnout I suffered for years.

For a long time, life was an uphill battle. Learning to love myself and recognising that it wouldn't mean I had any less to give anyone else – in fact, I was able to give more but differently – was a huge shift for me. I am still adjusting to it.

I now know I deserve a happy and fulfilled life and I don't have to hide my needs and desires behind those of others. In fact, I have come to realise that my happiness enhances the lives of those around me. Through working on myself and modelling self-love to those around me, particularly my children, I impart the hard-earned wisdom I have gained by walking a difficult path for so long.

I am not only a happier person for having learned to love and respect myself and my needs, but a stronger one. It is not indulgent to show myself love and compassion, but absolutely necessary *and* I deserve it; we all do.

I left the classroom four years ago due to burnout. However, it is now my mission and my passion to continue teaching others about the transformational impact of learning to truly love and understand yourself at heart level.

Have you ever felt so emotionally, physically and mentally exhausted that you cannot recover?

Have you been so drained, detached and unmotivated that you are unable to undertake everyday tasks?

Has the thought of starting work been so overwhelming that you cannot face it?

You may well be suffering from burnout.

At its heart, burnout is a state of emotional, physical and mental exhaustion. It develops when you're exposed to prolonged stress and feel constantly under pressure, without enough time or resources to recover.

While it's not classified as a medical or mental health condition, burnout is recognised by the World Health Organization (WHO) as an 'occupational phenomenon'. It is defined as a syndrome—a group of symptoms linked to ongoing, unmanageable, often unseen stress.

Although burnout is related to stress, the two are quite different. You have probably had a time when your level of stress affected your sleep, energy or mood. However intense this period was, you could probably keep going. Burnout, on the other hand, is deeper and longer lasting. You may also feel hopeless about your ability to improve your situation.

Burnout is often associated with work, but it can also be triggered by other long-term responsibilities—such as caregiving, parenting, studying, or managing a chronic illness. It typically arises when demands continually outweigh the time, energy or support available to meet them.

Whatever the cause, burnout can seriously affect your overall wellbeing, including your personal life and relationships. That's why it's important to spot the signs before it drains your energy, motivation, and hope.

I see people so consumed with the daily needs of others, be it family, colleagues, partners or children, that they forget their own needs, or even that they have any, until it is too late. Having experienced this myself, it is difficult to see them suffer and it frightens me to think of what they are doing to themselves by soldiering on.

Clever and resourceful as we are, we cannot outwit our basic imperative to care for ourselves, our bodies and our hearts. We are not robots. Living without love for ourselves results in broken wiring of the nervous system and an utterly confused body and mind. We can be hanging on by a thread and going through the motions of life because of the unrelenting pressure put on us both internally and externally, without recognising the potential threat to our health.

For several years, I have tried every physical solution imaginable to tackle my symptoms of chronic fatigue. My exhaustion impacted every area of my life and affected the way I showed up as a mother, wife and teacher. I was in fight, flight or freeze and struggled to prioritise my own needs. My weight was increasing and brain fog meant I found it hard to focus on anything. I was utterly exhausted and miserable.

However, I have always been a tenacious person and, despite being physically and emotionally drained, was determined to find out what was wrong with me.

I discovered that both burnout and emotional exhaustion are typically triggered by prolonged exposure to elevated levels of stress, whether at work, in personal life, or a combination of both. In fact, according to Mental Health UK, 'Burnout is a state of physical, mental, and emotional exhaustion. It can occur when you experience long-term stress and feel under constant pressure.'

Experts argue that 'anyone… who feels overwhelmed by repeated or continuous difficulties or has experienced severe or chronic emotional or physical trauma or illness is probably already suffering from some degree of adrenal fatigue.' (Wilson, 2017) It is also true that our ability to withstand stress varies from person to person. 'Repeated stresses, no matter what their cause, make a person more prone to adrenal fatigue. The effects of stress are cumulative, even when the individual stressors are quite different.' (Wilson, 2017) We are effectively burning out our adrenal glands through stress.

This resonates with me. I fell ill with a nasty virus at the end of 2016, the severity of which I had never experienced before, to the extent that I could hardly get out of bed. However, in the new year, I got on with things, looking after our two young children without having taken the necessary recovery time.

To compound the situation, my son started nursery school in January, at which point it became apparent that he was neuro-divergent and struggled hugely with the formal environment. I found it emotionally draining and triggering. I also had a horrible encounter with someone I thought was my friend, but who came into my home and verbally attacked me. This shocked and upset me hugely.

Then in April 2017, I fell pregnant with my third child, which naturally put my body into even more stress. It was the worst idea for my fragile body despite being the best news for our family.

All these separate but significant incidents were built on a foundation of continually managing 'little t' trauma from childhood, which set me up for complete burnout in adult life.

We can experience trauma in different ways, but burnout appears when we do not address the core of our issues and think we can rewire our brains to forget. The piece of the puzzle we are missing is the link to our heart. We falsely believe that we can out-think stress and trauma. We have long known that the body holds trauma, but we must consider that the heart – the most powerful part of the body – remembers it too.

In my own experience, although years of talking therapy and CBT definitely helped, I could still not get to the crux of my issues.

I discovered there are two types of trauma: 'big T' and 'little t'. 'Big T' Trauma is usually related to a life-threatening or life-changing event or situation, such as a natural disaster, serious accident or violent crime. 'Little t' trauma refers to events that typically don't involve violence or disaster but are often chronic or repetitive and create significant emotional distress. 'Little t' trauma for young adults might be a family or personal breakup, getting bullied, chronic feelings of inadequacy, being rejected by a friend group or a lack of sufficient emotional support from nurturing adults.

The truth of the matter is that we can be under enormous unseen stress through inner wounding and we often fail to recognise it until it is too late. Situations such as being criticised by a family member, undermined by a work colleague, gaslit by a partner or managing parenting alongside your own hidden childhood wounds can all contribute to this invisible angst we suffer. Other circumstances, such as facing red tape at every turn as you fight for the rights of your child with additional needs can also contribute to this unseen pervasive stress which seeps into every area of your life.

Women are especially adept at disguising trauma as the typical stress which everyone experiences, lacking compassion for ourselves. However, I have discovered that the heart of burnout is trauma and healing this trauma is the key to burnout recovery.

It is clear that there are links between trauma and fatigue/burnout. In addition, evidence is emerging of the correlation between unprocessed trauma and chronic/autoimmune illness in later life. The unprecedented diagnoses of conditions such as chronic fatigue syndrome, fibromyalgia, and other illnesses of which the exact causes are unknown, demonstrate the 'dis-ease' of the human body and mind under more stress than it was ever designed to endure.

No amount of talking therapy, psychoanalysis, supplements, homeopathy or nutrients can undo trauma. Although helpful, these things will only scratch the surface of a broken body and do little to fix a wounded mind.

We often have a way of belittling traumatic events which happen to us, especially those which happened to us as children. If no one died or was chronically abused, the assumption is that we should be able to 'get over it'. However, the meaning of trauma in its Greek origin is 'wound' and if we leave these wounds unrecognised and untreated it may be impossible to recover fully.

'Big T' traumas are often sudden and intense, leading to immediate psychological distress. 'Little t' traumas may seem minor individually, but their cumulative effect can be hugely damaging. Additionally, the fact that there isn't one big event can lead someone to think that they shouldn't have been affected by it and therefore demonstrate a lack of compassion for themselves in terms of dealing with the effects on their mental health.

Gabor Maté states that, 'Trauma is not what happens to you but what happens inside of you.' He argues that in both big T and little t trauma there is much overlap. They both represent a fracturing of the self and of one's relationship with the world. '*That fracturing is the essence of trauma.*' (Maté, 2022).

Clinical psychologist Dr Julie Smith presents trauma as much more than fear. 'It is often paired with a lack of control, deep shame, or rupture in our core beliefs in a way that shatters our view of the world, the self, or the people around us, creating a huge psychological threat.' (Smith, 2022). These feelings are particularly powerful around our teenage years when we are learning how to show up in the mature world and becoming who we will be in adulthood. Any doubts we have about ourselves during this period may often prove to be life-defining.

The key thing is that our nervous systems are unable to distinguish between a threat to our physical safety and an emotional threat.

Therefore, our bodies respond in the same way to both events and are flooded with cortisol in readiness for action far more often than it is needed.

Burnout is a severe form of chronic stress. Chronic stress causes a key hormone, cortisol, to surge in your body and your stress system becomes overloaded. If your body is on constant high alert, even with small everyday stressors, burnout can develop because your stress response stops functioning properly (McEwen, 2006). This is an example of unseen stress which permeates every aspect of your life even though you can appear to be 'fine' to others.

We often hear about the emotional responses of 'fight or flight' or even 'fight, flight or freeze'. However, it has become clear that trauma responses in adults and teens can have additional components: the six elements of Freeze, Flight, Fight, Fright, Flag and Faint. (The Newport Institute, 2022).

The lesser-known response of 'Flag' is when the body's systems begin to shut down, resulting in a numbing of emotions. This is dangerous as when the unhealed trauma in our bodies is allowed to go untreated it can lead to chronic fatigue, as the body is simply no longer able to cope with these unresolved emotions and shuts down in some areas.

Through experiencing and training in HeartHealing, I now recognise that I had unresolved traumatic experiences which led me to have a particular and not necessarily accurate view of myself. However, crucially, I also believed I was not worthy of resolving them; I was somehow responsible for my own unhappiness, and it was a cross which I had to bear. Altering this reality has been pivotal for me.

I have been anxious for as long as I can remember. I did not know the word as a child, but the feeling was real. It was a deeply unsettling knot in the pit of my stomach that I was not okay, and in fact no one was okay. Even scarier, perhaps I was the only one that realised it. My unconscious mind was telling me, 'The world isn't safe, and you need to be prepared.' My nervous system was put on alert and never stood down for fear that I could be hurt, or worse, be responsible for hurting someone else. That is quite a burden to shoulder.

I can see now that I was wounded and lacked trust in myself. I was operating from a place of fear, and my core belief was that I was not safe and neither was the world. Dr Julie Smith (2025) states that, 'the most intelligent and insightful of people can carry the most unsound core beliefs about themselves that will override logic. We base decisions on emotion and rationalize it afterwards.'

When my daughter was born and I was in my early thirties, that feeling was magnified. The unthinkable had happened: my beautiful baby girl had a congenital limb defect which had not been detected in pregnancy. It was confirmation that, as I believed, the world was unsafe and unfair. There was no evidence to suggest it was my fault, but my wounded heart and past traumas pushed me to believe that I must be responsible. This was unimaginably painful. I was always to blame, always. This was an enormous cross to bear.

It was a journey to get her through surgery. I kept my emotions to myself and rarely cried. I was always the strong one, the coper, the person that others went to when they had problems. I needed to power through and make it okay.

Again, when my son was struggling, I was driven like a motor to make things better, taking full control over managing the situation, feeling fully responsible for his happiness. It took an enormous toll on my wellbeing. Not that I cared, in fact I couldn't even see it until it was too late. My own wounds would not allow me to admit that I needed or deserved help.

It is this wounding which led me to burn out. I had taken as much as I could take and had no more space. It was time to unload the baggage which had accumulated over years and finally see what was lurking in there.

Although I had experienced talking therapy and CBT, which had been effective at the time, there were clearly still very unhealed parts of me that I couldn't remember. The brain is adept at hiding things which are too painful to resurface. It became clear that healing my trauma from the inside was the key to moving my life forward. Developing a spiritual practice, listening to my intuition, and tackling my fears head-on was the road to healing for me. I needed to value myself enough to know that I was worth the investment and that by valuing me and giving myself the time and space I deserved, I was able to be more present for the people I loved.

When I started looking at the power of healing my body from within, the natural first step was to focus on my inner child. This involved going back to painful childhood situations in which I could recognise patterns regarding my trauma response later in life. Pushing down emotions which were considered 'indulgent' or 'selfish' at the time led me to realise that I refused to give myself compassion when I was confronted with a difficult situation. I believed that I should have known how to manage it, and I was somehow faulty if I didn't.

I can now recognise that I had buried many traumatic incidents (little t) as a child and teenager, but these had remained in my brain and heart and informed my responses as an adult.

Through undertaking a HeartHealing package with Natasha Bray in 2023, I began uncovering some of the hidden wounds in my heart which I had not processed. I discovered thoughts and values which were so ingrained in my psyche I thought they were part of me rather than something which had been formed by life experience. Once I started to heal these my life began to change. I became more confident, more self-aware, and increasingly able to stand in my power.

I started to believe that it is possible to be a good person and be successful too. They are not mutually exclusive. It is possible to have money and love and be happy. I had always previously believed that this to be untrue.

Interestingly, it was also far less painful than talking therapy, which I had engaged in extensively in the past. Seeing the younger version of me in a safe and protected space meant that I could nurture her in the way I wished I had received in real life and could allow myself to recognise these feelings and, crucially, the ways they have formed my current reality. This was huge!

Discovering HeartHealing was the missing piece in my healing journey. It enabled me to take a safe yet expansive look into my childhood experiences of little t trauma and be clear about the way they had affected me as an adult.

Dr Julie Smith (2025) says, '...looking back on early experiences once you are no longer there and no longer dependent, revisiting them in a constructive way helps you to enhance your perspective on the consequences which you still deal with today.'

Travelling into my heart chambers and meeting wounded versions of myself as a child there meant I could safely remember parts of my childhood which I had chosen to forget because they were too painful. It has been revolutionary to unpick thoughts and behaviours that were so ingrained in me I thought they were part of me.

I didn't trust myself because I could never truly trust others to keep me safe. On top of that, experience had shown me that I was right. I can now see that good things don't happen in exchange for bad things. You can be happy and successful and be good and loved and everything you dreamed of without sacrifice.

Loving and prioritising myself doesn't mean that I am selfish; it means that I am preserving my health and energy. I no longer believe that I must pour to others from my cup leaving nothing for myself. I need a top-up too!

Leaning into my parasympathetic nervous system rather than my sympathetic nervous system has meant that I have been able to feel in control of my body rather than be controlled by it.

When a client of mine stepped back into her childhood and could acknowledge the damage caused to her by her hugely traumatic childhood, she was suddenly able to identify where negative patterns and beliefs in her life had begun and begin to question them. In a series of powerful HeartHealing sessions, we worked together to explore situations which formed her opinions about the world, her unrelenting drive to succeed and ultimately her identity.

It has been incredible to see her start to take her power back.

So many of her negative thinking patterns were established as a young child. Having the chance to revisit those situations as an adult has meant that she can understand it from a clearer perspective. She has had talking therapy on and off for years but through visiting her young self as her adult self in the heart has enabled her to accelerate this healing and truly start to plan her future as a healed version of herself. By acknowledging those feelings from a safe place, she can now recognise them as unhelpful and untrue rather than the reality she had always accepted them to be. By seeing these wounds and healing them she has taken the pressure off herself in her current life, stopped her relentless self-critical obsession with her career and reduced her risk of burning out completely which she was on course to do.

I decided to train in HeartHealing to enable me to serve other people, especially parents, who are trying to operate effectively in an adult world with very genuine issues but from the basis of an unhealed, wounded childhood. Often these people strive for perfection which is impossible to achieve by any standards but particularly if you are operating from a basis of trauma. However, by seeing our lives through the lens of ourselves as the vulnerable child we once were, we are able to feel compassion and identify where these, often wrong, beliefs have manifested from.

We are all still works in progress but moving forward through life as healed versions of ourselves is by far the most empowering experience we can have. Healing our hearts is a key component to relinquishing the pressure we unwittingly apply to ourselves on a daily basis as high achieving adults. We not only deserve to heal but we can lead much more fulfilling and happy lives by recognising and healing those wounds which no longer serve us and are slowly burning us out. As Natasha Bray herself says, 'Healing your heart is the "missing piece" that will help you find your missing peace.'

You can begin your own healing here with this simple yet powerful task. Place your hand on your heart and ask yourself, "What part of me believes I need to do more in order to be loved, safe or worthy?" How old were you when you first felt that way? What does that version of you need to hear to be able to rest and just be?

References:

Maté, G., & Maté, D. (2022). *The myth of normal: Trauma, illness, and healing in a toxic culture*. Avery.

McEwen, B. S. (2006). *Protective and damaging effects of stress mediators: Central role of the brain.* Dialogues in Clinical Neuroscience, 8(4), 367–381.

Newport Institute. (2022). *Big T vs. Little t Trauma in Young Adults: Is There a Difference?* Retrieved from https://www.newportinstitute.com/resources/mental-health/big-t-little-t-trauma/

Smith, J. (2022). *Why has nobody told me this before?* Michael Joseph.

Wilson, J. L. (2017). *Adrenal fatigue: The 21st century stress syndrome* (2nd ed.). Smart Publications.

ABOUT THE AUTHOR

LUCY LAMBERT

Lucy Lambert is a business owner, ex-teacher and mental health advocate who runs a tutoring business and writes workbooks for teens and young adults to support their well-being.

She has found a new passion in supporting other women who are experiencing burnout or can see it on the horizon.

Lucy helps them to prioritise their own needs amongst those of others whilst uncovering and healing the root cause of their need to please. She believes that we can be abundant in all areas of our life without personal sacrifice.

Lucy enjoys reading, Pilates and spending time with her family.

Lucy offers HeartHealing packages for professionals, looking specifically at causes of fatigue and burnout in mid-life, and healing these wounds. She also provides an online course on Self-Love for Women to accompany her workbook of the same name.

www.theabundanceevolution.com
lucy@theabundanceevolution.com
facebook.com/abundanceevolution
instagram.com/abundanceevolution
tiktok.com/@abundanceevolution

11

LAURA L. TRUESDALE

THE HEART OF ADDICTION

For twenty-seven years, I have dedicated my career to behavioral health as a social worker and addiction counselor, guiding individuals through their darkest moments and helping them rediscover hope and purpose. My professional journey has been one of service and compassion, and is intertwined with my personal journey that has shaped not only who I am as a practitioner, but who I am as a woman.

You might not think this chapter on healing the heart of addiction is for you if you have not experienced issues with addiction or know anyone who does: addiction can include more than the addictions we consider common, such as alcohol and drug use, gambling, or sex. Some behaviors are more socially acceptable and not typically regarded as detrimental, such as work, exercise, perfectionism, overachievement, social media, shopping/retail therapy, and self-improvement or personal development. These socially accepted behaviors can be ways in which we cope with negative emotions and core beliefs. At the core of all forms of addiction is the heart, which is the keeper of all the deepest wounds. These wounds create negative beliefs and perceptions about ourselves and the world around us and lead to unhealthy behavior patterns. I, personally, know the profound impact of perfectionism and overachievement.

As a behavioral care social worker and addiction counselor, I have witnessed how mental health and substance use disorders are often profoundly interconnected with trauma and relational wounds. Trauma, including adverse childhood experiences (ACEs), abuse, neglect, or significant loss, can dysregulate the nervous system and leave lasting emotional scars. These wounds often stem from fractured relationships, whether with caregivers, partners, or significant others, leading to a lack of self-trust, not feeling good enough, a lack of self-worth, fear of rejection and abandonment, feeling unlovable, and a lack of emotional safety. The impact of these wounds permeates all aspects of a person's life and can create life-altering consequences.

Common issues my clients experience include self-harm, eating disorders, substance use, depression and anxiety, and unhealthy relationships, all of which are tied to these relational wounds. They struggle with limiting beliefs such as, "I'm not good enough," "I do not deserve happiness," or "I'll never change," and these beliefs fuel behaviors such as poor decisions, procrastination, avoidance, staying in unhealthy relationships, and failing to prioritize themselves. They experience intense mood swings, emotional numbness, overwhelming anxiety, depression, and negative self-talk. They develop behaviors that often emerge as coping mechanisms to manage the emotional pain of feeling unworthy, undeserving, or unloved. Fear of abandonment and mistrust of self and others further compound the struggle, creating cycles of isolation and distress.

Clients challenged by mental health issues and addiction feel disconnected from themselves, their loved ones, and often their sense of purpose or reason for living. Unconsciously repeating patterns of childhood dynamics, they choose emotionally unavailable partners, become caretakers, and stay in unhealthy, abusive relationships, perpetuating their emotional suffering and sense of low self-worth. Adverse impacts on clients' lives include health decline, relationship breakdown, financial instability, lack of fulfillment in their lives, and pervasive low self-esteem.

Healing requires addressing core wounds, fostering a sense of safety, and rebuilding trust within oneself and others. We have to get to the *root* of the trauma. Left untreated, trauma can manifest as anxiety, depression, addiction, post-traumatic stress disorder, or other mental health challenges. A cyclical connection between trauma and relational wounds often perpetuates maladaptive coping mechanisms such as addiction. It is an attempt to numb emotional pain, avoid trauma and its effects, and seek external validation.

According to the World Health Organization (WHO, 2025), "Anxiety disorders are the world's most common mental disorders, affecting 301 million people in 2019, with more women being affected than men."

WHO also say, "An estimated 5% of adults suffer from depression globally with women being more affected…"

WHO statistics indicate that more than 720,000 people die by suicide every year, and reasons for suicide are often influenced by social, psychological, biological, and environmental factors.

About 296 million people aged 15-64 had used psychoactive drugs in 2021, and about 39.5 million are estimated to be affected by drug disorders. https://who.int/news

The Adverse Childhood Experiences (ACE) Study (Felitti et al, 1998) links childhood trauma to long-term health outcomes, including mental health issues and substance use. Bessel van der Kolk, MD, in his seminal work, *The Body Keeps the Score: Brain, Mind and Body in the Healing of Trauma* (Kolk, van der, 2014), emphasizes how trauma is stored in the brain, affecting the brain, physical health, and emotional regulation. He explains how unresolved trauma disrupts the nervous system, creating patterns of hypervigilance, emotional dysregulation, and chronic stress. These are often seen in individuals struggling with mental health and addiction.

Similarly, Gabor Maté, MD, in his work *In the Realm of Hungry Ghosts: Encounters with Addiction* (Maté, 2008), explores the roles of relational wounds in addiction, describing how feelings of unworthiness, abandonment, and emotional neglect drive individuals toward substances and behaviors to soothe unmet needs. Both authors underscore the importance of addressing the root causes of trauma and relational wounds to break these cycles. They say that healing begins with creating safety, connection, and self-compassion. The therapeutic relationship is key to creating the environment necessary for healing and transformation.

These frameworks provide evidence-based support for addressing relational wounds and traumas underlying mental health issues, substance use, and all forms of addiction. Their insights resonate deeply with my approach to therapy as I work to help clients uncover and heal these underlying wounds to achieve lasting transformation. As a result of reading Dr. van der Kolk's work and becoming a trauma-informed therapist, I changed my paradigm from focusing on the problematic behaviors of the individual to what has happened in the person's life that underlies the behaviors and issues.

Some clients pursue therapy seeking to address the problematic symptoms without understanding the subconscious origins. Each person has a conscious mind, which is what they are aware of, and an unconscious mind or subconscious mind, which is outside of awareness. The subconscious mind retains the underlying beliefs and narratives an individual has about themselves, and this guides how they engage in life. The subconscious mind does not attempt to correct or dispel beliefs; it takes them as truth. Unconscious beliefs manifest in powerful and subtle ways and contribute to the way a person perceives their world and their place in it.

Trauma therapies address the events that have happened and create a sense of completion of unresolved events. Traditional talk therapy addresses the conscious cognitive beliefs through reframing, which assists in changing the thoughts to more effective ones. HeartHealing beautifully heals the trauma and relational wounds that created those thoughts and unconscious beliefs. This method bypasses the analytical mind, allowing people to release deeply ingrained emotional blocks without the need to relive trauma repeatedly. HeartHealing works directly with the heart and subconscious to foster rapid and lasting change in self-worth, relationships, abundance, and overall well-being. It integrates love, forgiveness, and self-acceptance, helping people align with their soul's purpose and experience breakthroughs that traditional therapy may take years to achieve.

People who have been impacted by relationships commonly experience the core universal wounds that HeartHealing has identified, including the wounds of enoughness, love, trust, worth, and acceptance. These wounds can be at the root of any form of addiction and co-occurring disorders. HeartHealing unlocks the obstacles to treating people with complex histories and offers pathways to comprehensive healing.

HeartHealing creates a shift from merely coping with your challenges to fully transforming your inner world, unlocking new possibilities in love, success, health, and spiritual growth. Your heart holds the wounds of your past, including generational and ancestral patterns. It is also the source of true healing, which resolves the root cause of relational wounds and guides you to transformation. HeartHealing replaces subconscious patterns with empowering beliefs that align with your true self and fosters self-love and self-worth.

I incorporate my clinical background uniquely with HeartHealing, and my clients have regained connection to their bodies after severe sexual abuse, learned how to live substance-free lives to reclaim their most authentic selves, found a voice for their inner child, restored confidence, gained insight into maladaptive patterns, and changed how they engage in their lives.

Their results include unlocking the wounds of abusive patterns that left them feeling they were not capable or deserving of love, success, happiness, health, and financial stability. They gained insight into how their parents' words were the negative voice of their negative self-talk and how their parents' wounds were repeated in this generation. Some recognize how they exhibit the same avoidance of emotional pain as their parents and now embrace their emotions and understand they are breaking family cycles and modeling healthy coping.

Clients have shared that they gained more insight and relief than they achieved through other therapies; one client stated after his experience with HeartHealing, "I've made more progress with HeartHealing than forty years of therapy." I have worked with others as they healed wounds with deceased parents and reestablished a loving connection after years of a strained relationship, giving them a sense of peace. These clients have identified how the wounds of their childhood could be seen in their relationships and their work, tolerating abuse and failing to establish healthy boundaries. They gained the ability to confront verbal and emotional abuse and establish healthy boundaries and communication.

Clients have gained a profound sense of self-worth in their professional identities, building the confidence to pursue and secure roles that align more closely with their skills. These clients gained insight into how their core negative beliefs have kept them from seeking advancement in their careers, receiving higher pay, and tolerating unfulfilling jobs that did not allow them to utilize their skills and gifts. HeartHealing provided the transformation and reimprinting of their subconscious mind with a new narrative of knowing their worth and what they offer.

Others have recognized how the wounds of their loved ones influenced their struggles with body image and eating disorders, allowing them to heal and rediscover a deep appreciation for their bodies. They have reclaimed self-love, freeing themselves from self-punishment and limiting beliefs tied to their body and shape, hiding from their bodies to embracing their beauty.

Yet others have healed core universal wounds of enoughness, love, worth, trust, and acceptance. After years of not believing in themselves, sabotaging their goals, and not living their desired lives, they uncovered answers and took steps to heal. Healing each of these wounds has uncovered the relationship at the root of those wounds and has broken the emotional and energetic cords that have kept the client from achieving their innate potential. My amazing clients have found the bravery and courage to allow themselves to uncover the relational wounds and traumas that have blocked their paths to achieving wholeness, self-love, and acceptance. They have faced what they feared and realized their amazing potential.

I have used HeartHealing with long-term clients who had not made consistent progress with other traditional methods. Their results through HeartHealing have been profound and transformative. One of the most rewarding moments in HeartHealing is seeing a sense of peace and understanding on their faces and the energetic shifts in their being the most authentic versions of themselves. Training in HeartHealing transformed my practice as a therapist and transformed my personal life. Not only have I delivered these amazing shifts for my clients, but I have experienced them firsthand in my healing through this powerful modality.

Through my transformative healing journey, I faced wounds head-on and delved into the depths of self-discovery and self-compassion, unearthing layers of pain and limiting beliefs that had taken root over the years. The process was not easy, but it was profoundly rewarding. I learned to quiet the voice that told me I was not enough, replacing it with one of unconditional love and acceptance. I began to see myself as a whole, deserving being, worthy of the life I desired. Today, I stand in my truth as an authentic, confident woman who knows deep in my soul that I am worthy and deserving.

This transformation has not only enriched my personal life but has deepened my capacity to support others on their paths to healing by creating a safe space of unconditional acceptance. I bring the wisdom of my own experience into my work, creating a space where clients feel seen, heard, and empowered to rewrite their own stories of worth and possibility. My clients say they notice the change in me and how my passion for helping them has been more visible, showing the depth of my compassion for them and their journeys of healing.

A crucial part of being a therapist is engaging in personal healing and self-reflection to ensure that individual experiences do not interfere with the therapeutic process and client relationships. Throughout my life, I have experienced traditional talk therapy with a cognitive behavioral approach and have experienced EMDR (Eye Movement Desensitization Reprocessing) addressing trauma. I gained insight and felt I was navigating life and my symptoms of anxiety well. I was managing the problems. I was living, but I was not happy, and I had a nagging sense of not being enough, which has been present throughout my life.

As a young child, I believed my worth was more in my academics than in being myself. I received the validation and affirmation I needed primarily through my accomplishments. In high school, I was number fourteen in my class and a member of the National Honor Society and the French National Honor Society, but it did not feel enough. I struggled with perfectionism and would often have emotional breakdowns because my grades were not good enough. I was always anxious about doing things right, being a good student, and making my parents proud. School was my "job."

As early as twelve years old, I had the opportunity to serve as a mentor to a younger child. I watched her struggle with challenges at school and in her home life. I felt so helpful and needed. This sparked something in me, and I knew my purpose in this world was to help others, so I pursued education to support that purpose. I had once believed I would be a teacher, but something about listening, supporting, and helping led me to pursue being a therapist.

On the day of my college graduation, a comment rang in my ears – *so now what can you do?* – implying that what I had achieved by graduating with degrees in Psychology and Sociology were not valuable degrees that would allow me to have a successful career. My destination was graduate school, where I obtained my Master of Social Work degree. I finished the program with a 4.0 grade point average. I spent two years of grueling studies trying to be the best. I put everything into school, repeating the cycle of having to be perfect at the expense of my mental health. I could not balance school and life. I was missing out on life and having fun.

Upon graduation, I started working for a large hospital system and, after four years, became a Clinical Program Coordinator of an adolescent mental health and substance use disorder treatment program. I married and achieved my dreams of marriage and career. I worked so hard and gave more than required. I had this unrelenting work ethic. Do more, work more, achieve more, and now I realize work and achievement have become my addiction, my sole focus, and my way of being seen and valued. Still, I never felt I was meeting the expectations placed on me. I now realize that they were the expectations I placed on myself.

In my middle adult years, I had a failed marriage, was a single mom, and felt my life was over. How would I ever be lovable and find happiness? All I did was work and take care of my son. So, I took on a second job in private practice, once again trying to prove I was worthy and good enough. I overworked to fill the void. I gained more training and became more focused on getting more certifications. Despite all my training and certifications and having a successful private practice in addition to my full-time job, I still did not feel I was good enough or competent enough. I began dating again, and that was a period of profound doubt that I was lovable or would ever achieve happiness. Again, I was trying to fill the void and seeking external validation from relationships. I firmly believed that I could not have it all – love, family, career, success, or wealth – because something had to suffer.

And then something happened that changed my life forever. What a surprise when a mentor of mine compassionately shared that I needed to work on healing. I had done therapy for years, and I accepted my past and believed I was as healed as I could be; after all, I am a therapist, and I had done the work to make sure I was the healthiest I could be. I was introduced to HeartHealing by this wonderful mentor and was blown away at the insight I gained after one session.

I gained an understanding of why I never felt enough in my relationships. I explored why I believed I could not have it all: love, family, career, and success. I was shocked when I encountered a past life version of myself and came to understand this was the origin of the ingrained belief. My faith and spirituality began to take on a whole new meaning, especially after experiencing what I consider a moment with God in a HeartHealing session. At that moment, I knew I would become a trained HeartHealing practitioner.

HeartHealing has profoundly expanded my spirituality by deepening my connection to divine love, universal wisdom, and the limitless power of the heart. Through this work, I have healed ancestral and past-life wounds and gained a heightened awareness of how energy, emotions, and soul imprints shape our reality. It has allowed me to move beyond intellectual understanding into true embodiment-experiencing healing as a sacred, transformative force rather than just a process.

The importance of spirituality is paramount in healing and allows for a more profound experience of post-traumatic growth or the positive psychological change following a traumatic experience. This journey has strengthened my intuition, deepened my trust in divine guidance, and awakened a profound sense of purpose. HeartHealing has shown me that true transformation happens when we heal at the deepest level – within the heart – and align with the unconditional love that has always been available to us. Through this expansion, I have stepped into my highest calling: guiding others to rediscover their connection with their soul and their higher power, their self-worth, and their limitless potential.

When I embarked on my deep healing journey and explored my wounds, I became aware of how, in my early years, I carried the weight of relational wounds that left me feeling unworthy and undeserving. The belief that I was not good enough echoed through every area of my life, holding me back from fully embracing my potential and the joy life had to offer. These feelings created barriers in my relationships and fueled an unrelenting drive to prove my worth through professional achievements. No matter how much

I accomplished, it never felt like enough, making it challenging to show up as my authentic self.

Deep introspection made me realize that what I once saw as mere life events had left profound wounds. I uncovered the hidden reasons behind the patterns I kept repeating in my relationships, my treatment of myself, and my life choices. I had been my own worst critic, speaking to myself with cruelty, neglecting my body, and carrying immense guilt and shame for the mistakes I had made and the way my life had unfolded. Losing my identity as a wife left me feeling adrift, uncertain of how to navigate single motherhood, and terrified of financial instability. I felt incompetent – not just as a mother and wife, but even as a therapist.

As I healed, I uncovered the roots of my struggles. My mistrust of myself stemmed from an innocent childhood prank that left me questioning who I was and where I belonged. My tendency to fawn in relationships with men was traced back to early bullying by a male. My deep sense of unworthiness and fear of abandonment was shaped by my parents' divorce and my own painful romantic experiences. My negative self-image was influenced by watching the women in my life battle their own, as well as by the relentless societal messages linking weight to worth.

HeartHealing and its profound personalized imprints allowed my subconscious to rewire. I see my worth, love the woman I am, and believe that the desires of my heart are indeed attainable. I have gained newfound confidence, uncovered the wounds and beliefs that impaired my relationship with money and success, and finally understood my fear of embracing my authentic self. I kept myself small, afraid that success would bring judgment or distance from those I loved. I was addicted to achievement yet deeply afraid of success. But through this healing journey, I reclaimed my power, my self-worth, and the courage to step fully into the life I am meant to live.

I have a wonderful life filled with a loving relationship with my partner, and I fully embrace the love he showers me with daily. I am blessed with a beautiful relationship with my adult son and proudly embrace my changing role as a mother. I enjoy a balanced life and consider myself my highest priority. After all, you cannot pour from an empty cup. My passion for healing and healing others has ignited a bigger mission in my life, and I am excited to continue evolving as a healer. I am the happiest I have ever been and have a sense of peace I have never felt before.

By addressing subconscious patterns at their root, HeartHealing has empowered me and my clients to heal past trauma, break the cycles of self-doubt, and step into our fullest potential. My mission is to continue to create a safe, compassionate space where individuals can reconnect with their self-worth, rewrite their narratives, and embrace the abundant life they deserve.

Addictions show up in some of the most unexpected ways. Do you find yourself losing yourself for hours on social media? Do you feel you only feel good when you buy yourself a "few things" and realize it leads to financial strain? Do you spend long hours at work, impacting your relationships, because you want to show your worth to your employer? Ever feel you just have not reached your goals or achieved enough?

I invite you to take a deep, honest look at your life and dreams. What do you truly desire – love, success, fulfillment, inner peace? And what is standing in your way? Are you carrying old wounds, limiting beliefs, or patterns that no longer serve you? Often, we hold ourselves back without realizing it, trapped by subconscious fears of not being enough, fear of failure, or not feeling worthy of the very things our hearts long for.

What if those barriers aren't permanent? What if healing your past could unlock the future you have always envisioned? I encourage you to pause, reflect, and ask yourself: What would my life look like if I honestly believed I was worthy of it all? Because you are. Your healing journey begins the moment you decide to embrace that truth.

References:

Felitti, V.J., Anda, R.F., Nordenberg, D., Williamson, D.F., Spitz, A.M., Edwards, V., Koss, M.P. and Marks, J.S. (1998), Relationship of Childhood Abuse and Household Dysfunction to Many of the Leading Causes of Death in Adults. *American Journal of Preventive Medicine*, 14(4), pp.245–258. doi: https://doi.org/10.1016/S0749-3797(98)00017-8.

Maté, G. (2008),. *In the Realm of Hungry Ghosts: Close Encounters with Addiction*. Toronto: Vintage Canada.

van der Kolk, B. (2014), *The Body Keeps the Score: Brain, Mind, and Body in the Healing of Trauma*. New York: Penguin Books.

Who.int. (2025),. *News*. [online] Available at: https://who.int/news [Accessed 30 Mar. 2025].

ABOUT THE AUTHOR

LAURA L. TRUESDALE

Laura L. Truesdale is a Licensed Social Worker, Licensed Addiction Counselor, and Master Addiction Counselor dedicated to supporting adolescents and adults navigating mental health challenges, substance use disorders, and trauma. Laura previously served as the Clinical Program Coordinator for a partial hospitalization and intensive outpatient program for adolescents facing mental health and substance use challenges, and maintained a part-time private practice, specializing in trauma recovery for adults.

Laura is trained in Cognitive Behavioral Therapy (CBT), EMDR (Eye Movement Desensitization and Reprocessing), BLAST

(Bilateral Analysis & Stimulation Therapy), and is a Level 3 certified HeartHealing Practitioner. Her approach is compassionate and trauma-informed , focusing not just on behaviors but on the underlying experiences that shape them. Her goal is to help clients recognize their intrinsic worth, build resilience, and develop effective coping strategies to create meaningful change in their lives.

Laura enjoys spending time with her partner, her adult son, and their two beloved goldendoodles. She finds joy in the outdoors, especially at the beach.

truesdalecounselingservices.com
ltruesdaleLISWCP@gmail.com
facebook: Laura Love Truesdale
instagram.com/lltrue

12

HANNAH DARBY

THE HEART OF GRIEF

You hold grief in your heart and it changes you, as though your heart has broken. You can't run from it. You can play hide-and-seek with it, but it will always win. Grief has many different faces that stretch far beyond death, even beyond humanity, as animals have been shown to grieve in their own way, too (King, 2016).

Grief lurks in the dark corners of your mind, body, heart and soul unless you embrace it, acknowledge it, feel it, listen to it. Grief hides inside other emotions. You may recognise some as coming from grief, others you may not – despair, pain, hurt, loneliness, guilt, shame, love, passion, jealousy, apathy, fear… to name but a few. It never leaves you once it arrives, but you can learn to live with it, to accept it, and to find the love buried within it. It comprises a complex cycle of emotions all intertwined in stages – denial, anger, bargaining, depression and acceptance (Kübler-Ross, 2014, as cited in Bray, 2020).

I healed my heart of grief with the help of HeartHealing. I now accept it as part of me, my past, present and future. I live in harmony with grief and no longer fight it. This has given me a chance to grow, to feel the depth of my emotions. Grief has shown me my strength, my courage, my love, my passion, my devotion, along with my resilience, allowing me to enter the wisdom stage of The Healer's Journey (Bray, 2020).

Healing my heart of grief has allowed me to express safely and compassionately the emotions buried within my grief, free from guilt or shame. It comes from a place of love. I wake up every day and grab life with both hands. I am happy to be alive and glad to be me, even when my symptoms are screaming and the physical pain takes my breath away. I face whatever obstacles are sent my way without spiralling down a slide of despair. I've lifted my cloud of doom, seeing clearly without its fog for the first time in my life, thanks to HeartHealing.

Now my grief, not only for lost others but also for lost parts of myself, lives in peace inside my healed heart. I no longer fear grief, nor am I afraid of death. Death is a part of life that you have no control over. Once you embrace this, everything becomes easier. Grief is my friend, not my enemy, because it has taught me so much. It has helped me grow, shown me how much I care, how compassionate I can be, and how kind I am. The key to healing grief ultimately lies in feeling grief.

You may assume you only go through grief when someone dies. This is one of the most known forms of grief but it has many different faces and can enter your life in many ways. You can prepare yourself better for grief by learning about these faces and how they affect you.

Grief goes far beyond bereavement. You go through grief when you lose anything you care deeply about, anything that was important to you:

- Loss of a loved one
- Loss of yourself through accident, illness or bullying
- Loss of health
- Loss of relationships (loss of love)
- Loss through adoption
- Your parents divorcing
- Going through divorce yourself
- Never having met your parents
- Loss of a safe, happy childhood
- Loss of a child
- Going through a miscarriage
- Finding out you can't have children
- Loss of stability
- Losing your job/career
- Becoming homeless
- Losing a life you dreamed of
- Losing a pet

When you lose anything meaningful to you, it can cause you to grieve. My clients often say, 'I'm not grieving so I do not need to know/think about it.' You naturally want to hide from grief because it's painful, but hiding it away doesn't protect you from the effects – the creation of a wall around your heart. It allows the wall to grow taller. You must be brave, face your grief and break down the wall surrounding your heart. Grief never leaves once it arrives; you continue to travel through the cycle Külber-Ross described. Sometimes it can be quiet, sometimes loud, but it will come around again and again, knocking you flat when you least expect it.

Grief enters your mind, body and heart as a deeply personal journey. However, there are symptoms common to those who are grieving. It leaves you feeling socially isolated. You pull away from others, becoming withdrawn and excluding yourself. It leaves you feeling lost and confused, unsure how to move forward or what to do next with your life. You struggle to accept your new reality which creates an overwhelming inner turmoil. You can feel a multitude of emotions all at the same time. Anger is often the hardest emotion to cope with, maybe because we are taught not to speak ill of others. But anger is only a natural grief response, as Külber-Ross described, that will not leave you until you express it. All of these symptoms can create a negative mindset that may pull you into the depths of a clinical depression.

Grief also affects your body. It affects your sleep, leaving you weak and exhausted. When you do sleep, it can cause vivid nightmares. Sleep is so important for you that a lack of it exacerbates other symptoms. It leaves you feeling anxious and panicky, causing excessive sweating, clammy hands, body shakes, panic attacks. It creates a tightness in your throat and a dry mouth, making it hard for you to talk or even breathe. It leaves a hollow feeling in the pit of your stomach, making you nauseous. It affects your appetite; you stop eating healthily. It causes headaches, numbness and muscle weakness along with random aches and pains in your joints and muscles. Some people cry uncontrollably; others are unable to cry at all. Each is a normal response. If you don't cry, it doesn't mean it has affected you any less than someone who does cry.

Grief affects your heart. You build a wall around your heart to protect you from the pain. It affects how you feel your emotions, leaving you hollow hearted, like a pit has formed in your chest. You feel like your heart is broken into pieces.

Grief affects every aspect of your life. It changes how you interact with the world, and how you communicate with others and with yourself. It changes your daily routine and seeps into every corner of your existence. It affects your ability to look after yourself and others. A lot of my clients struggle with self-care after experiencing grief. You can lose even more from your life – friends, family, your job – creating the cycle of grief that Külber-Ross described, becoming self-perpetuating if you let it.

Grief even affects your ability to move, so you struggle with exercise. It causes addictions to numb the pain you feel inside your heart, perhaps an addiction to alcohol, recreational or prescription drugs, doom scrolling, binge watching, food, nicotine, sex, exercise, work or self-harm. However, these addictions just create another problem. They don't help you to heal. After the effects of your chosen vice wears off, you end up feeling lower than you did before, which fuels the depressive symptoms you experience.

You can be changed deep inside by grief. It changes how you think and feel about others, the world and yourself. It changes your heart and your soul, affecting your faith in yourself, the universe and the divine. It can make you question your religious beliefs and your relationship with whatever God you believe in, if you believe in one. It can be hard to heal from this without the help and support of someone who truly understands your grief.

You have changed. It is hard to accept that life has changed and you can never go back to how things were before, but you can never return to the old you and your old way of thinking and feeling. Accept the new you. Learn to love the new you. Learn to feel worthy as the new you. Learn how to feel enough as the new you. Learn to trust the new you.

The heart of healing grief is *feeling* grief rather than denying or burying it. HeartHealing heals the relationships of your heart, making it a powerful tool in healing grief. According to quantum physics, the heart's energetic field is thousands of times more powerful than that of the mind (Bray, 2020). Through healing your heart you can start to love again, trust again, feel enough again and accept your new world.

HeartHealing allows you to communicate through the heart safely, unapologetically and without judgement, and free from guilt and shame. Being able to safely express your emotions, especially anger, is essential to healing your heart of grief. Anger isn't always a negative emotion. It is an entirely normal part of the grief cycle and can be positive in some circumstances: it shows how passionate you are and how much you cared for what you have lost.

In Western cultures we tend to suppress our emotions. We are taught it is good to have a 'stiff upper lip' and that we should never speak ill of the dead. I prefer to approach the issue more like Mexico. On 'Dia De Los Muertos' ('Day of the Dead'), they celebrate the lives of those that are lost rather than mourning their deaths. When I am gone, I would prefer my loved ones to celebrate my life than to mourn my death!

The emotions of grief are intense and crash into you like waves. Experiencing them is not linear and we cannot put a timeline on how long we are supposed to feel them. If you try, you will never heal. Working in the heart, you are free from time. Your mind is able to catch up with the new reality, creating a space for true grieving and then healing to occur.

Your adult life is affected by your childhood experiences. A traumatic bereavement in childhood can leave you in a trauma response freeze state. This means you can't move forward, because you are unable to process your grief. This intense feeling travels into your heart, so you build walls to numb the pain. This serves a short-term purpose in protecting you, but as you grow older, it sabotages you. It stops you moving forward past your grief and leaves you unable to heal. When you work on the Receiving

Wounds of the Heart, you break down these walls and begin to heal your heart of grief.

I help people to build their hearts and souls back together with gold, just like the Japanese art of Kintsugi – that of repairing broken pottery with gold. The principles are simple and follow my HEAL approach:

- H – Healing the relational wounds of your heart
- E – Expressing your anger and pain
- A – Acceptance of your new reality
- L – Learning to live and love again

When you learn to accept the differences of your new reality, you can discover the gifts hidden beneath your grief. After all, there cannot be life without death. Grief is a natural part of the circle of life.

My Kintsugi programme allows people to move from pain to purpose, and they find a new love for life. When you incorporate the HEAL method, you free yourself from the effects of grief. People who have done this report sleeping better, and looking after themselves and others again. You can learn to notice the signs of grief within yourself, give it grace rather than ignore it, then confidently move forward again.

People come to me feeling as though their hearts are blocked but can't see why. They might have adoption wounds that left them with unseen grief and I guide them to heal these wounds. This healing allows them to speak freely with their partners, removing their fear of loss and enables them to love again as their true selves. If they are business owners, they become visible in their business for the first time.

When you heal the Receiving Wounds of the Heart through HeartHealing you can unleash the love that your grief has buried. Grief is rooted in love, and learning this brings peace to your soul.

Love, like grief, is unbound by time. Unconditional love transcends the separation of the worlds of the living and the dead. Healing your Love Wound sets free the love trapped in your grief so you can celebrate the happy times before your loss, which is one of the most transformational things you can do.

Your worth is tied into grief. A loss can leave you feeling hard done by, like the universe has punished you by taking away what you cared for and you are unworthy of success. Healing your Worth Wound allows you to feel worthy of life again and you can find peace. Grief is a natural part of life, not a punishment. You are worthy of success, worthy of carrying on after being forced to leave behind what you loved. You are worthy of the life the universe has destined for you.

You can also create emotional resilience to cope with future losses. By healing your Trust Wound you can trust that your grief is allowing you to grow. Your loss is not a punishment but a part of life to learn to live with.

By accepting your new reality, you can move forward. Healing your Acceptance Wound lets you break free from the grip of grief. You can ride the waves of grief without capsizing your boat. This allows you to accept what has happened, forgive the past and no longer let it control your future.

Healing your Receiving Wounds unlocks your grief and lets you express your anger without guilt or shame. Knowing it's a natural response and that whatever you grieve for will live in your heart forever.

The first experience of grief I remember was when I was five and our two cats died. They comforted me when I was sick, curled up with me whilst I slept. My world fell apart when they died. The death of a pet can hit just as hard as any other loss. Studies show (Cleary *et al*, 2001) that people who experience the death of a pet have feelings of grief just as powerful as with the death of a human. I have felt this, as the little me who lost her cats and again as an adult when my first dog died.

I am so glad my parents were honest with me about death right from the start. I advise you to do the same with your own children. When our cats got sick, we all went to the vet together for them to be put down. I was right by their side until the end. Being with them when they passed gave me the chance to say goodbye, the chance to grieve. I am thankful to my parents for giving me that closure.

The first thing I did when I got my own home was find two kittens to call my own. I now have four cats. They never replace the cats I lost as a child but they allow me to remember the happy times I had with them, rather than the pain left behind when they died. I plan never to live in a house without cats again!

A study which looked at children whose parents had died when they were between the ages of thirteen and twenty-one found that these children felt that adults didn't understand the longevity of their grief and that it intersected all areas of their lives (Abraham-Steele & Maya, 2024).

I agree with this because this was me. My father passed away in front of me when I was thirteen. He died suddenly of a heart attack on my grandmother's sofa. It was a long time before I was able to look at that sofa without seeing him there, grasping his chest. I resented the fact we were whisked away to a neighbour's house and didn't know what was happening. However, I am grateful that my mum stood up for us and allowed us to be present at his death certificate signing (even though the officials tried to shut us out).

Mum also gave me the chance to say one last goodbye at the funeral home. I wrote him a letter and placed it in his coffin along with one of my favourite soft toys. Thank you, Mum, for standing up for us in this way, for giving me the chance to say goodbye. My faith helped me get through too, as I know it was not the end of his journey, just a new chapter. I will see him again when my time is up, along with all the others I have lost along my life's path. This brings me a great sense of peace.

I had no outside support, no one to talk to. Mum was lost in her own grief, my peers didn't understand, and the school wasn't helpful. I carried this grief around with me until I healed my heart with HeartHealing. Healing my heart allowed the little me to go back and say all the things I never got to say to my father. I expressed my anger at him for leaving. I released the self-hatred I had developed for being angry at him. The little me did not realise this anger came from a place of love and was a natural response to grief. It allowed me to renew my faith in God and release the pain that it was somehow my fault that he had died. Davis (1973, as cited in Birtchnell, 1975) observed that following a parental death, a person becomes more likely to suffer severe depression. Remember, this can be a natural response to death but does not mean you will never be free from its grasp. I broke free; you can too.

Years of severe bullying and exclusion by my peers throughout my education, which worsened after my father died, left me feeling worthless and alone. This led me to years of numbing the pain with alcohol, drugs, self-harm and suicide ideation. This is why I studied Psychology and Criminology at University in an attempt to understand all the depression and anxiety I held inside. It helped me understand why I felt this way, but couldn't help me get past those feelings. It wasn't until I healed my heart that I managed to move these feelings.

I later experienced a different face of grief when I broke my back in a life-changing car accident. It left me living a life in chronic pain which fed my depression again. In fact Burke et al (2015) found that those living with chronic pain are more likely to develop depression and anxiety. This grief of self hit me again years later, when I developed ME/CFS. I lost myself and my future. I lost my dreams, my financial security, and I lost my mind again, drowning in a sea of depression.

The grief associated with this took me back to feeling like that little girl who lost her father. I was not prepared to experience this profound grief again. Alongside the symptoms of my conditions, it took me back to the dark place I had been hiding from. For the first time in a decade, I thought about self-harm and suicide ideation. The grief of living with chronic illnesses is raw, painful and soul-destroying. I now know I was living with prolonged grief disorder (PGD). A study found that those living with PGD and depressive symptoms are positively associated with suicide ideation (Sekowski & Prigerson, 2022). Finding this out made me feel less alone. I hope it does you, too.

Healing my heart of grief by feeling grief has allowed me to accept my past, live in the present, and look forward to my future. I embrace life without fear. It has lifted my depression and I talk freely about my darkest moments to bring inspiration to others living with grief. I embrace grief rather than running from it. I am better prepared for it to surface again. I am passionate about raising awareness of grief – it needs to be talked about more in our society.

It is rewarding to share this profound transformation with my clients. It helps them to recognise, acknowledge and feel their grief in order to start to heal. It gives them the tools to cope better with grief when they are faced with it again.

I will leave you with a piece of advice about the power of writing. When I was a teenager, I wrote a letter from my heart expressing the reality of my grief to my father. I took this to his grave, read it out loud and burned it. When I studied HeartHealing I discovered this is a therapeutic tool. I advise you to write a letter and address it to your grief. Tell your grief where it came from, how it affects your life and allow yourself to pour your feelings onto the page. Thank grief for showing you your caring nature. Let it know that you see it, hear it, feel it, but that it does not control you any longer. Then read it aloud, fold it up away from you, rip it into pieces and burn it outdoors. See how much lighter you feel afterwards.

Grief will enter your life at some point: it is a part of life. There are many faces of grief that go far beyond death. Do not be afraid, but embrace it, feel it and allow your emotions to flow unrestricted. Whatever you feel is valid and therefore important. Do not judge your grief by how others grieve. Do it your way, as your way is the best way for you. Allow yourself time, as grief does not follow a timeline. I urge you to think about it, plan for it, and then when it does come into your life, it will not make you fall into the depths of despair. You are not broken, just different now. You too can find your gold in this different you. Finally, embrace the new you with compassion and kindness.

References:

Abraham-Steele, M. (2024), *Exploring bereaved children's experiences of the death of a close relative and the ways they wish to be supported: an emancipatory repeated focus group study.* Other thesis, University of Essex & Tavistock and Portman NHS Foundation Trust. https://repository.essex.ac.uk/39073/

Bray, N. (2021), Module 1: HeartHealing® Introduction Level 1 - The Heart as the Missing Link. https://schoolofhealing-masteryprogrammes.mykajabi.com/products/hearthealing-mastery-certification/categories/2149889741/posts/2171307079

Bray, N. (2021), Module 1: Understanding the Healer's Journey Workshop. https://schoolofhealingmasteryprogrammes.mykajabi.com/products/hearthealing-mastery-certification/categories/2149889741/posts/2171307100

Bray, N. (2021), Module 11: *The grief workshop* - Kübler-Ross, E. & Kessler, D with an introduction by Shriver, M. (2014) *On Grief and Grieving: Finding the Meaning of Grief Through the Five Stages of Loss.* https://schoolofhealingmasteryprogrammes.mykajabi.com/products/hearthealing-mastery-certification/categories/2149889757/posts/2156127253

Burke, A., Mathias, J., & Denson, L. (2015), *Psychological functioning of people living with chronic pain: A meta-analytic review.* British Journal of Clinical Psychology, 54(3), 345-360. https://doi.org/10.1111/bjc.12078

Cleary, M., West, S., Thapa, D. K., Westman, M., Vesk, K., & Kornhaber, R. (2021), *Grieving the loss of a pet: A qualitative systematic review.* Death Studies, 46(9), 2167–2178. https://doi.org/10.1080/07481187.2021.1901799

Davis, D. R. (1973), *The death of the artist's father: Henrik Ibsen.* Br. J. nied. Psyhol. 46. 135-141 as cited in Birtchnell, J. (1975), *Psychiatric breakdown following recent parent death.* British Journal of Medical Psychology, 48: 379-390. https://doi.org/10.1111/j.2044-8341.1975.tb02346.x

King, B. J., (2016), *Animal mourning: Précis of How animals grieve* (King 2013). Animal Sentience 4(1) https://www.wellbeingintlstudiesrepository.org/animsent/vol1/iss4/1/

Millar, B., (2024), *Can Animals Grieve?*, Ergo an Open Access Journal of Philosophy 11: 17. doi: https://doi.org/10.3998/ergo.6157

Sekowski, M., Prigerson, H. (2002), *Associations between symptoms of prolonged grief disorder and depression and suicidal ideation.* British Journal of Clinical Psychology, 61(4), 1211-1218.

https://bpspsychub.onlinelibrary.wiley.com/doi/full/10.1111/bjc.12381

ABOUT THE AUTHOR

HANNAH DARBY

Hannah Darby GMBPsP SMACCPH is an award-winning trauma-informed therapist and coach who specialises in guiding clients on their personal grief journey. Her unique Kintsugi Method and H.E.A.L approach have been featured in international magazines.

Hannah is a General Member of the British Psychological Society, Senior Member of Accredited Counsellors, Coaches, Psychotherapists and Hypnotherapists, Reiki Master, HeartHealing practitioner, Masseuse and International Bestselling Author.

She spent twenty-six years in careers serving others and eight years as a registered healthcare professional. Hannah draws on her decades of professional and personal wisdom to help individuals H.E.A.L their heart, mind, body and soul, using techniques grounded in both science and spirituality.

Hannah has travelled the world but has been drawn back to the British countryside, where she now resides with her husband, four cats and two chihuahuas. Hannah enjoys reading and country walks.

Hannah is available for one-to-one healing therapies, group workshops, speaking and writing projects and wellness events.

www.healingwithhannah.co.uk
hannah@healingwithhannah.co.uk
facebook.com/hannahsdarby
instagram.com/healingwithhannahd
linkedin.com/in/hannahdarbyhealingwithhannah

13

AARON SWARTZ

THE HEART OF FALSE MASCULINITY

I am sixty-seven years old and loving life. After forty-six different jobs (yes, forty-six), I find myself working as a Psychotherapist. I love this work. Seeing other people become happy makes me happy.

I am at peace, and I love and accept myself just as I am. I no longer have to put on a mask and appear strong. I am genuinely strong, yet able to be vulnerable and share my feelings. I am imperfectly perfect.

I feel so grateful to be in a peaceful and loving relationship with my wife; we can share deeply with each other, just as we are. Don't get me wrong. We can have our bad days and get into difficulties. But we always 'stay in the room', listen to each other and eventually find a peaceful outcome.

For years, I struggled in relationships, primarily because I struggled with myself. I was at war within myself. I was never at ease.

Forty-six years ago, I was a very unhappy young man. I was in crisis and suicidal. Happily, things have changed.

For the past eight years, I have run two men's groups. I've got to listen to hundreds and hundreds of men's stories, and I have come to the conclusion that men are in crisis. They have false ideas of masculinity. They are at war with themselves.

They go to war, killing others and themselves. Just look at Gaza, look at Ukraine, look at the high rate of male suicide. Tragically, men currently commit suicide at a rate of thirteen per day in the UK (or one every two hours), a figure that's three times higher than it is for women.

Men account for eight out of ten people cautioned by the police; nearly nine out of ten people found guilty of indictable offences are men. Men are responsible for 97% of burglaries and 92% of violence against the person.

95% of the UK prison population is male and over 80% of homeless people in the UK are men.

We have a problem… a serious one. Why are men in this position? What is going on?

Men have the wrong idea about themselves. They are living out false ideas of what it means to be a man. How many times have men been told to *man up* or *be strong*? How about, "When the going gets tough, the tough get going," which conveys the idea that we have to do it all, be in control, and above all else, never show our feelings?

Where did these messages come from? Men? Women? Society?

These ideas are all false. We think we have to do everything, we need to appear strong, and we have to stay in control. We strive for power. We don't talk about what's really going on within ourselves. We are addicted to porn, phones and screens.

So often, men push themselves too hard to achieve and be successful. Or they lock themselves away, inside themselves. At some point, we forgot what it is to be a human being. We disconnected from our vulnerability. We became cogs in a machine – a machine designed to get things done, to achieve, to become successful.

Or sometimes we just give up and shut down. In short, we are disconnected from our deepest needs. We are depressed, overwhelmed, suicidal, uncomfortable, and unable to be calm and relaxed.

I too was like this. I never felt good enough. I became an actor. I thought if I was famous and rich, I'd be happy. But I was depressed and suicidal.

Since my teens, I fantasised about ending my life. And then one day, after a performance, I took an overdose. Fortunately, I survived.

Many of the men I've worked with have had equally challenging lives. Take John (not his real name). He was married with two toddlers. His marriage was on the rocks. He worked long hours, was paid well, but was unable to be happy. He felt trapped and just worked harder and longer. His health was suffering and he often felt suicidal.

Or Michael (again, not his real name). He was twenty-nine years old, unemployed and depressed. He was still living at home, addicted to his phone and his PlayStation. He struggled in relationships, couldn't sleep and had no hope for the future.

Both John and Michael were in crisis. 'Crisis' in Japanese is represented by two characters. One is 'Danger'. The other is 'Opportunity'.

Both John and Michael took this opportunity, came to me and did therapy. Both of them had the wrong ideas about what it is to be a man.

There's a great book by former professional footballer Joe Ehrmann called *Season of Life*. He explains how men's identities get so messed up in what he calls 'false masculinity'.

It starts in the playground at school when they play sports. The better athletes get elevated in the eyes of their peers, whilst those who are not so athletic become deflated. When they reach puberty and go to high school where their lives are measured by their ability to relate to and win the opposite sex. Success is measured on their ability to attract girls. Often, they are encouraged to be 'macho' in order to 'get' the girl. It can be very shameful if you don't feel that women are attracted to you. As these boys become adults there can be enormous pressure to be professionally successful and have economic success.

'It is as if one's whole value and worth as a man is based on job titles and bank account balances. Those who achieve and acquire the most are deemed to be real men. And those who do not grab the brass ring, well…' (Ehrmann)

So many men believe they do not have what it takes to be a man, that they are inadequate, and that they do not measure up. So often, men are told, "You're not good enough." This produces a sense of shame, and shame destroys a man's life.

But what if men have it all wrong? What if their sense of masculinity is rooted in a false belief? The brilliant French philosopher, Blaise Pascal, observed that the primary reason people struggle in life is that they have false ideas about reality. So many men are chasing an impossible, unattainable objective.

We are not machines; we are human beings with deep needs, but unfortunately, we are disassociated from our deepest needs.

Dissociation is a state in which a person feels disconnected from themselves and the environment. In a dissociative state, we cannot identify our needs. If we can't identify our needs, how are we going to attend to them? This is when we get stuck or locked in ourselves. We call this a 'freeze' state. The energy in our body is unable to be released.

The 'freeze' state is energy that is locked in the body. But energy is always in motion, and therefore needs to move. It is like a rubber band that gets twisted and twisted. If you keep twisting it, it will eventually snap, because the energy in the rubber band needs to go somewhere.

This affects our entire body, especially our hearts. Both John and Michael were in the 'freeze' state. Their hearts were frozen.

Human beings seem to be very good at keeping this energy 'locked up' inside. We do it for survival reasons. Many times, I've seen someone trip on the pavement and clearly hurt themselves. I go to help and ask, "Are you ok?"

They say, "I'm fine." They don't shout 'ouch' or make any sound. But it's clear that they have hurt themselves. Why didn't they ask for help or at least make a sound when they fell?

I reckon it's the part of the brain that doesn't want to appear vulnerable or weak. They want to appear strong… that false idea about masculinity. So they behave as if nothing happened.

If the energy in their bodies was allowed to be released, they would maybe cry, shake or make a sound. You see, crying, shaking and making sounds are called 'regulating functions' of the body that help us discharge this energy.

This can be helpful in certain survival situations. When the impala is chased by the cheetah, it knows it doesn't stand a chance of fighting the cheetah so it collapses, appearing to be dead. It is able to 'freeze' its energy. When the cheetah catches up with the impala, it amazingly smells like dead meat. It appears not to be breathing. Its body locks up all the energy and 'freezes' so it can survive.

The cheetah sniffs the 'dead' impala and picks it up by the neck, but then releases it, uninterested in 'dead meat'. After a few minutes, the impala shakes itself, releasing all the built-up energy. It has survived and carries on grazing. You can watch this clip on YouTube. (Search for 'impala escapes death'.)

Human beings are fundamentally animals, too. We also freeze this energy inside of us when we are under threat. But unlike animals in the wild, we can keep this energy frozen for a long time. However, this energy needs to be released if we want to be well.

So, how do we release this energy? How do we get our deeper needs met? I reckon 'unmet needs' and 'frozen energy' are the same thing.

Here is some good news! Although you may have unmet needs and you may feel 'locked up' (frozen) inside… your needs *can* be met and your locked-up energy *can* be released. It is what I had to do with myself. It was what I did with John and Michael.

I am going to explain the process we all went through before we could begin to heal our hearts. Sometimes, we need to understand what happened in our past in order to understand the present. I will use John as an example and perhaps you can relate to some of John's story.

John was brought up in a very busy family. His mother was depressed and his father was a workaholic. Both his parents had very little time to be fully available to him. John felt lonely as a child, and was sad and confused.

His father was often angry and frustrated. Often John was scolded and hit when he did something 'wrong'. He learnt in order to avoid punishment he had to be 'nice' or 'good' all the time. Every time his father came home, he also soon learnt 'to be seen and not heard'. As John grew up, he learnt that 'achieving' was the most important thing to do. As if that was not difficult enough for John, at five years old he was also sent part-time to boarding school. It was a difficult place where bullying was common and he soon learnt that in order to survive he had to be tough and never reveal his vulnerability. He learnt to 'fit in'.

Fundamentally, John was not getting his deepest needs met. Our deepest needs are:

- to feel safe
- to feel seen
- to feel wanted
- to feel heard
- to feel validated
- to have our realities validated
- to feel attuned to
- to feel emotional stability
- and most important of all, to feel unconditionally loved.

There are a million ways your deepest needs may not have been met by your parents when you were very young. Which ones do you relate to?

When John's needs were not met, his body went into 'disassociation'. His body got 'frozen' and 'locked'.

Just like the impala, John's body needed to 'thaw out' and be able to release all the held energy. As a therapist, my job was to help John thaw out and begin to relax. When that began to happen, he could gradually connect with his needs. This can sometimes take a long time, especially if a person has never had another adult in their life that they can fully trust.

Once John could finally trust me, his body began to relax naturally, and he was able to connect with his deepest unmet needs. I used a number of techniques to help him feel safe in his body. But the most important factor of all was that John began to reconnect with his heart.

In Chinese medicine, the heart is considered the Emperor. The Emperor rules the kingdom and if the Emperor is not well, the kingdom is also not well. If we are disconnected from our hearts, our lives will not be well either.

Did you know that the heart, like the brain, generates a powerful electromagnetic field that reaches about three feet outside the body?

Did you know that positive emotions such as love generate a harmonious pattern in the heart's rhythm that leads to coherence and emotional regulation?

That's amazing. The heart is our engine! So it is important that we heal the deeper root hurts and pains that are held in the heart. Your superpower is your heart. Amazing, isn't it?

When somebody hurts us, our hearts feel the pain. When we lose a loved one or we experience a relationship breakup, we feel 'heartbreak'.

Scans of people whose hearts have been broken show that muscles surrounding the heart have literally been torn. In order not to feel the pain, the muscular wall (the myocardium) around the heart will tighten. It can become very hard and rigid, and if this wall never comes down again, it means the heart is never open to love again. And that can become a very lonely place.

This was where John was. His heart was shut down and over-protected. This doesn't just happen when we lose someone; it can also happen when we are very young and a parent or caregiver hurts us. This protection may have been helpful at the time of the heartbreak, but if it persists into later life, we will eventually dissociate from our hearts.

If our hearts are damaged, they must be repaired. If the engine fails in a car, it doesn't matter if you fix something else that's wrong with the car; it still won't function. We are the same.

As John 'thawed out', he could also begin to access his heart. We did some HeartHealing sessions and over time, John's unmet needs could be met.

When our unmet needs are met:

- We feel safe
- We do not live in fear
- We allow life, people and things to be just how they are
- We are relaxed, calm and resilient, and enjoy being alive
- We feel seen for the 'whole' of who we are
- We know that we matter
- We feel heard
- We feel loved
- We feel validated
- We feel our reality is validated
- We are attuned to others, and others can connect to us through our feelings
- We feel a sense of emotional stability
- We feel hope
- We can have fun and play
- We love being alive
- We feel unconditionally loved just as we are.

When we feel the above, our needs have been met.

Eventually, John and Michael began to feel the above. Today, John and Michael's lives have changed. John's marriage is going well, he has cut back on his working hours and has actually found a job that he loves. Michael, too, has found a job he likes. He has made some new friends and joined a men's group, and feels positive for the first time ever.

Both have learnt to love themselves and are now able to prioritise their needs. They are healing their hearts.

This is the very same journey I too had to go on to heal my false ideas of masculinity. For years, I never felt comfortable with who I was. My soul desperately needed to be seen, heard, acknowledged and unconditionally loved.

I remember the moment I decided to become an actor. I was sixteen years old, at a party, and playing the clown as usual. I told jokes, trying to be funny. It was wonderful when people laughed. I felt good inside. I must have equated that with 'being loved'. This was how I attempted to get my needs of being seen, wanted, heard, validated and loved met. I decided to become an actor.

A couple of years later, I was at drama school in London. I had just performed the lead role in a play. Despite the audience loving our performance, I hated it. Clearly, 'being loved' by the audience wasn't enough.

I went home depressed, hating myself, life and everything. I self-harmed and took an overdose. I thought it was going to put me out of my pain, but I just felt more awful. I was taken to hospital where they pumped my stomach out, and I was sent away depressed and dazed.

That was forty-eight years ago. Despite this, I went on to have a 'successful' acting career for twenty-five years. It is amazing what a person can do even when their mental health is poor. But I was still depressed and had suicidal thoughts. This became the norm. I was in 'survival' mode, getting by but unhappy and hurting deeply.

I got married and we had a little boy. Suddenly, my life was jettisoned into overwhelm. Being a parent was a very challenging and painful experience. I couldn't take care of myself, even though I loved my wife and son so much. I was exhausted, trying to do it all on my own and moving fast towards a mental breakdown.

I was a nightmare to be with. I exploded into rages all the time, sometimes punching holes in walls and hurting myself. My poor ex-wife was scared of me. (I have since deeply apologised.)

I didn't realise it at the time but I was suffering from the trauma of my past. In order for us to survive as a family and for me to be a safe and loving parent, I would need to heal my own trauma history. My heart was broken and I needed to heal it. I was in 'crisis'.

Remember how the Japanese represent 'Crisis'? It was an opportunity. I was desperate for help but asking for help was difficult, as it is for so many men. We have been conditioned to do it alone and be 'strong'. But I had no choice but to seek help.

I saw an ad in a magazine for the 'Hoffman Quadrinity Process'. It said, "You can change your life!" I immediately got in touch. I knew my life and my family were at stake. Looking back, that moment of reaching out changed the whole course of my life.

During this retreat, I could completely focus on my early life and my unmet needs with my parents. I discovered that I was very angry with them and all this anger was bottled up inside of me. I always felt in my family that I couldn't really be who I truly was. No one would listen to me deeply. My parents, although they 'loved' me, were too preoccupied with themselves to be able to give me the deep listening and attunement that I realised I so needed.

In order to try to get the attention I needed, I developed another version of myself. This person was the 'handsome nice guy' who was always trying to be funny. So as I said earlier, I became an actor, both professionally and in life. But no matter how successful I was (I still get fan mail!), I was never happy. I was continually depressed.

I was able to release this anger inside of me in a healthy way, not a destructive way. We used bats to hit pillows while saying what we were angry towards our parents for. It was the beginning of getting my need to 'be heard' met.

I also realised that becoming an 'actor' was connected to being a 'false self': my false masculinity. I had to put on a mask in order to be somebody. Being an actor was a way of covering up my deep self-loathing and shame. I had no self-worth.

During a HeartHealing session, I was able to heal the 'Worth Wound'. It was a beautiful yet painful experience, where I was able to meet a young part of me that felt this shame and loathing and finally be able to release it and feel 'worthy' again, just as I am.

I didn't need to be somebody else. I could simply be my imperfect perfect self.

Through Psychotherapy, Somatic Experiencing (SE), Comprehensive Resource Model (CRM) and HeartHealing, I have been able to thrive in life instead of just 'surviving'. I now help others do the same.

It is a beautiful sunny day. The sun glistens through the trees. The birds are singing. I take my dog, Henry, for a long walk. I end up in a pub waiting to meet my wife. We share what's happened in our day. It is good to share with someone you love. I have her back and she has mine. It is a good day. We both feel immense feelings of gratitude.

I help people to realise that they can love themselves. When we heal our hearts, we can love ourselves and get our needs met. When we know, feel and experience this, we are free, happy and fulfilled.

Once men connect to their hearts, they can heal the wounds of their past. Once men heal their hearts, the world will be a safer place. War will end and, as Charles Eisenstein says, they can create, 'The more beautiful world that in their hearts they know is possible.'

The world needs healed people. The world needs healed men!

Right now, you have said *yes* to reading this book. Congratulations. I hope reading this has been helpful. When I said *yes* to therapy all those years ago, the mountains of pain and suffering began to slip away.

The time of the lone wolf is over. If you need help, reach out.

Are you ready for one last *yes*? I hope so. Would you like to feel more relaxed and connected to your heart? *Yes?* Great!

Take a few moments to get yourself comfortable… sitting, lying, whatever works for you.

> Notice whatever your body is in contact with.
> Notice your feet.
> Notice your breathing.
> Notice the air coming into you.
> Notice the inhale.
> Notice the exhale.
> Simply breathe.
> Simply breathe.
> Simply… breathe.
> Take your time…

Spend a few minutes doing this, even if your brain is racing away.

> Now, place your hand on your heart.
> Be patient and simply start to 'sense' your heart. Again, take your time.
> Can you feel your heartbeat?
> Now, be honest with yourself and ask: "What does my heart need?"
> Take a few moments to write down your response.

References:

Ehrmann, J., (2004), *Season of Life: A Football Star, a Boy, a Journey to Manhood*.

Levine, P., (1997), *Waking The Tiger: Healing Trauma.* North Atlantic Books,U.S.

McCraty, R., *The Energetic Heart: Bioelectromagnetic Interactions Within and Between People*, Ebook. https://www.psychologytoday.com/gb/blog/building-the-habit-of-hero/202011/the-hearts-electromagnetic-field-is-your-superpower

Morales, J., *The Hearts Electromagnetic Field is Your Superpower.*

Psychology Today, Posted November 29, 2020. https://www.psychologytoday.com/gb/blog/building-the-habit-of-hero/202011/the-hearts-electromagnetic-field-is-your-superpower

Pascal, B., (1995), *Pensees*, Penguin Classics.

ONS. (2019). Suicides in the UK: 2018 registrations. Retrieved from: https://www.ons.gov.uk/peoplepopulationandcommunity/birthsdeathsandmarriages/deaths/bulletins/suicidesintheunitedkingdom/2018registrations

Schmidt, S. J.,(2009), *The Developmental Needs Meeting Strategy: An Ego State Therapy for Healing Adults with Childhood Trauma and Attachment* Wounds.

Schwarz, L., (2018), *The Comprehensive Resource Model: Effective therapeutic techniques for healing of complex trauma.* Routledge.

YouTube. *Impala Escapes Death*, https://youtu.be/-QgglTik-6G4?si=MXv20NsvlDxOdCdk

A Band of Brothers. An award-winning charity helping young men grow and develop, https://abandofbrothers.org.uk

ABOUT THE AUTHOR

AARON SWARTZ

Aaron Swartz is a Psychotherapist, Teacher, Speaker, Facilitator, Painter and Healer with seventeen years' experience, specialising in Trauma. He weaves a unique blend of Psychotherapy, Somatic Experiencing (SE), Comprehensive Resource Model (CRM), Deep Brain Reorienting (DBR) and HeartHealing to help people transform their lives and live 'the more beautiful life they long for in their hearts'.

For the past eight years, he has run two successful men's groups where men can be their true vulnerable selves in the presence of other supportive men. Men have stayed in the group for up to five years.

Before becoming a Psychotherapist, he worked as a successful Actor, Film and Theatre Director. Although he loved this work, helping people work through their Trauma was the best contribution he could make to creating a better world.

www.aaroncounselling.co.uk
aaronswartz0@gmail.com

14

DIANE HUTCHESON

THE HEART OF ADHD

ADHD (attention-deficit/hyperactivity disorder) first came to my attention while working with people with substance abuse disorders (SUD). I owned a substance abuse outpatient treatment center, and I noticed quite a few people had symptoms that met criteria for ADHD, although their ADHD was undiagnosed. As I learned more about ADHD, I started to identify some of the same symptoms characteristic of ADHD in myself.

I probably had it, I thought. Why did no one say anything to me about it? But then I thought, no, wait, I can't have it: I held a Master's in Advanced Practice Nursing. So I denied thoughts about my own ADHD and only returned to the idea ten years later. I discounted the importance of it and felt it really did not matter.

I did not take into account, however, that it took me longer than others to obtain my Master's because my learning, focus, and attention were different. ADHD has to do with how you learn and accomplish things. It has nothing to do with your knowledge, and everything to do with how you use it and when you implement it.

I only sought help when things were no longer working. In menopause, the hormones that were protective previously were in decline. I was unable to function and use what I now know are workarounds. I was one of many women diagnosed with ADHD in perimenopause or menopause (Kooij, 2023). It turns out getting a diagnosis was crucial for me.

I truly did not understand until I got diagnosed with ADHD what it meant to have untreated ADHD. Life now is more fun, and I do more of the things I love that I did not do before. I am happy, and I have clarity and purpose in what I do. I am able to understand and share with others the possibilities and the journey of what life can be like.

Today, I have confidence that I know exactly what to do in any situation I may encounter. I have connected to myself at a deeper level than I knew existed. I am connected to my intuition more than ever before, and my perception of what life is like is very different. My hope is that you learn more about ADHD so you can recognise the symptoms in yourself and others, knowing there is a way to have an easier, more fulfilling life.

What Is ADHD?

Most people's picture of someone with ADHD is the typical boy child being disruptive in class. This is because much of the early research on ADHD was focused on school-aged boys who displayed obvious symptoms of excessive motor activity, inattention, and impulsiveness, mostly excluding girls and boys who experienced more internalized symptoms of ADHD or were better at masking their symptoms.

We now know that children do not outgrow ADHD. They continue with it their whole lives. Their symptoms and environment may change; the presentation may change – but it is still there. Men and women have the basic core symptoms of ADHD that I named above, but they look different in presentation. Also, societal influences and perceptions mean men and women are treated differently. Perceived gender roles influence how the person is brought up, which influences the presentation in each person as much as the DNA blueprint they are born with.

Attention deficit hyperactivity disorder (ADHD) is one of the most researched and treatable disorders in Mental Health. It is a neurological disorder, heritable from parent to child, or acquired, such as after chemotherapy treatment of a child or traumatic brain injuries. Intelligence (IQ) has nothing to do with ADHD. A lot of people with ADHD have high IQs which may enable them to achieve many things, but it may take them longer than other people or happen later in life.

It is not only children who are diagnosed with ADHD, but also adults. Adults with ADHD born in the 1990s or earlier were often not diagnosed. Women, especially, were only beginning to be diagnosed in the 1990s. There was a shift in the understanding of ADHD symptoms by then, and the inattentive symptoms, which women more often exhibit, were now in the forefront of diagnostic committees for the DSM.

There are two main dimensions of neuropsychological deficits in ADHD: hyperactivity-impulsivity and inattention.

- Hyperactivity-impulsivity includes: decreased motor inhibition, impaired verbal inhibition, impaired cognition, impaired motivation, emotional dysregulation, and restlessness (Barkley, 2018).
- The types of inattention which exist are: poor executive attention and functioning; poor persistence toward goals; impaired resistance to distraction; poor prioritization; poor initiation, continuation, and completion of tasks; poor working memory, both verbal and visual; diminished self-awareness (Barkley, 2018).

All of these are looked at for the diagnosis of ADHD. Evaluation for a diagnosis can be a first step with anyone who thinks they may have ADHD. To get an official diagnosis, you must do an interview with a provider who specializes in ADHD.

No single test can tell if you have ADHD. There are screening questionnaires and symptoms associated with ADHD, and people may have similar symptom profiles, but each person's ADHD is different. One must interview the person and ask about the symptoms and why they have sought help. Corroboration with others, such as employers or families, or school report cards, is also necessary. The impact on their function in daily life is also considered. Often, people come seeking help for other things, such as depression, worry, OCD or anxiety… not for ADHD. ADHD can be accompanied by or mistaken for mood disorders like depression, anxiety, tics, autism, learning disorders, C-PTSD or substance abuse.

The Impact of ADHD

Mood is not included in the diagnostic and statistical manual that we currently use for diagnosing ADHD in the US, although we know that people with ADHD often have fluctuations in mood depending on the influence of their environment and the people in it. The person who goes from zero to one hundred in rage with seemingly little provocation is exhibiting mood dysregulation; for example, the father who loses patience with his son who is learning how to hit the ball and screams at him to get it together.

In other cases, a mother or father might not allow the child with ADHD to do those things they know he will fail at, thereby robbing them of the experience of failure (which everyone needs) and learning resilience and how to be successful. This well-meaning parent often fuels the child's resentment and misunderstanding, making him want to escape quickly from that life. Going forward, this can cause a separation between child and parent. They are prevented from being able to connect with his emotions and feelings as well as impacting his ability to have a close relationship with a significant other in the future.

ADHD impacts how you learn and what you pay attention to. If you can't pay attention, you do not form a memory of something and therefore your learning is impacted. It is a misleading title for the condition, however. There is no deficit in the attention of a person with ADHD – they pay *too much* attention to everything, which makes them scattered and unable to focus on any one thing. The problem is screening the stimuli out, picking one thing, focusing on that, and sticking to it, maintaining the focus and completing the task even with other stimuli coming in.

I am describing executive function skills, the organizing that happens (or doesn't) in your prefrontal cortex. (Barkley, 2012) The ADHD brain is different in this way from the "neurotypical" brain. The prefrontal cortex is also where the dopamine and norepinephrine (or lack of them) are utilized (or not) to help pay attention, to remember what is next, and to modulate and regulate mood.

The effectiveness of ADHD medications can be influenced by hormones. Men may have testosterone issues which can affect energy, mood and interest indicating the need to be aware of hormones in men when prescribing medication for ADHD. Women are affected by hormones that change and cycle from the time of their birth and which peak during childbearing years. Each woman has her own hormonal pattern, which changes and then decreases during perimenopause not in a rational, even way but irregularly, depending on the person, their genes, the environment, and their exposure to toxins.

These hormones influence the production of neurotransmitters – primarily dopamine, norepinephrine, Serotonin, GABA and acetylcholine – which make the brain and body work together well. Neurotransmitter fluctuations, caused by these hormonal fluctuations, interfere with the effectiveness of ADHD medications, especially during peri-menopause and menopause (Eng *et al* 2024).

The Heart of ADHD

While ADHD is widely recognised as a neurological disorder that benefits from diagnosis and medical treatment, there is a growing body of research that explores the overlap and connections between trauma and ADHD.

For example, Szymanski *et al* (2011) found an increased risk of experiencing complex trauma (such as stress and attachment trauma) if you have ADHD and trauma worsening symptoms of ADHD due to the nervous system dysregulation it can cause. It is important to note that not everyone with ADHD has trauma, and not everyone with trauma has ADHD – but they often co-exist and they can impact each other. The experiences that a person has by living with untreated ADHD lead to worsening symptoms and these experiences are traumatic to them, leading them to be misunderstood by others, parents, teachers, and friends. This contributes to experiences that are traumatic. This can range from childhood abuse (physical, sexual, emotional, and psychological) and neglect, to experiences with substance abuse, or being what is known as small t trauma, not the big T trauma of a motor vehicle accident, but relational trauma that HeartHealing focuses on.

ADHD contributes to the vulnerability of the person, making them more likely to experience abuse from others who are supposed to care for them (Merscher, *et al 2025)*. This also means that parents or caregivers may have the same disorders diagnosed in the children, and that is what predisposed them to have an environment that contributed to trauma experiences.

This suggests that ADHD can benefit from a more holistic approach that recognizes the history of ADHD as a treatable mental health condition but also explores the healing possible for people with ADHD when we address the underlying trauma that has resulted in ongoing guilt, shame and embarrassment that continues to affect their wellbeing and relationships with others.

This more holistic approach is one that I am uniquely positioned to help my clients with because of my thirty-plus years of psychiatric/psychological education and extensive experience, along with my personal journey with ADHD and my training in HeartHealing.

The HeartHealing modality specifically uncovers and addresses the wounds and traumas caused by early childhood experiences, experiences in our adult life that enforce invalidation of us as a person and the people in our life that were not able to create safe spaces or environments. This is relational trauma.

HeartHealing allows me to help those men and women with ADHD who have been traumatized by poor relationships with their family while they were growing up to know and understand their own feelings. They learn to self-regulate their emotions and this allows them to have patience with significant others so they can have space to do their work and grow as well.

Men with ADHD are often more cut off from how they feel, unable to identify emotions and/or behave defensively when someone seemingly opposes their position, when really they are saying the same thing just in a different way. Relationships with self, spouses, and friends are what bring men to seek out help, since they want to keep the relationship and have more supportive friends than they may have now. Things are not going along like they had thought. Often there are no friends or few that can help with the isolation and ostracization that may have occurred due to estrangement from family.

HeartHealing can help connect us to ourselves that previously had been blocked due to being ashamed, angry and unable to understand what had happened. If you do not know something you can't change it and that lack of awareness makes us defensive and angry. This may be the same response or pattern that we learned from our family and was probably modeled by our families when we grew up. It is common to have other family members who have traits of ADHD not diagnosed or under the threshold to meet the criteria for diagnosis. This is important as it contributes to the continued dysfunction that is not as overt or noticeable.

Feeling safe is necessary to change; when it is not safe in your family, change will not happen. If that has been going on for generations of your family, then that influenced everyone to continue the same pattern of dysfunctional relationships. For me, the difference came when I did the Ancestral HeartHealing Safety wound. It was the biggest *aha* moment. What underlies all healing is feeling safe, and that can be from obvious and not so obvious causal relationships.

Women with ADHD often have difficulty trusting themselves to discern well and fall into the trap of believing someone is going to be there and take care of them. This level of betrayal is ultimately the repeated betrayal of themselves by themself: they depend on those others who promise to take care of them but fall short time and time again. The woman with ADHD does not trust herself and keeps trying to find the right man to take care of her, probably repeating the same scenario that played out in her growing up with her family. Sometimes a woman with ADHD feels like the odd woman out and that others are always excluding her or putting her down because she talks too much or is too loud. I had this experience. It is also about my perceived experience from the interactions. But I did not feel worthy enough, so why would I trust any of them?

Feeling enough is one of the most impactful HeartHealing Receiving wounds that needs to be addressed. When Enoughness is healed it can open the doorway for the person to take action to assert themselves and, for example, take charge in a serious situation with children involved. This can happen to the total surprise of the person. They might offer a solution that makes everything turn out for the best. Before the HeartHealing session, there might have been years of talking about the situation and very little action.

They might have felt that nothing would ever change so there was no point in bothering. They might not have trusted their intuition and were mistrustful of themself and second-guessed everything. But after HeartHealing, this person with ADHD would make a huge transformation and now shows up for themself where it counts and makes friends who are worthy of their friendship. These issues are much easier to navigate when using intuition and believing in themself so that they have improved relationships both with themself and children. They had been able to set boundaries and stick to them, successfully negotiating improved financial outcomes for themself.

My Journey with ADHD

I was diagnosed with ADHD at the age of sixty-four after knowing for almost ten years that I probably had it but was avoiding it. After all, I had two Master's degrees, I held a 4.0 GPA, and I am a psychiatric nurse practitioner who diagnoses and prescribes meds. Besides all that, how would it benefit me to get diagnosed? It really wouldn't matter, would it? Wrong!

Around the ages of fifty to sixty-four years old, I was going through menopause, which meant I was creating fewer hormones that are protective of the brain. This made it much more obvious that there was an issue with my attention span, working memory, initiating and completing tasks, and generally being able to pay attention.

If you can't pay attention, you do not have memory. Memory is everything for day-to-day things, especially if you are a provider. I somehow made it through, but things were not right. My mood felt depressed, but I wasn't really depressed. The usual quickness of my brain had disappeared; it turned sluggish, with difficulty retrieving information.

This had bigger implications than you might think. All along, growing up, I was saved by my memory and how smart I was but then it started not to work the same way anymore. Little things and then big things slipped. General life things became difficult. Traumatic things and problems with relationships happened. This led me to seek a diagnosis. Getting diagnosed was important for me because I kept questioning if there was something wrong with me. For myself and clients I work with, having someone else confirm ADHD can be life-changing.

That is when I started to get help for the ADHD symptoms. I started to realize what I had missed, not just for the last couple of years but for most of my life. Not being able to pay attention meant I did not have an opinion about things; I took whatever anyone gave me, and followed the next shiny thing. I did not so much decide to do something as just fall into things or I just couldn't say no to someone. This was big, I just didn't realize how big.

Now I am seventy-three and about five years ago I found HeartHealing and Natasha Bray. I often counted myself out before I tried anything leading to dropping out of things or not going to things I wanted to for a long time. These coping patterns hid those "flaws" in myself of feeling ashamed, not enough and guilty. HeartHealing identified the deeper wound of not feeling safe and healed that Safety Wound that had been passed on for generations.

These wounds are not unique to me, but what I did with them and how I handled them with ADHD are. HeartHealing worked in a deeper way than any other therapy I tried. The work I have done has been life-changing in that it has helped me peel back the layers of limiting beliefs and habits that no longer served me. I did not know what I did not know until after I got diagnosed and prescribed meds. I had always thought it was someone else's problem impacting me and my business. But through this work, I found it was not them: it was *me!* It is my responsibility to take care of myself; to learn and to teach myself and then to teach others how to be in this world.

I have taken many courses and learned advanced levels of EMDR, Lifespan Integration, Hypnosis (2006), and other world leading therapies. I have a Master's in Clinical Psychology (1990), a Master's in Advanced Practice in Psychiatric Nursing (1998), RN Diploma in 1974, and a Bachelor's degree in Psychology. Personally, not one thing really made a difference until after I got diagnosed, was treated and then started my own work with HeartHealing.

ADHD particularly skews your view of the world. Some of it you notice, some you don't, and some you notice too intensely. I had been looking for the missing piece of me and what was wrong with me. I always questioned why I did not fit in, why I always overworked, and why I always said yes when I didn't mean it. Why did I not know something that everyone else seemed to know? Simple things, such as the possibility that you can have lacy underwear, not just plain cotton.

I blamed my father, the way I grew up, the school, whomever, but the issues were with myself and how I saw the world; it was through a fog. I never had an opinion because I did not think I could have one, or even that there was something I could have an opinion about. Someone had always made the decision for me or rescued me from something.

The patterns developed not just from me but from the generational influences of my family (state, country, world), and the way of life that became entwined with my current life that I could not have foreseen.

I thought I had done a lot of work before I came to HeartHealing in 2019/20. Then Covid quarantine came and health problems came up for me in the middle of studying HeartHealing. I had to pause for treatment and reevaluate what I wanted to do. HeartHealing took off the layers of mistrust, unfamiliarity, lack of self-love, lack of self-worth and lack of self-acceptance.

The *aha* moment came with the HeartHealing Ancestral Wound around Safety that had blocked me from my full connection to myself and my purpose. The lack of feeling safe stemmed from generations of mistrust and lack of safety. I could not fully be myself if I always had to run and hide. This was the opening of myself to use my intuition and healing knowledge with others that I had not done before.

I decided I wanted to do things differently than I had. It meant confronting the habits that impacted from long ago to this present day. This realization about how far back the impact went led me to another level. I am constantly changing and growing and adapting to how I want to be, not letting others push me and pull me but standing up for what I know I want now.

It led me to be easily and smoothly confident in what I say and do with my clients, family, and friends. Most of the people I work with have ADHD. My own journey has helped me to intuitively know what will help the other person to heal and has brought more wonder and fun to my life and work.

If you think you have ADHD (you may have taken an online test) consider seeking out an evaluation from a qualified practitioner who is experienced in ADHD. Then, educate yourself, learn what symptoms you have of ADHD, gain clarity for you about your symptoms. Next, follow through (one of the biggest issues is not following through with recommendations) with treatment, medication, support of other people with ADHD (a group), begin to take care of yourself with sleep, nutrition, and seeing your medical practitioner. Find an experienced practitioner in ADHD who knows how to help you heal relational wounds and make changes. This is where HeartHealing's impact is the greatest as part of a holistic approach to ADHD.

It means the world to me that I get to help others with ADHD experience the same connection, safety and trust that has opened up for me. If anything I have shared here resonates with you, you are not alone. There is nothing wrong with you, and a better quality of life is possible for you.

References:

American Psychiatric Association. (2022), *Diagnostic and statistical manual of mental disorders* (5th ed., text rev.). https://doi.org/10.1176/appi.books.9780890425787

Barkley, R. A. (2012), *Executive functions: What they are, how they work, and why they evolved*. New York, NY: Guilford Press.

Barkley, R. A. (2015), *Attention-deficit hyperactivity disorder: A handbook for diagnosis and treatment* (4th ed.). New York, NY: Guilford Press.

Daucourt, M. C., Haughbrook, R., van Bergen, E., & Hart, S. A. (2020). The co-development of reading fluency and reading comprehension: A twin study. *Developmental Psychology*, 56(10), 1861–1874. https://doi.org/10.1037/dev0001126

Eng, A. G., Nirjar, U., Elkins, A. R., Sizemore, Y. J., Monticello, K. N., Petersen, M. K., Miller, S. A., Barone, J., Eisenlohr-Moul, T. A., & Martel, M. M. (2024). Attention-deficit/hyperactivity disorder and the menstrual cycle: Theory and evidence. *Hormones and Behavior, 158,* 105466.

Kooij, J. S. (2023). Hormonal sensitivity of mood symptoms in women with ADHD across the lifespan. *European Psychiatry*, 66(S1), S23. https://doi.org/10.1192/j.eurpsy.2023.92

Merscher, J., Barra, S., Xander, A.M. *et al.* Adult ADHD predicts intimate partner violence perpetration and *victimization irrespective of gender and age. Sci Rep* 15, 4914 (2025). https://doi.org/10.1038/s41598-024-74222-w

Szymanski, K., Sapanski, L., & Conway, F. (2011). Trauma and ADHD – Association or Diagnostic Confusion? A Clinical Perspective. *Journal of Infant, Child, and Adolescent Psychotherapy, 10*(1), 51–59. https://doi.org/10.1080/15289168.2011.575704

Resources:

https://www.additudemag.com/category/adhd-add/symptom-tests/

https://chadd.org

ABOUT THE AUTHOR

DIANE HUTCHESON

Diane Hutcheson's approach as a Healer involves the whole person, using body, mind and spirit to transform and achieve wellbeing for men and women.

Before she focused on HeartHealing, Diane was a RN, working in psychiatry for twenty-plus years. Extensive experience as a Psychiatric Nurse Practitioner allowed her to formulate her current practice of providing evaluations, prescribing medications and using therapeutic tools with a focus on HeartHealing to fine-tune what she does. Always looking for what works, Diane combines her education and experiences in practice with HeartHealing, bringing them together powerfully.

Diane lives in Seattle, WA, and focuses on having fun; this includes line dancing, walking her dachshunds and doing what she wants and likes to do.

Diane is available for Consultation, HeartHealing packages, and various programs related to ADHD, such as the Amazingly Awesome Women with ADHD Group/Program.

diane@dianehutchesonarnp.com
facebook.com/amazinglyawesomewomenADHD
instagram.com/diane.hutchesonadhd
facebook.com/diane.hutcheson.79
instagram.com/dianehutcheson1

15

DARCY BAILEY

THE HEART OF SELF-MASTERY

Owning My Story:
The Heart of True Freedom and Self-Mastery

I own my story—every single part of it. I trust that every experience in my life has been intelligently designed to support my greatest growth and expansion. Because of HeartHealing, I am deeply connected to my knowingness that I am worthy. That I matter. That I am enough. Not because of what I do but because of who I am.

I accept all parts of who I am with compassion and humility because I accept me. No one and nothing can change that. I trust myself—my voice, my intuition and my decisions. I have released fears around being seen or heard and truly authentically known. I take up space and let my voice be heard. I won't shrink to fit in nor hide behind who I thought I needed to be.

I no longer live in survival mode with deeply embedded patterns of vigilance, protection, and control so that I could feel safe. I have surrendered the exhausting grip of perfectionism and relentless self-judgment, and released the pervasive beliefs about not being enough, which caused persistent self-doubt and self-criticism. I resolved the exhausting pressure to get it right, the fear of failure and making mistakes. I have transformed the need to prove, to earn, to strive for worthiness or to search outside myself, for wholeness, worth and acceptance.

I healed and have forgiveness for the relationships that taught me to be so.

I know now that I have always been enough – not because of anything I do, but just for being me. My worth is intrinsic. My power is within.

I have come home to myself. My true self. And stepped into the freedom of simply being me. My heart is open. My mind is clear. I am present. I live with peace and a sense of calm. I live more fully, freely, and on purpose. I feel connected and my relationships are deeper. Love has expanded. I wake up curious, inspired and eager—not because I have it all figured out, but because I trust that I will.

This is the Heart of Self-Mastery. It is not just intellectual understanding, nor just mindset shifts. It is a deep, embodied knowing.

Freedom comes from healing core trauma wounds, wounds of the heart which create unconscious patterns of limitation and keep us from a life we want. Freedom comes from the connection to the truth of who we are and our incredible capacity.

Now I have the freedom to live, love, and create from a place of sovereignty rather than survival: from contracted to expanded; from fractured to whole; from searching to knowing; from hiding to being fully expressed; from surviving to personal sovereignty. And I tap into the power within so I can be a powerful creator of my life.

This is the Heart of Self-Mastery.

The Root Cause of Survival Patterns: Self-Mastery as the Path to Freedom

To highlight what Self-Mastery is, it is helpful to identify what it is not. The opposite of Self-Mastery is self-sabotage, self-abandonment, and unconscious living. These are sources of inner conflict that people experience when they want more from life but can't find a way. It is a pervasive source of stress and dis-ease.

How do people end up in these patterns and ways of being?

At the core of every human experience is the drive for safety and connection. We are social, relational beings. Our earliest relationships shape how we experience life by imprinting how we see ourselves, others, and the world, and how we come to understand who we are, how relationships work, and what to expect from the world around us. When early attachments are secure, we internalize the belief that we are worthy, loved, and safe. But when those attachments are fractured, often through emotional inconsistency, conditional love, neglect, or abuse, those wounds leave an imprint that becomes the framework through which we interpret and create the narrative of our lives.

It is in the heart our true sense of Self resides—our connection to the essence of who we are, our Soul or Spirit. When wounded, the heart bears the deepest impact, driving a wedge between our true self and a "false self" developed for protection. These protective patterns shape our personality—our perceptions, beliefs, thoughts, feelings, and behaviors—becoming the lens through which we see ourselves, others, and the world, and dictating how we navigate life.

The ego and personality form a system of parts in response to trauma, attachment wounds, and the need for safety and connection. These wounds imprint in the nervous system and mind, becoming unconscious core programs—survival strategies born of protection. Over time, these mechanisms become habitual and feel like our identity, especially shaping how we see ourselves. But these patterns are not our true selves—they are strategies meant to protect the wounded heart. When we react instead of respond, we're acting from the false self. The patterns are symptoms; the root cause is the trauma to the heart—the injury to the essence of who we are.

Though they once served a purpose, these protective patterns become habituated into unconscious cycles of limitation and self-sabotage. Over time, they paradoxically perpetuate the very pain they were meant to shield us from—keeping us stuck in fear, limitation, disconnection, and unworthiness. The root of these unconscious programs lies in wounds of the heart. While they show up in various ways, they are often tied to nervous system responses of Fight, Flight, Freeze, and Fawn. These are automatic survival states wired through our nervous system to protect us from perceived threats.

Through my work, I've developed a framework of five core cycles that help people identify how these unconscious patterns formed in response to early wounds to identity. These cycles tend to repeat until resolved. People may relate to one or several or have a dominant style.

1. The Cycle of Proving: Chasing Success to Feel Worthy (Fawn and Fight)

This cycle ties worth to achievement and doing. People overwork, overperform, and struggle to rest without guilt.

- Rest feels unsafe; productivity becomes self-worth.
- Mistakes trigger shame and self-criticism.
- Success never satisfies—the goalpost keeps moving.

Core Belief: I'm only valuable if I achieve something. Achievements define my worth and value.

2. The Cycle of Hiding: Playing Small to Stay Safe (Flight and Fawn)

Fear of judgment or failure leads to shrinking back, people-pleasing, and avoiding visibility.

- Visibility feels threatening; self-expression is suppressed.
- Growth opportunities are missed due to fear.
- Frustration and a sense of invisibility.

Core Belief: If people see the real me, they'll judge and/or reject me. I'm not ready yet – I need more time.

3. The Cycle of Avoidance: Fear of Action, Fear of Change (Freeze and Flight)

This cycle replaces action with overthinking and planning. Fear of getting it wrong keeps people stuck.

- Action feels unsafe; over-preparing and procrastination tendencies.
- Temporary relief of avoidance leads to long-term regret.
- Fear of failure. Not taking action reinforces feelings of inadequacy and stagnation.

Core Belief: If I make the wrong choice, everything will fall apart.

4. The Cycle of Disconnection: Losing Yourself in Survival Mode (Freeze and Fawn)

Overgiving and emotional numbness lead to disconnection from needs, desires, and purpose.

- Emotions feel flat; needs are chronically unmet.
- Identity feels blurred; life becomes a checklist.
- Leads to emptiness and quiet resentment.

Core Belief: Other people's needs matter more than mine.

5. The Cycle of Overdrive: When Hustling Becomes Your Identity (Fight Response)

Work becomes self-worth. Slowing down feels unsafe, and success is never "enough."

- Constant push to do more; rest triggers guilt.
- Joy and relationships get deprioritized.
- Burnout and emotional depletion follow.

Core Belief: I'll rest when I've made it—but I never feel like I've made it. I'm not as far along as I should be.

Self-Mastery is the path of healing core imprints, releasing heart-held wounds, and reclaiming the true self buried beneath conditioning. People aren't broken and don't need fixing: they simply forgot who they are beneath the patterns. Self-Mastery is not about improving the ego but softening its grip so the True Self can lead.

It is the unwinding of resistance and the shedding of limitation to live from safety, connection, and truth. It requires healing the heart, shifting the mind, and regulating the nervous system. It is a return to wholeness—where we are no longer ruled by survival cycles but led by our higher self.

As we align with who we truly are, we awaken the power to consciously create our lives. In this alignment, we step into resonance and are open to receive—to be, do, and have what we deeply desire.

Self-Mastery is the key to everything.

The Missing Piece: Why The Heart Is the Key to Self-Mastery

The heart is more than a symbol of emotion, it is the center of wisdom, intelligence, and connection. For over five thousand years, civilizations across cultures have regarded the heart as the seat of the soul, the bridge between mind, body, and higher intelligence. Modern science is now validating what ancient traditions have long understood: the heart plays a central role in shaping perception, cognition, and emotional regulation.

As early as the 1960s, researchers like John and Beatrice Lacey, and later Dr. J. Andrew Armour, demonstrated that the heart has its own nervous system, actively shaping emotion, cognition, and decision-making. Subsequently, they introduced the concept of the "heart brain" (Rozman, 2022, p.36).

The HeartMath Institute, established in 1991, has become a leading authority on heart-brain communication. Their studies on 'heart coherence' show the heart's signals reach the higher centers of the brain, such as the cortex and influence emotional balance, cognition, and nervous system regulation. This means that the heart is intricately involved in how we think, feel and respond to the world (Rozman, 2022).

Research by the HeartMath Institute also confirms that the heart emits an electromagnetic field one hundred times stronger than the brain's and up to five hundred times according to Salem—affecting our own system and those around us. It even appears the heart senses and signals future events before the brain processes them, linking us to intuitive intelligence beyond time and space (McCraty, 2022). Science has helped us understand that the physical and energetic heart work together, giving us access to deep, inner and intuitive guidance.

My professional work is influenced by neuroscientist Allan Schore and physician Gabor Maté, who have explored the profound impact of early attachment wounds on brain development. Maté says, "Trauma is not what happens to you, but what happens inside you." These inner ruptures—wounds of the heart—are what foundationally shape identity and create unconscious survival patterns that disconnect us from our True Self. Since identity is formed through early relationships, wounds to the heart become the root cause of emotional, psychological, and physiological distress.

Again, science is affirming ancient wisdom—the heart is the bridge that connects the mind, body, and soul. And yet, it remains the missing piece in many healing modalities. Top-down approaches like cognitive reframing increase awareness but rarely reach stored emotional wounds. Bottom-up methods like somatic work support regulation but may not fully resolve deep-rooted emotional patterns. Many focus on external context, not the primary relationship that has shaped how we see ourselves and the world. On their own, these approaches don't address the root cause of unconscious self-limiting patterns.

The heart is the key—where emotion, perception, and nervous system regulation converge (McCraty, 2022). It is the gateway to true integration and transformation. As I like to say, "Where the mind questions, the body reacts, and the heart knows—it is the bridge that harmonizes all."

Self-Mastery is a journey of inner transformation back to wholeness. It frees us from self-limitation by healing the heart, clearing the mind, and rewiring the brain and nervous system so we can fully own who we are, align with our True Self and wisdom, and create a life of purpose, freedom, joy, and fulfillment.

The path to Self-Mastery moves us beyond survival cycles and into higher wisdom. As we align with our True Self, we step into our innate power to consciously shape our reality. In this state of alignment, we release root-level blocks, healing the wounds of the heart to fully receive all we desire—to be, do, and have.

Self-Mastery is the key to everything. If you want success, master yourself. If you want a better relationship, master yourself. If you seek better health, financial stability, or a thriving business—it all begins with mastering yourself. Any desired change, whether in how you think, feel, or in your external world, requires Self-Mastery. All change begins within.

Self-Mastery is wholeness—in mind, heart, body and soul. And the key to Self-Mastery is healing your heart.

I know this to be true, not only from my own story but from witnessing transformation in others who have healed the wounds of the heart. They had patterns of overworking, hiding, procrastinating, disconnecting, and endlessly proving themselves. Beneath the surface were unconscious patterns—root causes that kept them stuck in patterns and cycles. These patterns developed from early relationships that shaped beliefs around self-worth, safety, trust, acceptance, and what it meant to succeed. As they healed their core wounds, which fundamentally was their relationship with themselves, everything began to shift. Internally, they felt more peace and clarity. Externally, their relationships, businesses, health, and finances transformed.

Some of the women I worked with were exhausted, frustrated, and resentful—stuck in overdrive and doing it all themselves. Patterns of control and overachieving were common, where worth was tied to performance and driven by fear of failure. As they released survival responses and healed their self-worth wounds, they became more relaxed, trusting, peaceful, and confident. Some watched their businesses grow and their relationships thrive.

Others struggled with disconnection. Always putting others first, they became the caretaker, peacekeeper, fixer—believing their needs didn't matter. Through healing, they released that belief and reclaimed their worth. They set boundaries, became present with themselves, and naturally deepened their connection to others.

Imposter syndrome is another common experience. They doubted their expertise, feared being seen or heard, and procrastinated—waiting until they felt "ready." Stuck in avoidance and indecision, they battled perfectionism and self-doubt. Through healing fears of judgment and acceptance, people learned to embrace their imperfections, stopped waiting for permission and found their voice, which allowed stepping into leadership. As this was healed, the drive to strive and prove ceased and was replaced with showing up fully, as themselves.

Transformation is possible for anyone willing to do the work. The patterns that keep you stuck can be rewritten by healing the root—the unconscious programs formed in early relationships that shaped your identity and life path. Healing is about releasing old narratives from the mind, body, and most profoundly in the heart, so that you can reconnect with the truth of who you are. When you do, you come home to your True Self, where you are free, empowered, and fully alive

My Journey to Self-Mastery: Transformation Through the Heart

Too often, the pursuit of success, fulfillment, and happiness has an undercurrent of self-doubt, fear, and unconscious limitations. Like many, I lived with inner whispers of not being enough – pushing harder, achieving more; yet still feeling something was missing.

My mind constantly questioned my worth, although not always directly or consciously. I feared failure, second-guessed myself and developed perfectionism to always get it 'right'. Despite building a successful career, I worked tirelessly to prove my value; my inner reality didn't match the confidence I projected. My nervous system operated in a near-constant state of tension and anxiety. I was high-functioning, yet always on the edge of burnout.

The rupture began with a childhood trauma – not from my parents but impactful enough to rewire how I perceived safety and connection, and my nervous system into long-term survival and decades of dysregulation. I learned to protect myself through silence, internalized deep shame and the belief that something was wrong with me, that I was inherently not enough. I hid my true self and became who I thought I had to be to feel safe and accepted. My parents loved me, but they didn't know. My needs went unmet—not out of neglect, but because I never let them see. And their own relational patterns shaped mine: I learned to stay small, people please, keep the peace, and fly under the radar.

Despite years of personal and professional growth, I still cycled through exhaustion, overwork and self-abandonment, reinforcing the belief that I wasn't enough. Over time, this adaptive self became high-achieving, perfectionistic, self-critical, hyper-responsible, and emotionally guarded. Work became my coping mechanism and my identity – a way to prove I was worthy and to feel whole. Often, helping others all this time even while I still hadn't mastered myself was humbling. Those patterns weren't flaws – they were survival. My nervous system had been doing its best to protect me all along.

When I finally faced the relational wounds at the root, another level of deep transformation began. Through HeartHealing, I reclaimed my voice, allowed myself to be authentically seen, heard and known. I released the belief that my worth needed to be earned. Previously, I knew this intellectually but hadn't embodied it.

The turning point wasn't marked by a single event but a series of awakenings during my HeartHealing journey. A profound shift came with the unexpected passing of my father. I was devastated, and this loss amplified the emotional exhaustion I had carried for years. It created a sharp awareness of what really mattered. I stepped back from a six-figure position and gave myself space to rest, process and metabolize what I had held in my body.

A question from my coach pierced me: "What if you were as loyal to yourself as you are to your work and others?" That began a shift from striving to source from within.

I understood that while my mother's death decades earlier left unresolved grief that fueled my pursuit of enoughness, working through the grief of losing my father awakened me to finally begin to feel the truth: I already was enough. This period became a portal for deeper self-discovery. It became clear that my greatest work wasn't in striving for success but in learning to source within—to know, trust, and accept myself fully, without external validation. I began to heal my heart.

HeartHealing unlocked transformation. Patterns of people-pleasing, hypervigilance, and perfectionism became clearer, including the invisible standard of 'enoughness' I had chased. I saw how my inner critic kept me playing small, dimming my light to avoid making others uncomfortable. I realized my fear of being seen, heard and known was less about others and more about my own relationship with myself.

One profound shift came through public speaking, which terrified me. As a kid, I sometimes refused to speak. Again, silence was my protection. On this occasion, I presented on a large stage. After bombing a large talk, something broke open. I remembered the original feeling of not having a voice. I began to release what had been frozen and trapped in my unconscious. That failure became liberation. It was a gift, albeit the ultimate cosmic irony.

During this time, HeartHealing gave me deep insights into the patterns that shaped my life and brought me to the root and the heart of the matter—core wounds around love, worth, acceptance, and trust. Healing meant dissolving the old narratives that kept me from my true potential. It revealed the unconscious beliefs I had internalized, especially the fear around being seen and heard, which I came to understand as fear of being truly known. I carried an unconscious shame, a sense that something was deeply wrong with me. These weren't just insights—they were embodied experiences. I began to own my worth, not from achievements or approval, but from within.

HeartHealing helped me reconnect with and heal the younger version of myself who had learned to stay quiet and invisible in order to stay safe—and the adult who had exhausted herself chasing worth through achievement. It released trapped emotions in my body and nervous system that had been frozen in time.

I moved from self-doubt to self-trust, from over-giving to honoring my own needs and boundaries with self-loyalty. I released the patterns of control, hustle and stepped into alignment, where my actions flowed from truth instead of pressure. Fear gave way to inner safety. I stopped chasing external validation because I had reclaimed my worth from within. Burnout dissolved as my nervous system found regulation and peace. I no longer performed a role—I began living in authentic presence. I released the shame that had quietly shaped my identity and reclaimed my voice, my worth, and my right to be seen—by first truly seeing myself.

In accepting all of me—light and shadow, strengths and struggles—I found a freedom I had never known. Healing hasn't been about becoming someone new but remembering who I was before the world taught me to hide. That integration was the real magic—a transformation that showed up not just in my thoughts but in my presence, relationships, boundaries, and ability to receive. Each healing peeled back layers I no longer needed. With every layer shed, I came home to more of who I truly am. This transformation didn't just shift my internal experience, it radically altered my outer world.

Healing my heart impacted my business, too. As an overachiever, I have my own business and support another. When I started making choices from a place of alignment not fear, the external results reflected it: I exceeded revenue goals, crossed the million-dollar mark, and had my first six-figure month. More than the numbers, I felt different. My success was no longer tied to proving anything. It became a natural result of alignment. I could finally receive it because I had become someone who could hold it.

That said, I know that the outer world is simply a reflection of the inner experience. I am present to my life and my relationships in a different way. My life is fulfilling. In my fifties, I feel like I've trained my whole life for this moment—to truly live. My heart is open. My nervous system is regulated. My mind is clear. My relationships are meaningful. I meet challenges with ease, not fear. Healing has given me sovereignty—the ability to lead myself, trust my path, and be anchored in who I am.

This isn't just my story. I see it in so many brilliant, capable women who are held back by invisible chains. I've witnessed the same transformation in others: Women reclaiming their voices, stepping into their power, and breaking free from self-doubt and fear. The ripple effect of HeartHealing shifts not just the individual but relationships, businesses, and entire lives.

Many wait to feel 'ready.' But transformation doesn't come from waiting—it comes from healing. This is self-mastery. It's not about controlling life—it's about being guided by who you are. A deep knowing that you are already whole. Already worthy. Already enough.

If you resonate with this, know this: the power to change is already within you. The key to your freedom, success, and fulfillment—

it's not 'out there.' It's within your heart where the true path to self-mastery lies.

So, I invite you to pause, take a deep breath and gently ask yourself the questions below – not to get it 'right', but to listen deeply to your heart's truth.

- What do you truly desire, not just in your life but in your heart?
- Where are you still holding yourself back, and why?
- If fear or doubt weren't in the way, what bold moves would you make today?
- What part of your story needs compassion, not fixing?
- What would become possible if you fully owned your worth and fully accepted yourself?

Healing isn't about becoming someone new. It's about remembering who you truly are. The magic is in the being, not the doing.

Be the change. The world needs your light. And most importantly, you deserve to shine.

References:

HeartMath Institute (no date) *Science of the heart: Energetic communication*. Available at: https://www.heartmath.org/research/science-of-the-heart/energetic-communication.

McCraty, R. (2022), *The Intuitive Heart.* In: Childre, D., Martin, H., Rozeman, D., and McCraty, R., eds. *Heart Intelligence: Connecting with the Heart's Intuitive Guidance for Effective Choices and Solutions.* 2nd ed. Waterside Productions, pp.49-72.

McCraty, R. (2022), *Heart Coherence: Access to Heart Intelligence.* In: Childre, D., Martin, H., Rozeman, D., and McCraty, R., eds. *Heart Intelligence: Connecting with the Heart's Intuitive Guidance for Effective Choices and Solutions.* 2nd ed. Waterside Productions, pp.161-184.

Rozeman, D. (2022), *Attributes of Heart Intelligence.* In: Childre, D., Martin, H., Rozeman, D., and McCraty, R., eds. *Heart Intelligence: Connecting with the Heart's Intuitive Guidance for Effective Choices and Solutions.* 2nd ed. Waterside Productions, pp. 29-48.

Salem, M.O. (no date) *The heart, mind and spirit: Perspectives from Islam*. Royal College of Psychiatrists. Available at: https://www.rcpsych.ac.uk/docs/default-source/members/sigs/spirituality-spsig/spirituality-special-interest-group-publications-professor-mohamed-omar-salem-the-heart-mind-and-spirit.pdf.

ABOUT THE AUTHOR

DARCY BAILEY

Darcy Bailey is an experienced Therapist, Master Coach and HeartHealing Practitioner with a thriving group therapy practice who helps high-achieving women and leaders break free from unconscious patterns that keep them stuck to consciously create a life of fulfillment, purpose, happiness, and success.

Her journey of continued learning and personal healing led her to HeartHealing, where she personally experienced profound healing by addressing the root cause, which opened her to receive so much more success in her life. Consequently, Darcy became a Level 3 Certified HeartHealing Practitioner. Her transformational therapy and coaching is a fusion of psychology, neuroscience, spirituality and quantum principles in a proprietary blend of HeartSet. MindSet. SoulSet.

Darcy is available for Transformational Therapy and Coaching.

www.darcybailey.com
Darcy@darcybailey.com

16

DONNA HICKLIN

THE HEART OF LIMITLESS POTENTIAL

My life changed dramatically when I learnt one simple but powerful universal truth: *Human potential is limitless.*

What I'd thought possible for myself and my family was blown out of the water, and my life has never been the same since.

I smile as I think about how my thoughts, beliefs and life have changed since learning and *living* this truth. The first thing that comes to mind is staring me in the face right now: me sitting here writing this chapter. I would never have thought this possible a few years ago. I would have been too concerned about a few raised eyebrows to be so open, real and vulnerable about my life, how I help people as a healer, and my journey to get here.

Right now, I'm reflecting on my day. I finished work, feeling alive and buzzing, as I dashed downstairs from my home-based therapy room to see my beautiful eighteen-month-old boy and my husband. I've had an amazing day working with clients, and my guides, angels, fairies, goddesses (the list goes on), by my side, supporting me and my clients.

I feel aligned, knowing I'm working towards my purpose and making a difference, using my gifts and talents. I'm not saying this is my permanent state of existence. I'm human, not an ethereal being without earthly, worldly and very real problems. This is, however, normal for me now. It's a feeling I never used to have, even when I loved what I was doing. There's a subtle difference as to why.

Back then, I wasn't pushing myself to my next level and had 'selective hearing' to my gut instinct; that voice making helpful suggestions as to what to do or say next. It was so hard to hear that voice. Instead, I listened to the fearful voice whispering in my head - telling me I wasn't worthy of more, that this was all I was capable of, and all I should expect. So moving forward felt more like a slow shuffle than a bold leap. I would select what felt safe, in my comfort zone and what I felt worthy of.

Now that I have done some incredible healing, I feel love towards myself and I feel worthy. Not only am I happier, more confident, peaceful, driven and courageous, but I am tapping into my potential, and my life is starting to change. I want to expand myself, my skills, and my impact, even when it feels tough. I know I have amazing gifts and talents that the world needs, just as *you* do. You are also unique, talented and have incredible, untapped potential. None of this comes from thinking I'm perfect. It's also not that my life is trouble-free. We are humans living the human experience, and life does tend to throw us curveballs!

I have, however, a deep sense of knowing behind any mind chatter that I am love, I am worthy, and supported by the universe. I know that keeping myself small and not taking the steps I am divinely guided to, will not fill my heart or others' hearts with love and joy. I know that the more I feel love, passion and alignment with myself and the universe, the more that will positively impact others and create success for myself.

We can all learn, grow, and evolve. Your potential is the untapped higher version of you, your next level, then the next after that, waiting to be unlocked. This could be a hidden skill, talent or strength; or a trait like willpower, passion or determination. Everything about you can be up-levelled and that is *your potential.*

Tapping into your potential opens the floodgates of possibility in all areas of your life. Your work, health (emotional and physical), relationships, finances; everything. There is no ultimate point; no final destination where we reach our potential.

Our potential is limitless, as our souls are limitless.

We all have an innate power to expand. We were put on Earth that way, and that will never change. We just sometimes forget.

Life would be pretty boring without anything to aim for, wouldn't it? It's so easy to get caught up in life, forget the passion, the excitement, the drive, and the talents born within us. There is nothing like the feeling of achieving something new and expanding ourselves. We are wired to aim higher, to push for more, and to connect to our divine gifts and strengths. Think about achievements you've made in life and how amazing you felt doing them. Would you like to feel this more often?

Picture a toddler taking their first steps. They feel so happy. Now imagine if they looked at you and noticed you could run. They might think, "I can't do that. I'll stick as I am and not bother. I'm clearly not good enough to be a walker." Sounds funny? If they were like most adults, they could easily decide this.

Would you encourage a child to take those next steps, to try new things? *Yes.* You wouldn't let them accept that they are doing okay, and stick as they are? *No.* So why, when it comes to ourselves, have most of us lost connection to our natural drive to explore our uniqueness, gifts, and potential?

When you're eighty, will you say you pushed yourself out of your comfort zone, it felt scary but amazing, and you created the most wonderful, exciting life for yourself? I hope so. I certainly want that for myself and I'm trying my utmost to crack on with it. We don't know the extent of the gifts we have and the possibilities for ourselves. They get hidden. We hit adulthood and think we know ourselves, our downfalls, and our limits.

Do you ever hear yourself saying things like:

I wouldn't be good at…
I can't… because…
I'm not… enough.

Question those things you 'think' you know about yourself. Is there really zero chance you could change those things? Is there any evidence of anyone in the world who was, for example, anxious, who now lives a happy, content life? Anyone who procrastinated and is now extremely decisive and proactive? If you look, you will find that evidence, and you won't have to look far.

If they've up-levelled their lives, emotions, and possibilities for themselves, then why can't you?

We become confined and restrained in our identity because it feels safe. We worry about who we are without this identity we are used to. I've noticed a common thread in every client who walks through my physical or online door. I see or sense a box around them; an energetic box made of limiting beliefs, keeping them only as big as they feel comfortable being. I know it deeply affects how they show up in their career, relationships, health, fitness and even social life. There's nothing in our lives that isn't touched by our limiting beliefs.

Limiting beliefs are the thoughts and things we are *certain* about. If we are certain we are not capable of something, why the heck even try? What are your limiting beliefs?

Would you love *more* for yourself, but you don't feel capable? Or do you try to improve things but feel pulled back by bungee straps? I know this so well. Our box walls are made from the beliefs we have about ourselves, who we are and our capabilities. We love to stay within the confines of our cosy belief boxes. They have been emerging since birth (as well as from past lives and ancestry, but that's a conversation for another time). The boxes are built from what you are told, your wounding/trauma, and what you experience and see. All this paints a picture so vivid, it becomes embedded into your subconscious. It feels so real. Mistakenly we feel: *This is who I am.*

Imagine fleas put into a jar with a lid on for three days. They learn they can only jump as high as the lid. When the lid is removed, they can jump as high as they want. Yet, they confine themselves within the jar - and only jump to the height at which the lid once sat. Not only do *they* do this, but their *offspring* do the same too. This is us! What we have been made to believe about ourselves is keeping you in your box (your flea jar). What if there is more to your story than that? What if you too can jump way higher than you think? Would you love to jump higher? I smile as I write this, feeling my own soul shouting, '*Yes!*'

I want to share something *huge* with you now.

If you felt enough, fully worthy, and unconditionally loving towards yourself... If you were able to tap into your own wisdom and connect to the support of the universe... *your box would have its lid blown right off!*

How? By healing your heart. Your heart is where your trauma, wounding, thoughts and beliefs about yourself hide out. It's like that junk cupboard where you throw things you don't know what to do with - then quickly shut the door. No-one sees inside, rarely even you.

It is becoming widely recognised that the heart has a brain, known as the heart-brain. This is where our beliefs and trauma lie. The HeartMath Institute has proven that between the heart and the brain, 80-90% of the signals actually travel *from the heart to the brain* - and only 10-20% from the brain to the heart (McCraty, 2023). In other words, the heart is calling the shots!

We have been led to believe we just need to understand why we feel the way we do, and that we can just *think* differently to fix ourselves. This data proves this isn't the case.

Imagine your wounds, hurt or limiting beliefs as a big weed. The soil is your mind, and the roots are your heart. You might pull out that weed, but if the deep roots are left underground, it will keep growing back. We can keep pulling the weed out as it grows, but to fully remove it, we have to get the roots - the heart. This is why mind-based healing alone may not be enough.

To return to those pesky energy boxes around us. I've always seen and worked on them during my energy healing sessions, and I am now able to break them down even further through HeartHealing. Within HeartHealing they are described as heart walls; energetically, they are the same thing. These boxes are created through our thoughts, beliefs and trauma to protect us, and keep us small.

Your heart isn't just the storeroom for your limiting beliefs and wounding. It is way more magnificent than that! It is the portal to your soul, the gateway to your divine wisdom; it connects you to your spiritual support team and is the locker room for your gifts and talents. This amazing organ holds such power. Spirituality has known this wisdom for decades and I'm so happy that science and the world are finally catching up. Hand me the key, I hear you say? Yes, I hear you, your key is right here!

Over two decades as a therapist have blessed me with a rich and diverse healing toolkit through training and experience. This includes channelled energy healing, reiki, crystals, massage, aromatherapy, shamanic techniques, channelled meditations, coaching and HeartHealing. At the heart of everything I do in all my one-to-one sessions, group and self-guided programmes, retreats, workshops and meditations, is my most treasured tool – the connection to my spiritual support team. They are always there, guiding my sessions and passing on clarity and messages to my clients. My team even helps me to develop my own techniques and treatments.

It is wonderful to have so many tools to guide my clients from *limited* potential to *limitless* potential!

I use HeartHealing to guide people to heal the wounds within their hearts in order to activate self-love, limitless potential and soulful success. The wounds may have been formed in a younger version of themselves (as a child or adult), or they may be ancestral or past life wounds that unconsciously limit them. I shine the light on old thought patterns and beliefs, allowing them to transform. The walls around the heart/belief boxes are then broken down. This allows so much more into their life. They then listen to personalised imprinting audios for twenty-five days, allowing the mind and heart to transform and align with their next level of potential. Not only that, but I connect them to their higher self and their spiritual support team, who guide them forward through their next steps, and stay by their side forever.

Sometimes I work with fairies, but what I am saying isn't a fairytale. I have experienced vast change in my life, and I've seen it for my clients too.

Amongst others, I have worked with many female entrepreneurs and ambitious women. Every one of them has had a common thread. They are aware that, in some way, they don't feel good enough or fully loving towards themselves. They desire a life that feels joyful, healthy, peaceful and fulfilled. They want to feel in alignment with their values, purpose and passion and make an impact, whilst being well financially rewarded.

They want to nourish their soul whilst reaching their goals; they desire soulful success.

However, they felt an invisible forcefield stopping them from moving forward.

A past client (we'll call her Lisa) had been running her business for a couple of years. It was important to her and everything was going okay, but she was working so hard and wasn't moving forward as she wanted. She felt she didn't have the time to focus on her health or work on her relationship, which wasn't doing so well.

During our time together, she became more visible on social media and even enjoyed it. She started to take steps forward too, making bolder decisions without overthinking, and she felt inspired. She began taking better care of herself, eating healthier and adding exercise to her routine. She realised that her relationship wasn't healthy for either of them, so she ended it.

After her transformational journey with me, she told me she had met someone and was very happy. She was her authentic self with him, and her business also continued to fly. All of this happened because she now feels good enough and fully worthy, so she expanded what she thought was possible, and took action.

For me, it's taken four decades to get where I am now. I know what it's like to have huge limiting beliefs. Those beliefs were my identity. Because of this, I know anxiety, self-doubt, procrastination and excuses, and know drowning in the pain of feeling not good enough.

I felt like a misfit throughout my life. I was loved, but I felt like I wasn't 'right' somehow. I thought I needed to change. To be slimmer, more confident, know more, be funnier, less sensitive, and look different. I tried so hard to be the person I 'thought' everyone wanted me to be.

Feeling this way was the result of not feeling good enough, lovable or worthy, just for being me. I felt I wouldn't be accepted as myself. Growing up the signs of my feelings started to show up more. As a teenager, I suffered from an eating disorder, which I recovered from over time. It reared its head again in other forms as an adult, with body dysmorphia, severe anxiety, panic attacks and physical tics. I felt so uncomfortable within myself.

Fortunately, before these low points, I started my own business; something I'm very proud of. I provided beauty and holistic therapies from my serene home-based therapy room. Holistic therapies were my true passion and fascination, though. These therapies help clients on a mind, body and soul level. Even through my beauty treatments, I always wanted to help people more; I wanted to lift them up through their problems. Clients often mentioned how much I helped them - in more ways than just the treatment they had booked. Being a healer has always been who I am.

Over time, things got to a significant low point. Some days, I didn't want to get out of bed. I spent hours in front of the mirror and trying to work out how to fix the problems I saw. Or I went to the other extreme, avoiding even slightly shiny surfaces for fear of catching sight of myself. The anxiety was off the scale. I felt alone and afraid. I thought I wasn't lovable or good enough. I just wasn't worthy, and it was painful and lonely.

In my lowest, darkest moment there was a little voice that told me that my life could go in one of two directions. The first was escalating to a worse place - wasting more hours and days in despair, disconnected from my husband and family, not moving forward with my business, and certainly not starting a family.

How could I nurture a tiny human when I couldn't nurture and love myself? Or, path two, I could somehow heal from this.

I chose the latter; *I chose me.*

I think that somewhere deep inside, I knew I could get through it, and I had the support of the universe. As impossible as it felt, I was determined and felt like there was something or someone guiding me behind the scenes. I knew this was not only for myself, but for my family, as I knew how deeply my struggles were impacting them.

I looked for support. I went for CBT, which was helpful because they told me that I had body dysmorphia, and that's why I felt this way. I felt less alone knowing that other people felt the same as me. But this didn't really help me *heal.*

I then came across a HeartHealing online programme after attending a free taster session. Something inside me pushed me to say, 'yes, do it' - even though I wouldn't normally spend money on myself. Through the sessions, I really started to change my thinking. As a group, we went through healing our Enoughness Wounds (the reason we don't feel enough), and it planted a seed within me that started to blossom.

Then, I was intuitively guided to Cathy Heller. Listening to her words during an online course I attended, I had a moment of clarity and vision! She said that:

We only reach for the highest branch we can see.

This was like a mind explosion for me. I had never questioned the possibility that I could have *more* and achieve *more*, as I had never really seen *more* around me. She showed me evidence of women like myself who have become hugely successful, in business and personally too, even through adversity. These were also women who were mothers, which caught my attention. For years, I'd felt uncertain about having children. I was afraid I wouldn't be good enough, and I worried I wouldn't be able to work - and work has always been a true passion of mine. I now saw these amazing women working minimal hours, making a big impact and a large income, and spending lots of time with their children. So something shifted - I saw that I *could* do this too, and felt the truth at my core.

At that moment, the journey of expanding my potential really started, and I wanted everyone else to come along too. It somehow felt like the privileged knowledge of only a few, and I wanted this 'secret' to be known. Most people around me just accepted their current life situation, their stress and anxiety, and didn't try to move forward or improve their lives, or themselves. Many would comment that they couldn't complain as they should be grateful; things could be much worse. I understand that, and having gratitude for where you are now is wonderful... if you are *truly* feeling grateful. Not because you *should* feel grateful, that is very different. Feel grateful, yes, but don't be blind to opportunities for *more for yourself* too.

Let's be grateful *and* aspire for more.

With this newfound passion, I was naturally guiding my clients to expand their potential.

Small changes for myself snowballed into huge shifts. I said *no* to the constant barrage of negativity in my mind. I spoke to myself with much more kindness and compassion. I began to dress differently (finding what I actually *felt good* in), felt more confident, looked after myself better, and my relationships improved. As I felt better, I made changes in my business too. I slowly shifted my offer suite, gradually phasing out the beauty therapy treatments until they were completely gone, and I increased my prices as I began to feel more worthy and deserving.

I was becoming more aligned with what I knew was my path.

I went deeper and hosted women's 'inner calm outer confidence' retreats, and loved them! I could see the impact I was making on my clients. Then the ultimate in alignment happened. I was blessed with becoming pregnant. There is nothing like preparing to be a mum to make you want to get your life in order. I decided to advance my training and chose HeartHealing. I knew I wanted to make even more impact and create a better life for us, and this was it. Through the initial year-long immersion, I received so much healing on my own heart wounds. My beliefs about myself and my potential have continually up-levelled ever since.

I see so many transformations in my clients and myself. Less stress, anxiety, mind chatter, overwhelm, and infinitely more confidence, love, peace, worthiness, joy, passion, connection and motivation. This all impacts how they show up for themselves. Because of this, they can bring about huge shifts in their work, relationships, health and finances. Their lives as a *whole change.* This is what I call 'soulful success'.

Your beliefs are setting the stage for your life. They affect how you speak, listen, hold yourself, the action you take, and the action you *don't* take.

Your beliefs are running the show, so make them amazing, beautiful and limitless.

As you uplift yourself and your life, you will naturally take others with you. You will inspire them and impact their lives with your energy, passion, love and talents.

This may sound amazing, but a lot to take in, so where can you start?

Take a breath, put your hands on your heart and *feel* these words. Say them out loud, if you can.

I am beautiful.
I am worthy.
I am love.
I have incredible talents and limitless potential.
I have passion, power and courage to move forward.
I am supported by the universe, my guides and angels.

Use these affirmations every day if you want to start to make changes.

Also, start saying *yes* to opportunities and inner nudges that *feel* right. Every yes is another step forward. Say yes to yourself, yes to your journey and yes to your dreams!

Moving forward, allow yourself to look, to explore, to quiet the voice in your mind and turn up the volume in your heart. You will then tune into the wisdom of your soul and follow your path to *Limitless Potential.*

Don't let this be just another interesting read - let this be the start of the next incredible chapter of your life. You have the power to unravel old beliefs, activate self-love and your potential, and create soulful success.

You are incredible.

With love.

References:

McCraty, R. (2023), *Science of the heart: Exploring the role of the heart in human performance*, HeartMath Institute. Available at: https://www.heartmath.org/research/science-of-the-heart/heart-brain-communication/

ABOUT THE AUTHOR

DONNA HICKLIN

Donna Louise Hicklin is a transformational healer devoted to guiding ambitious women and female entrepreneurs to break free from limiting beliefs and step into their limitless potential.

Using a powerful blend of HeartHealing, intuitive energy healing, journey massage, channelled guidance and meditations, she creates profound transformations for her clients. Through her unique approach, she helps women activate self-love, embrace self-worth, and live a life filled with success, peace, love, vitality and joy.

Donna loves hiking, adventures and travelling with her young son and husband.

Donna is available for in-person and online one-to-one healing, group programmes and retreats.

www.donnalouisehealing.com
hello@donnalouisehealing.com
facebook.com/donnalouisehealing
instagram.com/donnalouisehealing

17

SHEETAL VITHLANI

THE HEART OF CONSCIOUS EVOLUTION

My story is one of immense gratitude, strength and resilience. I have faced cultural stereotypes, gender discrimination, defied the norms, and pushed boundaries to live life on my own terms by following my intuition and my heart as I heal and evolve.

I am blessed and grateful for all the setbacks, opportunities, successes and learnings along the way. I feel the most connected and aligned that I have ever felt. However, I know this is not the end of my journey, it's just the beginning of a magical adventure. I still don't know the destination, but I vow to learn, grow, evolve, be true to myself and have fun along the way, no matter what life throws in my path.

However, it was not always like this. I felt lonely and I was unable to trust. My walls were so high I would push away love and not let anyone in; what I yearned for the most was also my biggest fear. It was a fear that kept me stuck in this dark place with a need to control everything and do everything myself and alone. What would happen if I let go? What if I tried something new? What if I failed and disappointed my family? What would people say? I would be judged; I would be a failure. I played it safe and stayed stuck for far too long.

I did not find true love until I was thirty-five, got married when I was thirty-seven and never thought I would be able to conceive and have children. He arrived when I was forty-one, my miracle baby. I thought at this point I would have it all figured out, but I really didn't.

When life gets hard, you have two choices: it can make you or break you.

There are days I cried myself to sleep, questioning my purpose, and thinking, "Why me?" At times like this, I felt like giving up.

I *didn't.*

I am still standing; I keep pushing forward. I am stronger than I think or realise.

I am a fighter, a warrior, a go-getter: I refuse to give up. I learn, I grow, I heal, I evolve.

There will always be things you cannot control: setbacks, obstacles, heartbreaks, burnout, overwhelm, exhaustion and anxiety, just to name a few. The only thing YOU can control is how YOU react, what YOU do, how YOU choose to show up for yourself, and how YOU keep pushing forward even when it feels impossible.

There have been days when I wanted to hide under the duvet and curl up into a ball and be invisible, and you know what? I did. I cried, I slept, I felt sorry for myself, I reflected, I picked myself up, and I kept pushing forward, refusing to give up. In my heart of hearts, I knew I needed to keep going even if I didn't fully understand why or the destination, I trusted that my heart knew best. When you feel like this, remember: you are alive, keep going, anything is possible, keep believing the best part of your life is waiting for you to show up.

The reality is that growth doesn't happen in the comfort zone; it happens in moments you feel broken. It is about how you pick yourself up when you think you have given it your all, and then you dig a bit deeper and find a little more strength and courage. Don't let fear stop you; don't let doubt win. You don't need permission to chase a dream or to be who you are meant to be.

It is ok to start over. Take back your power and this time choose to consciously evolve. Instead of having change happen to you or be done to you. I chose to change and transform on purpose, knowingly and willingly, and you can too.

Historically, evolution has always been about changing biologically from apes into humans, as outlined in Darwin's Theory of Evolution (*On the Origin of Species*, 1859), driven by fear and the notion of survival of the fittest.

Humanity is becoming more conscious, more enlightened in the way we are evolving. This leads me to the theory of conscious evolution. Let's start by breaking this down into its components:

1. To be conscious means to have a sense of knowing, an awareness of information both internal and external.
2. Evolution is the process of developing through gradual changes; people and things change over time.

Conscious evolution, therefore, is the ability to look deep within yourself, searching for answers while expanding your awareness of your choices. It means choosing to be adaptable and making aligned decisions by setting clear intentions to change, grow and transform over time. It entails creating a life about meaning and purpose for your existence, lifting you out of your current darkness and pain. It is about choosing who you want to be and how you want to show up in the world.

You might have reached your tipping point. You could be at a time when you feel lost, broken or at the point of giving up; you have this innate knowing that something is not right, something has to change, you can no longer carry on like this. This is the tipping point.

This tipping point can present in your life in many ways, such as (but not limited to):

- Poor mental health
- Feeling of overwhelm
- Stress and anxiety
- Exhaustion and burnout
- No longer feel like yourself or know who you are
- Trauma of abuse
- Trauma of a narcissistic relationship
- Feeling stuck, trapped or like something is holding you back
- Judgement from cultural or social acceptance
- Not feeling good enough or feeling like a failure
- Not feeling worthy of success or good things
- Isolation
- Paralysis
- Financial struggles

During this time, you may find yourself wondering: Who am I? What am I here to do? What is my purpose? Will I find the light at the end of the tunnel? You may even experience a deep yearning for inner peace and a connection with yourself, your purpose and your unique way to contribute to the world. You might know or feel like something is missing, but you don't know what. You lack empowerment, freedom, courage and free choice.

Humanity is evolving and experiencing a major shift from being mind-led to being heart-led, as shown in the table below:

Mind-led	Heart-led
Fear based	Love based
Logical	Intuitive
External validation	Inner evolution
Struggle	Ease and in-flow
Separation	Unity
Competition	Collaboration
Scarcity	Abundance
Survival	Growth

This shift is not restricted to us as individuals. I am noticing more and more that this occurring with my corporate clients, in the language they use, subtle changes in behaviours. It is now being reflected in corporate values, vision and mission statements. Corporate organisations now talk about the importance of concepts such as Emotional Intelligence, Conscious Leadership, environmental sustainability, being kind to each other, being mindful, empathy, collaborations and partnerships.

There has also been a major shift in promoting workplace wellbeing, wellness and mental health with the introduction of courses, workshops or even support in the form of healing therapy. It is becoming normal to have meditation courses, trauma release support, energy healing like Reiki, tapping techniques (EFT), encouragement of work-life balance, healthy eating and healthy habits.

Most corporate Change and Transformation programmes have a significant focus on evolving from working in silos to working in unity across the organisation. They look to answer fundamental challenges such as: "How can we work better together?", "What is the change impact of this transformation?", "How can we make things better?", and "How can we make this a better place to work?" Whether they realise it or not, corporates are also choosing to consciously evolve and become more heart-led.

Individuals and corporates are all searching for the same thing – for that something that is bigger than them, the connection, unity, global networks and growth in some shape or form. This is a shift to a heart-led higher collective consciousness and it impacts how we approach personal growth, better relationships, personal and business success. The more we align with the heart, the greater the connection with our highest potential. This in turn supports the evolution of humanity.

Healing the heart and becoming heart-led is not just about personal transformation; it is a catalyst for global conscious evolution at every level.

Traditional psychotherapy research and therapies such as Psychoanalysis, Jungian therapy, Counselling, Hypnosis, Neuro Linguistic Programming (NLP), Cognitive Behavioural Therapy (CBT) and Rapid Transformation Therapy (RTT) are all mind-led. They focus on healing the conscious and unconscious mind. These therapies can require multiple sessions over a prolonged period of time and, from my experience, are effective in the short term. However, the trauma or issue will most likely return. I always found they made a difference, but I felt like something was missing: the healing was not deep enough. I discovered the heart, the heart was the missing link.

The journey to this point of realisation is different for everyone. When we create and develop our own behaviours, values and model of the world, we are driven to take intentional and conscious action. This enables us to consciously evolve, making us more adaptable and more likely to succeed and thrive. When we make conscious choices, we have the power to evolve to fulfil and exceed our potential. To do this, we must not only expand and heal our minds; it is crucial for us also to open and heal our hearts.

The heart is very special. It has the power to enable you or the power to disable you. When your heart is full of happiness and gratitude, it enables you. The heart is open, it is in flow, it is in balance, therefore it expands. It is able to give and receive love, which in turn fills your internal cup and you will find you attract more possibilities and more abundance. However, when the heart experiences trauma, pain or heartache, it disables you: it contracts. The heart is closed and unbalanced, therefore creating self-doubt, limiting beliefs, and is unable to receive love.

Healing the heart is integral to consciously evolving and becoming more heart-led. By healing at the heart level, we naturally expand into a higher state of consciousness, greater wisdom and love. This enables effortless personal and spiritual evolution aligned with our highest potential.

As we enter this new era of consciously evolving, we are becoming more self-aware and turning to ancient wisdom, techniques and rituals which include grounding, meditation, healing, aligning and clearing energy centres (chakras), breathwork, and yoga in order to expand our consciousness. It is about how we evolve and heal spiritually, emotionally and energetically with intent, with empathy, with love, with unity and with wisdom, moving us away from a place of fear and separation.

Physically, the role of the heart is to keep us alive, pumping blood, supplying oxygen and nutrients to all of our organs and cells, and removing metabolic waste. As we consciously evolve, we are discovering that the heart plays more than a physical role. It is also an energetic and emotional centre that ancient traditions considered to be the Seat of Higher Consciousness, forgotten by modern society, which is now being rediscovered and re-learnt.

For example, the Sanskrit word *Anahata* refers to the heart chakra, which represents love, compassion, balance, calmness and serenity. Hindus and Buddhists believe the heart is the door to the inner temple, the soul and infinite parts of ourselves, a bridge between two worlds, the gateway to higher consciousness and divine connection. In Christianity, this is referred to as Christ consciousness. In the Sufi teachings of Rumi, the heart *(Qalb* in Arabic; *Dil* in Persian) is considered to contain the divine spark that leads to spiritual awareness and in Taoism, people are taught to live in their heart. It is no coincidence that teachings throughout the ages in different cultures all say the same thing.

The HeartMath Institute *(heartmath.org)* is a not-for-profit organisation that has developed scientific evidence from studies, creating tools and techniques that show the alignment of physical, mental and emotional systems and how they work in sync. HeartMath Studies include findings such as:

- The heart sends more signals to the brain than the brain sends to the heart.
- The heart generates an electromagnetic field sixty times stronger than the brain's, influencing emotions, thoughts, and even reality.
- When in heart-brain coherence, we experience enhanced intuition, faster problem-solving, and emotional balance.
- This suggests that our intelligence isn't just mental—it's emotional and energetic.

This all points to how powerful and important it is to heal your heart in a journey of change and transformation.

Barbara Marx Hubbard, an American futurist thinker and co-founder of the Foundation of Conscious Evolution in the 1990s, paved the way and introduced the idea of conscious evolution. Deepak Chopra described her as, "the voice for conscious evolution of our time."

In her book *Conscious Evolution: Awakening the Power of Social Potential,* Hubbard talks about her futurist ideas to make a better society, as well as about what the conscious mind can do if it is aware of its power. She saw a special role for women in the emerging new consciousness: "An evolutionary woman is activated by an inner impulse to create, to love more, be more, create more and give more... The evolutionary woman is able to love what's being born in her – the creative feminine – and able to love giving her gift to the unknown world."

Natasha Leigh Bray, founder of the School of Healing Mastery, realised as part of her research that the heart was the missing link and created HeartHealing therapy. It is a powerful guided meditation which takes you on a journey inside your heart to release fear, trauma and self-sabotage patterns.

I have absolutely loved training and qualifying in this modality. It is a simple yet powerful technique which is personalised to the client and the trauma they present. I always tell my clients to trust the process and not to overthink it; you never know who you will meet in the heart. You will heal subconsciously and any emotional blocks that have been holding you back.

I have seen clients repair relationships with their parents by forgiveness and letting go of negative emotions or emotional baggage. Others have experienced more success and growth in their businesses or careers, feeling more aligned with their purpose, increasing self-confidence, increasing self-worth, and overcoming grief. After the sessions, clients say they feel lighter, happier and experience more clarity.

My personal healing journey started back in the late 1990s, initially with holistic therapies such as massage, reflexology, acupuncture and tapping to heal physical ailments and release trapped trauma and physical blocks that had manifested in my body. During this time, I also started to use affirmations and explore manifestation, visualisation and meditations.

In 2005, I started exploring more mind-led therapies which worked with the subconscious mind, gaining a deeper understanding of triggers, reframing and anchors. I explored and trained in therapies such as hypnosis, NLP and energy healing therapies like Reiki. These gave me greater insight into understanding the behaviours of myself and people around me, and why we all did what we did. This played a key role in expanding my emotional intelligence. It became easier to navigate my complex maze of emotions and trauma. I learned that not everything is personal or about me. I understood, appreciated and respected that everyone is navigating their own challenges. This gave me a whole new perspective. I no longer felt triggered and I was able to empathise. With this awareness, feelings of hurt and trauma dissipated and were replaced by warmth, love and openness.

While these were great tools and they helped me evolve, after a while I found these were short term results and I needed to go deeper. At the end of the session I would be asked, "How was that? How are you feeling? What came up for you?" I genuinely felt better, like a weight had been lifted; there was both an energetic and emotional shift. However, I found I was revisiting some of the same traumas and healing them at the next level, the next layer and the next and the next. There was something missing and a dull pain I felt in my heart. It felt like those therapies were never deep enough or that they had healed the root cause. I would always have this feeling that there was something else and something more but I couldn't quite put my finger on it.

I continued to search and yearn for that inner peace, that inner calm where I would no longer feel that dull pain. I would fill my time with things to do, keeping busy, yet never feeling enough. I launched new businesses; I created a range of healing chakra candles as part of my healing journey; I travelled and found myself in some of the most powerful energy centres of the world trying to reconnect with what my soul once knew, hoping to remove this pain that was holding me back and keeping me stuck.

In 2020, I was overwhelmed with emotions after having my son. It was like I had a secret Pandora's box of trauma, emotions hidden away containing events that I had no conscious recollection of and all of a sudden, this box was opened and all these memories came flooding back. I had subconsciously been carrying these my whole life and now I was piecing together how these unresolved events had shaped me. I made a decision I didn't want history to repeat itself and for this pain and trauma to be passed down to my son or any future generations. I worked with Natasha Leigh Bray to heal myself and in turn my heart.

At this point, my emotional intelligence had evolved. I was already self-aware and had an awareness and appreciation for others. I had an awareness and understanding of these events, what the triggers were, why people behaved in certain ways and that they were carrying unresolved trauma and pain from their lives.

During the HeartHealing sessions Natasha took me on a journey into my heart to release these traumas. There were relationship traumas with family members I thought I had healed in the past but these resurfaced in the heart, as well as other traumas and meanings I had attached to past events. After the session, Natasha would send me a recording of the imprint, the personalised guided meditation, to listen to every day for the next week. I would get to experience the healing again and again, reinforcing the release of trauma on multiple levels.

There were times before going into a session I would identify an event or trauma that I thought I needed to heal, but when I entered the heart, something or someone else would be presented to me by my heart. I never questioned why this had happened and just observed; hindsight would show that what was presented to me in the heart was what I needed to heal.

I found there was something different with HeartHealing. I made peace with the events at a deeper level. My heart no longer ached, and there was a noticeable expansion in my already expanded awareness. I felt this inner peace, a pure bliss I had been yearning for. I had honoured the past and I was able to move forward and embrace the beacons of light by releasing the wounds of the past. HeartHealing has played a significant role in helping me evolve.

I am always get excited by journeys into the heart for myself and my clients, as you never know who you will meet there. I recall one client who came to me because of issues in her marriage as the relationship with her husband had completely broken down and they were on the verge of divorce. I took her on the journey into the heart and when she got there, she met her mother. We healed the relationship trauma with her mother during the session. As a result, over the coming months her relationship with her mother improved, and slowly but surely her marriage made a U-turn and they were no longer talking about separation or divorce but on resolving the issues and staying together.

During my personal healing journey to date and twenty-plus years working in Corporate Change and Transformation, looking at people, process and system, I have noticed that all the processes are mind-led following a set methodology and do not take into account the human aspect or lead with the heart. Whether I talk to individuals or corporate entities, I have to meet my client at the starting point in their change and transformation journey and establish how we can expand their awareness to consciously evolve.

This led me to develop the C.R.E.A.T.E. Principles™, creating a different way of consciously being, leading and living.

C	Calibrate and communicate
R	Realisation and Ripple Effect
E	Emotional intelligence or empathy using HeartHealing techniques
A	Alignment for growth
T	Transition and transform
E	Evolve and expand

These principles work on both a mind and heart level. I use this framework when working with individuals and corporate clients, and we go through each of these steps to create a personalised plan. I use this holistically to bring together the wisdom and understanding gained during the sessions to release blocks and to improve relationships, personal and business growth, abundance and much more. This process requires a willingness commitment to improving mental wellbeing and self-reflection, which can be a gradual and ongoing process of choosing to consciously evolve, transform and grow.

I invite you to take a moment, find a quiet space and simply be aware of how you are feeling, acknowledge any happiness or hurt you are feeling, acknowledge any pains and niggles in your body. Ask yourself, how does your heart feel? Be aware of any blocks or limiting beliefs that are stopping you from aligning to your highest self and creating the changes and results you desire.

Look to quieten the mind and ask your heart any questions that you are searching for answers to or seeking clarity on.

The first step is always the hardest. If you feel that something is missing and you are looking for something more, something deeper, then as the famous Zen saying goes, "Leap and the net will appear."

Are you ready to take that leap to heal your heart and consciously evolve?

ABOUT THE AUTHOR

SHEETAL VITHLANI

Sheetal Vithlani is a highly experienced Strategy, Change and Transformation Specialist Consultant who helps professional, business owners and corporate organisations consciously evolve during their Change and Transformation journey.

Sheetal has a passion and mission to seamlessly integrate science and spirituality both personally and professionally to create a positive impact and consciously evolve society. She leverages the power of science, spirituality, intuition, and energy healing; she aligns mindset, passion and ambition to create results, provide clarity and overall wellbeing.

Sheetal is a self-confessed adrenaline junkie (skydiving anyone?). She is on her own journey, consciously evolving through learning and pushing herself and her boundaries to grow. Her mantra is, "Leap and the net will appear."

Sheetal is available for private consultations as well as corporate Change, Transformation and Wellbeing projects.

www.sheetalvithlani.com
info@consciouslyevolve.com
instagram.com/consciously.evolve

18

EMMA MASON

THE HEART OF FEMININE LEADERSHIP

I find myself on the other side of a crossroad. For the first time since I lost it in the process of becoming a grownup, I have a deep sense of peace, satisfaction and joy. Rather than work defining the focus of my life, my identity, and the lens through which I measure my value, it has become something I *do* rather than something I *am*. This fundamental shift has freed me from the expectations – my own and others' – of who I must be to achieve success.

This means I have surrendered to the ebbs and flows of life. I understand that leadership in life and in work isn't about balance sheets and profit and loss statements. It is about living an inspired life that includes choice, rest and peace. It is ok to have a down day, to lounge around and do nothing. To eat ice cream at the movies. Sleep in. Have loose plans. To work the hours that match my natural rhythms, regardless of the time, day or night.

Perhaps most importantly, I now live and work aligned to my identity, to my values and to who I am, not to the title I used to hide behind.

Instead of a title, I have a drive and a sense of purpose that inspires the work I do. I work with incredible leaders who shape the world around us. They do this not from fear but from a deep understanding of the responsibility they hold and the power they wield. They know leadership is so much more than doing a job. It is a calling, an understanding of the interconnectedness of ourselves and the living world around us.

I work as a success coach for senior women leaders who find themselves at the same crossroad. These women, like me, have a deep yearning to change the world around them. These leaders understand they have an important contribution to the restoration of balance in a world that's lost its connection to life. They understand that when we embody and bring forth our feminine power, we re-establish balance around the boardroom table, that table where big decisions with big impact are made.

Feminine leadership is the understanding that as women we have something different to offer than the traditional construct of leadership we see on display. We source our power and influence differently from men, so it makes sense that we approach leadership differently as well. We bring our own gifts to the table.

I have come to understand that the current construct of leadership is highly masculine. It is outwardly oriented and focused on getting things done. It is about productivity and efficiency. It wields a power that belongs to some but not others. It is exclusive and hierarchical.

Feminine leadership is more inwardly focused. It is based on relationships. It understands that success happens through collaboration and an appreciation of the unique experience and expertise that everyone brings to the table. It is not linear but adaptable, inclusive, responsive and organic, modelled on mother nature herself. It is a shared model of leadership, within which leaders share power with others rather than exert power over them.

This is not to say that feminine leadership is better. But it *is* to say that we need it alongside the masculine model to restore balance into the big decisions that shape the lives of those they are made for. This balance is possible.

Gen X female senior leaders are the first generation of women to experience what others before us fought for – "to have it all" – the family, the career and the success. The problem is that this lies within the paradox of opportunity and reality. We are the sandwich generation – not only because we are looking after our parents at the same time we are looking after our children, but because we are living a "new" future in a society that's holding onto the past.

Many women in senior leadership positions today are at this juncture right now having taken advantage of the opportunity to build a career and have a family. Many are peaking in their careers with the perfect balance of experience, expertise and authority. They find themselves at a seniority level where they can have real influence and make meaningful change for the communities they serve.

But for many women, instead of this being the doorway to their legacy, it marks the arrival at their crossroad. This crossroad has them questioning whether they *can* in fact have it all and whether the sacrifice to do so has been worth it. Instead of stepping into this phase of their career empowered and energised, many women feel exhausted and overwhelmed. The pressure to continue to prove themselves over and over feels relentless, even though they have a career of achievement and success behind them.

Many women, even with this solid track record, still feel undervalued. They are exhausted from the never-ending pressure to justify their decisions and rationalise their thinking. They over-deliver for their work to be seen as enough. They reinforce their commitment to their organisations by making themselves always available and setting poor boundaries. The undertone that they are somehow less reliable than their male counterparts persists, particularly at these senior levels.

This feeling of not being good enough to belong in these places of power and influence is reinforced by the language we use to describe how women arrived here in the first place. As Mary Beard explains in *Women and Power: A Manifesto* (2017), metaphors such as "smashing the glass ceiling" and "breaking down barriers" suggest that women are somewhere they don't belong, taking something they aren't entitled to. It's no wonder they feel exhausted from pushing against social norms and deeply ingrained beliefs about what it takes to be successful and therefore entitled to the power and influence it affords.

When we work in an environment that isn't built for us, we will inevitably lose part of ourselves along the way. It is the ultimate sacrifice a woman makes as she climbs the career ladder. The higher she climbs, the more masculine traits she adopts to survive and the further away she strays from her true nature. While quotas and gender equality initiatives have been helpful, they haven't addressed the real issue of inclusion. They have opened the door to more women in power, but they haven't changed the room those women enter into.

This has led to a generation of women disconnected from their real source of power: their bodies. In a world that values intellect over intuition and consistency over change, this suppresses the natural blueprint for success that lives in every woman. This disconnection leads women to look outside of themselves for validation. The problem is it's never enough. And so, the cycle of overwork, perfectionism and people-pleasing continues. It's no wonder women question whether the price has been worth paying when they reach these career crossroads.

But here's the main issue. We need women in these senior leadership roles. We need women who bring the heart of feminine leadership to restore balance around the boardroom table. Women who aren't afraid to question decisions that make logical sense but don't *feel* right and who encourage their colleagues to check in with their moral compass too. Women who dare to put their ideas forward even though they're unlikely to be adopted, knowing they've planted a seed for change. Women who have the confidence to speak up when they witness something they disagree with and pave the way for others to do the same.

In other words, we need women with the internal resilience and fortitude to do things differently, daring to do the inner work to return to their natural feminine state, remembering what it means to be a woman deeply connected to her heart and her conscience. This connection is formed through the intelligence of her monthly menstrual cycle, the seasonal cycles of life and the female archetypes she passes through over her lifetime. This connection to her own rhythm and infinite wisdom reveals her individual, unique blueprint for success.

Let's look at the seasons and how they are reflected through a woman's body.

Spring is represented by the Maiden Archetype, the symbol of youth. She is energetic, creative and curious. She is out in the world experiencing all it has to offer. It is the pre-ovulation phase of her menstrual cycle; the time she emerges from the darkness of winter, full of hope and possibility; a time to get excited about bringing the ideas and visions received in the previous seasons to life. It is the time to play, experiment and connect, the time for the *innovative leader* to emerge, test new ideas and concepts, and get a sense of how those ideas will be received and what needs to be done to build upon them.

Summer is represented by the Mother Archetype. This is the age when a woman is fertile, her confidence is high and her energy is through the roof. It is the ovulation phase of her menstrual cycle.

She experiences a state of flow, fortuitous timing and synchronicities. It is the time life mirrors back what she holds in her heart. As the *impactful leader,* others hang off her every word as she draws others to her with her magnetic presence.

Autumn is represented by the Wild Woman Archetype. It is the time she starts the inward journey back to herself as her shadow side starts to emerge. This is the premenstrual phase of her menstrual cycle and the perimenopausal stage of her life cycle. It is the time when the areas of her life she has neglected, ignored or rejected come to the surface seeking recognition and integration. Her tolerance is low and her demand for the truth is high. She is the *inspirational leader* as she bravely says no and sets a new standard for herself and those around her.

Finally, winter is represented by the Crone Archetype, the mature woman who surrenders to what will be. It is menstruation in the menstrual cycle and the post-menopause stage of her life cycle. This is when she connects with her deeper, wiser knowing. It is the time she lets go of what no longer serves her and makes space for what is yet to come. As the *intuitive leader,* she is divinely guided and supported because this season represents both the beginning and the end of a cycle of renewal. She trusts herself completely.

This cycle and the infinite wisdom of its seasons is available to all women. In fact, ignore them at your peril: they aren't optional. They demand that you grow, evolve and mature. For many women, this comes in perimenopause, the season of life when women peak as senior leaders. This is the time they are perfectly positioned in their career to make a real difference and leave a legacy.

Therefore, it's no surprise that this career crossroad intersects with this hormonal highway! This is why your usual go-to strategies suddenly don't work. Intellectual, fact-based pros and cons won't cut it. Your heart yearns for more. The world is begging for more.

Humans are one of the few species whose females live beyond their reproductive years. There is good cause for this, as mature women have an important role to play beyond nurturing and raising children. The social narrative that women lose their power and slip into irrelevance as they age is simply not true. Women become more powerful with age. It just happens to be a power that isn't recognised (Pope & Wurlitzer, 2022).

Hilary Hart in *Body of Wisdom* (2012) recognises nine spiritual powers of women. She states that women's powers serve the whole in ways distinct from men's, quoting Dr Sun, who claims that, "women's hearts communicate with the heart of the earth… which is our planet's seat of consciousness." She notes women's powers are activated in the body and come to us so naturally that we often don't recognise them as powers; the rest of the world doesn't either.

Dr Sun so eloquently describes our heart connection to the earth. Women cycle through the seasons just as Mother Nature does. Therefore, it makes sense that perimenopause is a universal calling, an initiation to a greater purpose and meaning in our lives. It is our opportunity to transition to the next season of life. Like any initiation, it is a rite of passage. It is challenging and takes us to the heart of who we are. Unresolved issues, wounds and trauma come to the surface, and demand attention, resolution and release. We reconcile the past, wipe the slate clean, and enter the next season of life.

Powerful work is required to reconcile the past. This is the work of the senior leader who wants to transcend where they are now and get where they want to go next. The training, the strategies and the tools that got them to the crossroad are not the tools that will get them to the next season of their lives and, therefore, their careers.

The journey is an inward one and the doorway is found in the heart. I love Elizabeth Lesser's (2020) concept of innervism. It sits right next to activism. She defines innervism as the act of inner change and healing, and activism as the act of healing and changing the world around us. They are not mutually exclusive, she explains. Rather, they keep each other in check. We focus on what needs to change *out there* while also doing the very real work *in here*. For senior leaders, this is an important concept as we work towards creating real change in the world without becoming that which we are fighting against.

Staying connected to our heart is central to our ability to do this. After all, leadership is a relationship game. It requires us to understand who we are, our relationship patterns and our behavioural cues. One of the first questions I ask my clients when they relay their story is, "When have you experienced this feeling before?" They always recall an experience from their childhood and get a glimpse into a pattern they hadn't recognised before.

It could be the role they played in their family: the peacekeeper, the negotiator and the nurturer are common ones. Or it could be a relationship dynamic they are stuck in, preventing them from connecting and showing up the way they want to. They might be looking for protection, for example, or waiting for someone to rescue them, or seeking permission, to name a few.

Our earliest and primary relationships happen within our family units. It is here we learn how to relate to others and, most importantly, who we need to be to be accepted by others. It makes sense that we adopt their beliefs and values because our desires to belong, be accepted and stay safe are strong. As we head out in the world, we are influenced by other significant figures in our lives such as teachers, friends and community members. But we also absorb the cultural norms of what it means to be a girl and then a woman.

Elizabeth Lesser (2020) amplifies this message, showing us how, throughout history, all the way back to the origin story of Adam and Eve, women have been vilified for speaking up. How we've been ignored, ridiculed and punished even for voicing our opinions. How we have been silenced and disempowered, accused of thinking too much, feeling too much and being too much. It's no wonder women start to crumble as we gain more power and influence through advancing our careers. After all, deep within our psyche, our survival is at stake. We are being asked to change our ancestors' lived experience, a story deeply ingrained in the cells of every woman.

I have worked with many senior women leaders who long to change the narrative. They have tried rationalising their way through their past and used logic and reason to understand why they are the way they are. Intellectually, they know their past has shaped their current beliefs and behaviours. Some have acknowledged the wounds of their childhood and are determined to be a better parent than their own, for example. Others don't believe their pain is that bad. They minimise it by comparing it to others' and pacify it by acknowledging they come from a loving and caring family who did the best they could. They have locked away their pain and thrown away the key. They believe any weakness or vulnerability that comes from their past is a distraction, taking energy and focus from where it is needed. They stay stoic, alert and focused on the future.

This works for them until they reach the crossroad. For some, their career then unravels, leaving them exposed and in a state of emotional turmoil as they lose control of the narrative of who they are and what value they hold. For others, they experience increasingly intense murmurs of discontent. They no longer recognise the woman reflected in the mirror. They are so lost in an outward pursuit of success and recognition that even when they've achieved all they thought they wanted, the meaning and the satisfaction elude them.

This was me. I sacrificed so much to have a career I loved only to leave it all behind, burnt out and broken. I was on an upward career trajectory in the government sector. I had made it into the senior executive ranks with the promise of more opportunities to come. I'd navigated my way through many difficult and complex situations in both my personal life and my career before. So, when faced with yet another, I threw everything at it that I knew had worked in the past. But this time it didn't work. Instead of feeling empowered and in control, I felt lost. I was in such a state of distress that I felt I had no option but to leave. Of course, I did have options. In fact, I even had opportunities, but paralysed by the shame and inertia of what was happening around me, I couldn't see another way out. So I walked away.

This led me on a quest to understand what happened to me. I reread the self-help books that had lined my shelves for years. While I had understood their concepts, I hadn't internalised their lessons. Like many Gen X women, I'd hardened my heart to show up at work as anyone other than who I really was. I was too busy to stop and reflect and too afraid to feel my senses. My hormones were raging and it took every ounce of extra energy I had to contain them. Weakness was the enemy in life and at work. As a result, I was completely disconnected from my body. My logical, intelligent, smart mind was well and truly in charge.

As time passed and with the pressure of work relieved, I started to soften and to feel again. I began to understand that my true wisdom lived in my body, not my head. I cried my way through a series of therapeutic yoga sessions and enrolled in a transformational embodiment coaching course, which taught and showed me the power that resides within.

I began my business teaching what I'd learnt through small group courses, connecting with like-minded women. The results were impactful. The clarity my clients received was life changing. They opened businesses, healed relationships and gained a greater understanding of who they were and what they wanted. I felt a whole lot better too.

Then, eighteen months after I left my career, I came face to face with a former colleague who had helped orchestrate my demise. All the shame, confusion, pain, disappointment and regret came flooding back. My body completely shut down as I processed this viscerally. I was an emotional and physical wreck. I sought help and was told I was experiencing post-traumatic shock. It was time to process the emotional trauma I'd conveniently locked away that had triggered me leaving a career I loved.

I understood something was holding me back in my business. I had a sense it was this but after poor experiences with counsellors and coaches in the past I was sceptical about where to find help. And so, I enrolled in Natasha Bray's Ultimate Uplevel Academy. I was expecting new insights, things to think about and a new perspective on business. What I wasn't expecting was to feel so seen and understood. I was sure I was the only person hiding in my corner of the universe feeling the way I did. This was my first experience of HeartHealing. It opened something in me that I didn't know was there. I have very few memories of being a child but this process allowed me to connect the dots between my adult life and my childhood life. So many seemingly disconnected events were tied together by a belief, a shared history, a memory.

I knew the course was the perfect piece to complement the work I was doing with my clients. It gave me the confidence to face my fears and show up to help the women I really wanted to help. They were the women who also worked within the government sector. Women who were perfectly placed to influence the big decisions that affect us all. The policy makers, the service delivery specialists, the technical architects. Those who impact the lives of millions as they go about innovating, impacting, inspiring and intuitively leading with an open heart.

The greatest gift my clients and I receive from HeartHealing is peace. We know that despite the challenges and the setbacks, we can handle it. We believe we are resourceful enough to navigate tough and complex issues. We replace the pressure of being perfect and getting everything right with permission to change our minds and change course. We understand that the work we do is so much bigger than us and that by softening our hearts, we increase our access to the feminine version of power that shapes us into the leaders we want to be. We have lost the heaviness of having to prove ourselves. Just as importantly, we role model a different version of leadership to a new generation of women.

The heart of feminine leadership is a felt experience. Take a moment to reflect on where you are in your leadership journey. Which season do you resonate with most: spring (innovation), summer (impact), autumn (inspiration) or winter (intuition)? Journal about how this phase shows up in your life and what wisdom it has to offer you.

Return to your body. Lead from the heart. Change the world.

References:

Beard, M. (2017), *Women & Power: A Manifesto*, Profile Books, London.

Hart, H. (2012), *Body of Wisdom: Women's Spiritual Powers and How It Serves*, John Hunt Publishing, USA.

Lesser, E. (2020), *Cassandra Speaks: When Women Are the Storytellers, the Human Story Changes*, Harper Collins, USA.

Pope, A. & Hugo Wurlitzer, S. (2022), *Wise Power: Discover the Liberating Power of Menopause to Awaken Authority, Purpose and Belonging*, Hay House, UK.

ABOUT THE AUTHOR

EMMA MASON

Emma Mason is a Success Coach for senior women leaders at a crossroads in their career to decide on the next move so they can rewrite the rules about what it means to be a woman with power and influence.

As a former senior executive government leader, Emma understands the challenges of navigating a public sector career. She was involved in large organisational change projects, managed multiple million-dollar budgets and led large teams of people through significant transformations. Despite being qualified, capable and experienced, she found herself burnt out and broken and left a career she loved. If she knew then what she knows now, she may have decided differently.

Emma is a passionate zero waster and loves gardening.

Emma is available to work one-to-one with clients, runs regular online programs, and offers self-paced learning options.

www.emmamason.com.au
emma@emmamason.com.au
linkedin.com/in/emma-mason-coach

RESOURCES

Receiving Wounds® Online Assessment:
https://schoolofhealingmastery.com/receiving-wounds-assessment/

Find a HeartHealing Practitioner in our official directory of qualified, supervised HeartHealing Practitioners:
https://schoolofhealingmastery.com/practitioner/

Practitioners listed operate independently. Please do your own due diligence. The School of Healing Mastery Ltd accepts no liability for their services.

Email:
info@schoolofhealingmastery.com

If affected by any of the topics of this book, you are encouraged to reach out to the relevant support services (or appropriate alternative in your country) listed below.

UK Support

Samaritans (emotional support for all issues including suicidal thoughts):
Website: www.samaritans.org
Free Helpline: 116 123

NAPAC—National Association for People Abused in Childhood (supports survivors of all forms of childhood abuse, including physical, sexual, emotional, abuse, neglect and peer-to-peer abuse):
Website: www.napac.org.uk
Support Line: 0808 801 0331
Email Support: support@napac.org.uk

Women's Aid (support for women and children experiencing domestic abuse):
Website (LiveChat support available): www.womensaid.org.uk

Mind (mental health support):
Website: www.mind.org.uk
Infoline: 0300 123 3393

ADHD UK (Information and advocacy to support with ADHD):
Website: https://adhduk.co.uk/

National Suicide Prevention (to help with mental well-being or thoughts of suicide):
Website: https://spuk.org.uk/
Help Line: 0800 587 0800

National Debt Line
Website: https://nationaldebtline.org/
Help Line: 0808 808 4000

Alcoholics Anonymous (to help with alcohol addiction):
Website: https://www.alcoholics-anonymous.org.uk/
Help Line: 0800 917 7650

National Bullying Helpline (to give support around bullying whether an adult or child):
Website: https://www.nationalbullyinghelpline.co.uk/
Help Line: 0300 323 0169

Miscarriage Association (to help with pregnancy loss):
Website: https://www.miscarriageassociation.org.uk/
Help Line: 01924 200799

Marie Curie (for bereavement and grief support):
Website: https://www.mariecurie.org.uk/
Help Line: 0800 090 2309

Eating Disorders Support
Website: https://www.eatingdisorderssupport.co.uk/
Help Line: 01494 793223

Narcotics Anonymous (for help with drug and substance abuse and addiction):
Website: https://ukna.org/
Help Line: 0300 999 1212

A Band of Brothers (Award winning charity helping young men grow and develop):
Website: https://abandofbrothers.org.uk/

USA Support

988 Suicide & Crisis Lifeline (to help with suicide prevention and crisis management):
Website: https://988lifeline.org/
Help Line: 988

National Sexual Assault Hotline (to offer support for sexual assault and violence):
Website: https://rainn.org/
Help Line: 800.656.4673

National Alliance on Mental Illness (NAMI) (for mental health support to help with dealing with tough challenges, ADHD):

Website: https://nami.org/
Help Line: 1-800-950-NAMI (6264)

Stop It Now (to help prevent sexual abuse of children):
Website: https://www.stopitnow.org/
Help Line: 1.888.PREVENT

Crisis Text Line (for support with depression, anxiety, suicide, self harm, gun violence and eating disorders):
Website: https://www.crisistextline.org/

The Hope Line (for support with grief):
Website: https://www.thehopeline.com/

National Alliance for Eating Disorders (The Alliance) (to help with eating disorders):
Website: https://www.allianceforeatingdisorders.com/
Help Line: +1 (866) 662-1235

National Drug Helpline (for substance abuse and addiction):
Website: https://drughelpline.org/
Help Line: (844) 289-0879

AA (to help with alcohol abuse):
Website: https://www.aa.org/

STOMP Out Bullying (for Bullying, Cyberbullying, Racism, Hatred, LGBTQ+ Discrimination and Homophobia support):
Website: https://www.stompoutbullying.org/
Help Line: 877 602 8559

Postpartum Support International (for support with baby loss, miscarriage, postpartum depression):
Website:https://postpartum.net/
Help Line: 1-800-944-4773

Childhelp National Child Abuse (for help with child abuse):
Website: https://www.childhelphotline.org/
Help Line: 800.422.4453

National Domestic Violence Hotline (to help with domestic violence and abuse):
Website: https://www.thehotline.org/
Help Line: 1.800.799.7233

Samaritans USA (emotional support for all issues including suicidal thoughts):
Website: http://www.samaritansusa.org/
Support Line: 1 (800) 273-TALK

Child Welfare USA:
Website: https://www.childwelfare.gov/
Support Line: Call or text 1.800.4.A.CHILD [1.800.422.4453]

Debt Advice (USA):
Website: https://www.debt.org/
Help Line: (866) 612-9971

NEXT STEPS

If you would love to further your healing journey and change your world and the world through healing hearts, there are two main ways you can do this:

Want to Heal Yourself?

HeartHealing® is a revolutionary healing approach used within the subconscious state which expertly and uniquely combines scientific, spiritual, and energetic principles for deep, fast and safe transformation in as little as one hour.

If you would like to experience HeartHealing® for yourself, we invite you to visit the online directory of HeartHealing® Practitioners, to find the right practitioner for you.

It is important to note that practitioners will come from a variety of backgrounds and experience levels, and we would encourage you to do your due diligence before deciding which practitioner to work with. Practitioners listed operate independently. The School of Healing Mastery Ltd accepts no liability for their services.

https://schoolofhealingmastery.com/practitioner/

Want To Heal Others?

Become part of our mission to heal ten million hearts worldwide with the HeartHealing Mastery Certification. Join our award winning, pioneering ACCPH Accredited Certification & Level 4 Diploma, which equips you with the revolutionary HeartHealing methodology, self-mastery, business tools and unwavering confidence to facilitate deep, fast and safe transformations for your own clients.

This pioneering approach combines psychology and spirituality, using the heart as a portal to holistic mind-heart-soul transformation that our practitioners and their clients often describe as "more powerful than years of therapy".

Find out more at:
https://schoolofhealingmastery.com/hearthealing-mastery-certification

ABOUT THE SCHOOL OF HEALING MASTERY

The Home of HeartHealing®. Founded in 2021 by multi-award-winning healer and visionary Natasha Leigh Bray, the School of Healing Mastery is setting a new standard in transformational healing. We exist to train the most confident, ethical, and deeply embodied healing professionals in the world — equipping coaches, therapists, doctors, psychologists, and professionals with the revolutionary tools and personal mastery needed to become powerful and safe healers.

At the heart of our work is a mission to heal ten million hearts and break generational cycles of wounding and self-sabotage, so that future generations can thrive in love, peace, success, and emotional freedom. We believe that when hearts heal, everything changes — and that more people like you can open to receiving the love, money, peace, and fulfillment that you are destined for.

The School of Healing Mastery is proud to be known as the gold standard in the healing industry, offering high-touch, high-integrity training and supervision that prioritises emotional safety, depth, and real-world impact. Our work honours and integrates the best of both psychology and spirituality, bridging science with soul to create truly holistic transformation.

Our HeartHealing® qualification has attracted doctors, psychologists, psychotherapists, and trauma experts from around the world, many of whom hold decades of clinical experience and advanced certifications. Why do they choose us? Because HeartHealing® is the method that finally brings everything together.

Our practitioners consistently report breakthroughs in both their clients' results and their own personal healing, often describing HeartHealing® as "the missing piece" they've been searching for. With hundreds of graduates trained globally, and more joining our mission every year, we're proud to be leading a new paradigm of healing.

Learn more or join us at: www.schoolofhealingmastery.com

Printed in Dunstable, United Kingdom

63671028R00198